The HUMONGOUS Book of PRESCHOOL IDEAS 2

Group

Loveland, Colorado

group.com

Group resources actually work!

This Group resource incorporates our R.E.A.L. approach to ministry. It reinforces a growing friendship with Jesus, encourages long-term learning, and results in life transformation, because it's

Relational
Learner-to-learner interaction enhances learning and builds Christian friendships.

Experiential
What learners experience through discussion and action sticks with them up to 9 times longer than what they simply hear or read.

Applicable
The aim of Christian education is to equip learners to be both hearers and doers of God's Word.

Learner-based
Learners understand and retain more when the learning process takes into consideration how they learn best.

THe HumonGous BooK of PReScHooL IDeas 2

Copyright © 2009 Group Publishing, Inc.

All rights reserved. No part of this book may be reproduced in any manner whatsoever without prior written permission from the publisher, except where noted in the text and in the case of brief quotations embodied in critical articles and reviews. For information, e-mail Permissions at inforights@group.com or write Permissions, Group Publishing, Inc., Product Support Services Dept., P.O. Box 481, Loveland, CO 80539.

Visit our website: **group.com**

Credits

Chief Creative Officer: Joani Schultz
Senior Developer, Children's Ministry: Patty Smith
Children's Ministry Champion: Christine Yount Jones
Senior Editor: Jan Kershner
Senior Project Manager: Pam Clifford
Art Director: Andrea Filer
Print Production Artist: Coffee Bean Design Company
Cover Art Director: Andrea Filer
Cover Designer: Illustrated Alaskan Moose and Andrea Filer
Production Manager: DeAnne Lear
Illustrator: Illustrated Alaskan Moose

Unless otherwise indicated, all Scripture quotations are taken from the *Holy Bible,* New Living Translation, copyright © 1996, 2004. Used by permission of Tyndale House Publishers, Inc., Carol Stream, Illinois 60188. All rights reserved.

Library of Congress Cataloging-in-Publication Data

Group's The humongous book of preschool ideas 2.
    p. cm.
 ISBN 978-0-7644-3813-4 (pbk. : alk. paper)
 1. Christian education of preschool children. 2. Bible--Study and teaching (Preschool)--Activity programs. I. Group Publishing. II. Title: Humongous book of preschool ideas 2.
  BV1475.8.G75 2009
  268'.432--dc22

                        2008030538

10 9 8 7 6 5 4 3 2 1   18 17 16 15 14 13 12 11 10 09

Printed in the United States of America.

Contents

New Testament

Introduction

You asked for it! And we listened!

We kept hearing, "Please create another *Humongous Book of Preschool ideas!* It's so easy to use, and my kids love the activities!" So here it is: *The Humongous Book of Preschool Ideas 2*!

Like its predecessor, *The Humongous Book of Preschool Ideas 2* is packed with ideas to build or enhance any lesson. Because preschoolers need different ways to actively explore God's Word and learn life-transforming truth, this book is filled with age-appropriate, sensory-filled learning experiences.

That's why this is the perfect resource for your preschoolers!

Humongous *ideas.* This book is full of humongous-impact Bible stories, from both the Old and New Testaments. Each Bible story uses active-learning where preschoolers actually become part of the story as they sing, dance, make sound effects, or cheer to bring the Bible story to life. After the story, you'll find a variety of humongous ideas that will help children remember the story and apply it to their lives.

Humongous *learning.* Every activity uses an active-learning approach, helping kids learn in their own unique ways. Whether it's acting out a Bible story, moving around in a game, singing a song, or creating a craft, little children will dig deeper into the story because they're learning as they learn best—by doing! And that sets the stage for humongous learning!

Humongous *life change.* Children will remember the Bible stories and life applications because you've chosen the ideas that work best for your children, in your setting, and with the message you want to share. As a result, children will continue to get to know Jesus better and better.

Easy to use! Each story is followed by humongous activity ideas, divided into easy-to-find categories. After each story, you'll find most or all of these categories: Bible Experiences, Crafts, Games, Prayers, Snacks, and Songs. Use the Bible story as your foundation, then add to your preschool learning experience from there!

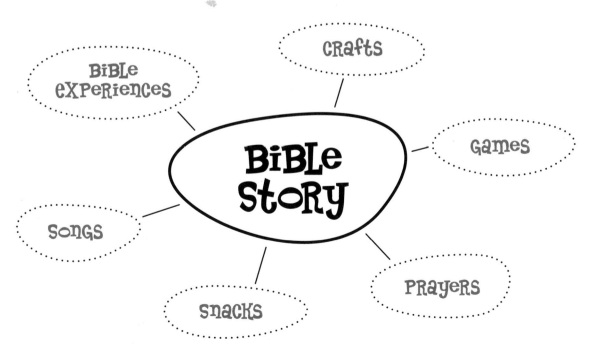

Since the Bible stories contain fun snack ideas to enhance your teaching. Keep allergy awareness in mind when using food with your preschoolers. Every time food is used, you'll see the Allergy Alert icon as a reminder.

Be aware that some children have food allergies that can be dangerous. Know your children, and consult with parents about allergies their children may have. Also, be sure to read food labels carefully, as hidden ingredients can cause allergy-related problems.

So are you ready for more adventures with your preschoolers? These humongous Bible ideas will help your preschoolers grow closer to Jesus in humongous new ways! So use these humongous ideas to make a humongous impact on kids' lives!

Choking Hazards

Be aware that small objects can be choking hazards for younger children. Supervise children as they work with small objects such as dry cereal and wiggly eyes. If you have several really young children in your class, you may want to substitute a larger object for the craft.

adam and eve sin

Bible Basis:

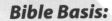 Genesis 3:1-24

Supplies:

Bible, poster board, apple, washable markers, wet wipe, smiley-face stickers, fine-tipped marker, tape

Before class, tape the poster board to a wall at kids' eye level.

Open your Bible to Genesis 3, and show children the words.

say ▶ **Today's Bible story teaches us that Adam and Eve, the first people God made, sinned. That means they disobeyed God. Let's draw a picture of Adam and Eve in the Garden of Eden, where they lived.** Have one volunteer help you draw a picture of Adam and another volunteer help you draw a picture of Eve on the poster board.

Let other children draw their versions of fruit trees, berry bushes, and shrubs.

say ▶ **Adam looked at all the beautiful trees he could eat from. Then he remembered that there was special fruit in the middle of the garden that God had said he wasn't allowed to eat.** With your marker, quickly draw a simple outline of a bigger tree. Choose a few more kids to draw colorful fruit inside your outline.

say ▶ **God told Adam and Eve they could eat all the fruits they wanted except special fruit from the tree of knowledge of good and evil. But someone else was very sneaky and wanted Adam and Eve to disobey God. It was a snake, who lied to Adam and Eve and told them it was OK to eat the special fruit. Let me show you what that might have been like.**

Draw two eyes and a mouth on the tip of your index finger with a washable fine-tip marker. Pretend that your finger is the snake. Wiggle your finger up and down when the snake talks. Use a soft, devious voice.

As the snake, **say** ▶ **Good morning, boys and girls. My name is Temptation. What kinds of rules do your parents have at home? What kinds of things aren't you allowed to do or eat?**

Let kids respond. **What if I told you it was OK to disobey your parents? What if I said it was OK to eat candy before dinner? Or what if I told you it was OK to hit your brother or sister. What would you say to me?**

Let kids respond. **Well, no matter what I said, it still wouldn't be OK to disobey your parents. But Adam and Eve didn't make a very good choice. They decided to disobey God.**

Take the apple and, with the Temptation voice, continue.

say ▶ **First I got Eve to disobey and eat some of the special fruit. Then I got Adam to disobey, too. Oops! Someone's coming! I better go before I get caught.** Set the apple down, and put your hand behind your back and wipe it quickly with a wet wipe to remove the snake's face.

ask ▶ • **Why do you think Adam and Eve disobeyed God?**

• **How do you think God felt when Adam and Eve disobeyed him?**

• **What do you think happened next?**

say ▶ **Adam and Eve felt so bad that they ran away and hid from God. But God found them, and God knew what they had done.**

God was sad that they had disobeyed. Because of the wrong thing Adam and Eve did, God had to make them leave the beautiful garden God had made for them. It made God sad that Adam and Eve had to leave, and Adam and Eve were sad that they had to leave the garden. Sin makes everyone sad. Let's draw sad faces on this poster to show that sin makes everyone sad. Encourage children to use markers to draw small sad faces on the poster.

Just like Adam and Eve, we all do bad things sometimes. But God still loves us. In fact, God loves us so much that he sent his Son, Jesus, to die for us. When we believe in Jesus, God forgives all the wrong things we do, and we can be close to God again! That makes us happy! Let's put these smiley-face stickers over our sad faces to show that we're happy that Jesus took the punishment for our sins! Encourage kids to cover up the sad faces on the poster with the smiley-face stickers.

crafts

Caring People Collage

Supplies: colored construction paper; glue sticks; old magazines, comic books, or picture books; hole punch; yarn

Give each child a piece of colored construction paper and a glue stick. Encourage children to look through the old magazines or books that you brought. Tell kids to tear out pictures of people who are caring for others, such as someone feeding a child, a child hugging an elderly person, or someone rescuing another person from danger.

Have kids glue the pictures onto their construction papers to make a collage. Encourage kids to glue as many pictures as they can fit on the paper. Punch holes in the top of each child's paper, and tie a long piece of yarn through the holes so kids can hang their collages.

Say that God cares for us, and we can care for others.

ask ▸ • **What caring actions did you find in the books and magazines?** Let kids describe their collages.

• **What's one caring thing you did for someone this week?**

• **What's one caring thing that God has done for you and your family?**

say ▸ God cares for us. God gives us food to eat, clothes to wear, homes to live in, and people who love us. When we help others and care for them, we are showing them God's love. God loves us, and we can love others!

Games

Mission Impossible

Supplies: crown (either make one or pick one up at a party store), masking tape, 2 adult volunteers

Place the crown at one end of a long masking tape strip on the floor. Have kids line up at the end of the masking tape opposite the crown. Encourage children to each jump one time as far as they can to try to reach the crown. The crown will be too far for any of the kids to reach.

ask ▸ • **How did you feel when you couldn't jump far enough to reach the crown?**

say ▸ We couldn't reach the crown because we're too far away. We all sin and do wrong things. Those wrong things keep us away from God.

But God loves us so much that he made a way for us to get close to him. He sent Jesus to take the punishment for the wrong things we do. When we believe in Jesus, God forgives our sins. Then we can be close to God.

Repeat the game. This time, after children jump, have two adults carry them to the crown. As the crown is placed on each child's head, **say** ▸ **Everyone has done bad things, but Jesus brings us close to God.**

After everyone has had a turn to wear the crown, **say** ▸ **Because we've done wrong things, we can't get to God on our own. But Jesus loves us, and believing in Jesus brings us close to God!**

- -

Hold Your Tongue!

Supplies: paper plates with "X's" cut out for the place of the mouth, noisemakers (the kind that extend when you blow them), markers, yarn, glue sticks, scissors

say ▶ Adam and Eve got into trouble by disobeying God and eating something he told them not to eat. God knew what was best for Adam and Eve because God cared for them. It made God sad when Adam and Eve chose not to obey him.

ask ▶ • What would happen if you disobeyed your parents and ate something they said not to eat?

say ▶ Our mouths can get us into trouble when we eat something we shouldn't, like Adam and Eve did, or when we say mean things to someone. But our mouths can also do good things, like say nice things to people, or tell people about Jesus. God made our mouths to do good things, not bad things. Let's make some silly masks to remind us to do good things with our mouths!

Give each child a plate mask. Explain that the spot where the X is will be the mouth.

Encourage kids to decorate their masks by drawing facial features and gluing yarn around the plate as hair. Demonstrate how to turn over the plate and put the mouthpiece into the mouth on the mask. The masks may not fit directly against kids' faces, but the masks will stay in place as long as kids keep their lips around the noisemakers.

Tell kids that you're going to say some actions they can do with their mouths. If you say a good action, kids can blow out their noisemaker "tongues". If you say a wrong action, kids should hold their tongues and not blow them out. Begin listing actions such as eating all your dinner, saying something mean to your sister, and saying "I love you" to your parents. Encourage kids to blow their noisemakers for each good action. Be sure to end the list with a good action.

ask ▶ • What are some good things you can do with your mouth this week?

say ▶ Those are wonderful things to do with our mouths! Let's use our mouths for good and not for bad. God cares for us, and wants us to obey him. God knows what's best!

PRayeRS

Care Prayer

Supplies: stuffed animal

Gather the children in a circle. Hold the stuffed animal up high where kids can't reach it.

say ▶ Just like Adam and Eve, we all do bad things. When we do something wrong, we get farther away from God. Have children try to touch the stuffed animal.

Just like we can't touch this stuffed animal, when we do wrong things we can't be close to God. But God loves us. He sent Jesus to take the punishment for the wrong things we do. When we believe in Jesus, we can be close to God.

Pass the stuffed animal around the circle. Then have the kids join hands in a circle and pray:

Dear God,

Thank you for sending Jesus so we can be close to you.

Thank you for loving us.

In Jesus' name, amen.

snacks

Cookie Crumbs

Supplies: cookies, resealable sandwich bags, snack cups of ice cream or pudding, spoons

Place a cookie inside a resealable sandwich bag for each child. Have kids wash their hands before beginning the snack activity.

say ▶ **When God made Adam and Eve, there was nothing bad in the world. No one was mean. No one disobeyed. Everything was perfect.** Give each child a snack bag, and point out the nicely shaped cookies. **God wanted the world to stay perfect, but Adam and Eve chose to do something that was wrong.** With the bags sealed, have the kids break their cookies into small pieces.

Adam and Eve sinned—they disobeyed God. When they did that, the world wasn't perfect anymore, just like your cookie isn't perfect anymore. When we sin, we're far away from God.

ask ▶ **• How was the cookie better before it was broken?**

Ask the kids whether the cookies can be put back together again.

say ▶ **We can't put the cookies together again. And when we sin, we get far away from God and can't get back to him by ourselves. But God loves us so much that he made a way for us to get back to him. He sent Jesus to take the punishment for the bad things we do. When we believe in Jesus, God forgives us. And then we can be close to God again.**

It's good to believe in Jesus! Let's make something good out of these broken cookies to remind us that God loves us even when we aren't perfect.

Let someone pray and thank God for his love and for the snack. Pass out spoons and snack cups of ice cream or pudding, and have the kids sprinkle the cookie crumbs on top. As children enjoy their snacks, have them talk about ways God cares for them each day.

"All Have Sinned" Rhyme

Supplies: none

Remind children that God sent his Son, Jesus, to take away our sins. Then lead kids in this action rhyme.

Everyone has done wrong. (Have kids point around the room.)

I know it's true. (Point to head.)

I've been bad. (Put face in hands.)

Haven't you? (Point to others.)

Jesus died (hold arms out to the side)

To take away (brush off body with hands)

The wrong we've done. (Cross pointer fingers.)

Believe today! (Stretch both arms up.)

Sin Keeps Us Away From God

Supplies: none

Choose two children to hold up their hands to form a bridge for the rest of the class to walk under. Sing "Sin Keeps Us Away From God" to the tune of "London Bridge."

When we choose to disobey (children walk in line under bridge)**,**

Disobey, disobey,

When we choose to disobey,

We get caught in sin. (Arms of bridge drop around one child.)

Sin keeps us away from God (gently rock caught child)**,**

Away from God, away from God.

Sin keeps us away from God,

But Jesus frees us. (Arms of bridge lift, freeing child.)

GOD FLOODS tHE eaRtH

Bible Basis:

 Genesis 7:1–8:22; 9:8-16

A Faithful Man

Supplies:

Bible

Have children sit in a circle. Open your Bible to Genesis 7, and show children the words.

say **Once there was a man named Noah. Noah loved God and trusted God. But he was the only person who did! Let's do an action rhyme now as we hear the story of Noah.**

Lead children in this fun action rhyme about Noah. Say each verse while demonstrating the actions that accompany it.

say **Noah was a faithful man who listened to what God said.** (Cup hand to ear.) **Not like the others who pushed God away and did what they wanted instead.** (Push hands away from body, and then put them on hips.)

So God said to Noah, "Please listen to me, this is what you should do. (Cup hand to ear, and hold one finger up.)

Build me an ark. Make it really big because the sky will no longer be blue! (Pretend to hammer, and then stretch arms wide.)

It's going to rain for a really long time, and I want you to be ready." (Twinkle fingers from high to low to imitate falling rain.)

So Noah built the ark. He worked long and steady. (Pretend to hammer, and then cup hand over eyes and look out.)

Then God said to Noah, "See? I am sending the animals two by two. (Hold up two fingers and "walk" them in the air.)

Bring the animals on board with your family. That's what I want you to do." (Wave hand in toward body.)

Then it rained for 40 days and nights, and the water rose up to their heads (twinkle fingers high to low to imitate falling rain, and then show a high level of rain by stretching out one hand high)

because God was angry at people who pushed him away and did what *they* wanted instead. (Make an angry face, and push hands away from body.)

When the rain finally stopped, Noah sent out a dove to see if the dove could find land. (Flap arms like a bird.) **The water had dried up, and up in the sky was such a beautiful sight!** (Spread arms out to show God's beauty.)

A rainbow from God, a promise he made, to never cause us such a fright! (Make a wide arc with hands in the air.)

ask ▸ • **How did God take care of Noah and his family?**

• **When has God taken care of you and your family?**

• **Why do you think God takes care of us?**

say ▸ **God saved Noah, his family, and all the animals in the ark. God will take care of us, too!**

BiBLe eXPeRieNCes

A Rainbow of Color

Supplies: two or three 30-inch crepe-paper streamers in different colors per child, packing tape

Before class, cut the crepe paper into 30-inch streamers, then tape a loop at the end of each streamer to form a handle.

Give each child two or three streamers of different colors. Lead the children in singing "The Lord Will Keep His Promises" to the tune of "The Muffin Man." Encourage kids to walk or skip around in a circle, waving their streamers from side to side to the rhythm of the music. During the last line, "God never tells a lie," have the children hold the streamers high above their heads as they spin around.

The Lord will keep his promises, promises, promises.
The Lord will keep his promises.
God never tells a lie.

Noah obeyed and built the ark, built the ark, built the ark.
Noah obeyed and built the ark.
God never tells a lie.

Animals on the ark came two by two, two by two, two by two.
Animals on the ark came two by two.
God never tells a lie.

God shut the door when the rain came down, rain came down, rain came down.
God shut the door when the rain came down.
God never tells a lie.

It rained and poured for 40 days, 40 days, 40 days.

It rained and poured for 40 days.

God never tells a lie.

The boat hit land when the water dried, water dried, water dried.

The boat hit land when the water dried.

God never tells a lie.

The Lord will keep his promises, promises, promises.

The Lord will keep his promises.

God never tells a lie.

say ▶ We can always trust God to keep his promises. God never tells a lie!

Crafts

The Rainbow

Supplies: white construction paper, washable markers, rubber bands, spray bottle with water

Give each child a sheet of white construction paper, and write children's names on their papers. Let each child choose three or four washable markers, and help him or her place a rubber band around the markers. Demonstrate on a separate piece of paper how to use the banded markers to create an arch-like rainbow. Provide a small spray bottle with water in it, and have kids take turns lightly spraying the page. Let the page dry, and observe the effects of the blended colors.

ask ▶ • What do you like about rainbows?

say ▶ God made the rainbow as a promise to never flood the whole
earth again. God keeps all of his promises, and every time we see a
rainbow, we can remember God's promise.

Rainbow Bags

Supplies: packing tape; blue, yellow, red, and white tempera paint;
1 sandwich-size resealable plastic bag per child

Before class, fill a sandwich-size resealable plastic bag with a half cup of white paint for each child.

Give each child one of the resealable plastic bags that you prepared before class. Encourage children to add drops of colored paint to their bags. Then seal the bags with packing tape so the children can squish the colors together without opening the bags. Talk about the colors they are creating as they squish the bags.

say ▸ The colors in your bags are like the colors of the rainbow. The rainbow is a sign that God puts in the sky to remind us that he promised never to flood the earth again. God keeps his promises!

ask ▸ • How can we thank God for keeping his promises?

say ▸ Let's thank God right now for keeping his promises! Lead kids in clapping and cheering for God.

Shoe Box Ark

Supplies: shoe box, brown paper, modeling dough

Before class, cover a shoe box with brown paper to represent the ark.

As children arrive, give them modeling dough to create animals to go into the ark. Remind children that in today's Bible story, God told Noah to build an ark so he and his family and lots of animals would be safe during the big flood God sent. God saved Noah, his family, and lots and lots of animals.

Rainbow Mural

Supplies: red, orange, yellow, green, blue, and purple poster board; hole punch, string

Have kids make rainbow murals to decorate your classrooms. Cut one arch each out of red, orange, yellow, green, blue, and purple poster board. Punch a hole in the top of each arch, then help kids lace a string through each hole, starting with the purple arch on the bottom, then blue, green, yellow, orange, and red. Tie a knot after you put each arch on the string—this will keep the arches separate. Leave a long length of string above the red arch so you can attach the mural to the ceiling. If you have a larger class and several volunteers, set out supplies so each volunteer can help a group of kids make a mural.

PRAYERS

Action Prayer

Supplies: none

Use this action-rhyme prayer to help children be thankful for God's promises.

pray ▸ Thank you, God (fold hands in prayer),

For your promises true. (Cross heart with one finger.)

Thank you, God (fold hands in prayer),

I love you, too. (Point to self, cross arms, point up.)

In Jesus' name, amen.

snacks

Bread of Many Colors

Supplies: 1 piece of white bread and 1 clean paintbrush per child, small bowls, milk, food coloring, toaster, butter

Before class, fill several small bowls with milk. Use red, blue, yellow, and green food coloring to color the milk. Place the bowls of milk in a refrigerator until you need them.

Give each child a slice of white bread, and place the small bowls of milk colored with food coloring on the table. Have the children use clean paintbrushes to paint rainbows on their bread. Lightly toast and butter the bread, then let the children snack on their rainbow bread.

ask · Have you ever seen a rainbow? What was it like?

say God put the rainbow in the sky as a reminder of his promise to never flood the earth again.

ask · What can you think about every time you see a rainbow?

say It's wonderful to know that God keeps all his promises. We can remember God's promise every time we see a rainbow.

Songs

Only God Can Make a Rainbow

Supplies: none

This song will help children remember the importance of the rainbow. Sing it to the tune of "Did You Ever See a Lassie?"

> **Only God can make a rainbow,**
>
> **A rainbow, a rainbow.**
>
> **Only God can make a rainbow**
>
> **To shine in the sky.**
>
> **Red, yellow, green, blue,**
>
> **God's promise is true.**
>
> **Only God can make a rainbow**
>
> **To shine in the sky.**

The People Build a Tall Tower

Bible Basis:

Genesis 11:1-9

Supplies:

Bible, small blocks, a brick

Open your Bible to Genesis 11, and show children the words.

say ▶ **Today's Bible story teaches us that we need God.**

One day some people in the Bible decided to build a really tall tower that would reach to the heavens. As you tell the story, have the children use small blocks to build a tower on the floor.

The men said to each other, "Come, let's make bricks." Show the children the brick, and explain how people made bricks from straw and mud. Encourage children to continue building their tower. **The people said, "Let us build ourselves a city with a tower that reaches to the heavens, so we'll be more important than God."** Have children continue building. **And then they said, "If we can build a tower to the heavens, we'll be the most important people in the world. We won't need God to take care of us; we'll be able to take care of ourselves."**

But (have the children freeze, stop building, and look at you) **soon the Lord came down to see the city and the tower that the people were building.**

ask ▶ • **What do you think God thought of this tall tower they were building?**

say ▶ **The people thought they could do things better than God. So God had to remind them that he is more important than building the biggest tower and that we need all God's help. God mixed up their languages and scattered the people all over the earth. From that time on, the unfinished tower was called the tower of Babel.**

We need God, don't we? Let's say that together. Have the children repeat that with you: **We need God. When we are weak and need his help, God comes to us. God is strong. God knows we need him, and God sent Jesus to earth to die for us and forgive our sins. We can get to know Jesus and spend time with Jesus. We can ask Jesus for help, and Jesus will help us.**

BiBLe eXPeRiences

Language Tower

Supplies: objects that can be stacked such as paper cups, books, blocks, and toy cars

Set out several piles of objects that can be stacked, such as paper cups, books, blocks, and toy cars. Invite children to work together to try to build a tall tower using the objects. The only rule is that they can't use any words to talk to each other; they can only talk by saying "ba ba ba" or "bel bel." Let children work on their tower for several minutes, then tell them they can go back to using regular words. Encourage kids to tell you about their experience of trying to build the tower without being able to talk to each other.

Confusing Conversations

Supplies: none

Invite two guests to your class who speak other languages. Have both guests speak in another language at the same time as you are talking to the kids, and note the confusion. Now have each guest, one at a time, say something to the children in his or her language and then translate what was said. Tell children that there are many different people and different languages in the world, but that everyone needs God. Have each guest teach children how to say "We need God" in another language.

CRafts

Helping Hands

Supplies: paper, colorful tempera paints, paintbrushes, smocks, wet wipes, paper towels, or a large washable stamp pad instead of paints

Distribute pieces of paper, and write children's names on them. Set out colorful tempera paints, paintbrushes, wet wipes, and paper towels. Or try using large washable-ink stamp pads instead of paints. Have the kids put on paint smocks and paint the palms and fingers of their hands. Then encourage kids to put their hands on their pages to leave handprints. Remind kids that we need God's helping hand.

ask • How can you ask God for help?

• When do you need God?

say We always need God, and God always wants to be with us and help us. We need God.

Games

What's That You Say?

Supplies: none

Have the children sit in a circle. Explain that you are going to play the game of telephone. Tell children that you will whisper something in the first child's ear, and then that child will whisper the same message to the next child, and so on, until the message gets back to you. Remind kids that they need to whisper very quietly so that only the person they are telling the message to can hear them.

Using a foreign language, whisper "We need God" into the first child's ear. You can use Spanish: "Necesitamos a Dios"; French: "Nous avons besoin de Dieu"; German: "Wir brauchen Gott" or another foreign language that you are familiar with. Encourage the child to pass the message on as best as he or she can to the next child in the circle. When the message gets back to you, the following questions:

- **Who can tell me what the special message was?**
- **Why was it so hard for you to understand the message?**
- **Why did God make the people in our story speak different languages?**
- **Who would like to play again and hear our special message?**

Play the game again, and this time say, "We need God."

 • **Why was it easier this time to understand our special message?**

 In our story today, the people forgot who was the most important; they tried to be more important than God. They didn't think that they needed God. We must remember that God is the most important and that we need God.

- -

Friendly Helpers

Supplies: none

 We need God to help us. Let's play a game to show us that we always need God's help.

Group the children into threes. Have one child of each trio sit cross-legged on the floor with arms folded stiffly across the chest. Have them try to get up without uncrossing their arms or legs. Then have the other two children in the trios stand on either side and gently lift the child by the elbows. Let each child try to get up and then get help from the others.

 • **How did you feel when you couldn't get up?**
- **How were your two friends like God?**
- **What can you ask God to help you with?**

 Your friends gave you a "helping hand" the way God does. We often need helping hands, and with God's help, anything is possible. We need God.

PRAYERS

"We Need God" Prayer

Supplies: none

Teach children this prayer about how much we need God. Sing "We Need God" to the tune of "This Old Man":

> **Thank you, God!**
>
> **This is true!**
>
> **We need you in all we do.**
>
> **If it's night or day;**
>
> **If we sleep or play—**
>
> **We need you in all we do.**

After the song, have the children close the prayer by saying together, "In Jesus' name, amen."

- -

With God's Help

Supplies: none

Ask kids what they want God to help them with. Have the children who want to pray aloud during the prayer take turns asking God to help them. Have them pray the following:

> **Dear God,**
>
> **Please help me** [the child's words]**.**
>
> **In Jesus' name, amen.**

SNACKS

Brick Stackin' Snacks

Supplies: pound cake cut into cubes, whipped topping, chocolate syrup

 In our Bible story today, the people forgot they needed God. But we always need God. We can always pray to God and ask for his help.

Have children wash their hands before they prepare the snacks. Then ask a child to pray, thanking God for his help in our lives. Encourage kids to build small towers using the cake cubes for bricks and the whipped topping for mortar.

As the kids stack the cake bricks on their plates, have them tell ways we need God, such as "We need God to forgive us" or "We need God to show us how to live." When the towers are finished, have the kids squirt chocolate syrup on their treats. Then let the children eat and enjoy!

 **aLLeRGY aLeRt**

View From Above

Supplies: bowls, yogurt, bananas, granola

Give each child a small bowl of yogurt and half a banana. Help children peel their bananas and then place them in the bowls of yogurt so the bananas look like towers. Then give each child a small cup of granola to spread around the base of the banana to represent the people scattering from the tower. Invite one child to pray and thank God for the snack.

 ask
- **Did the people want God's help when they were building the tower at Babel? Why not?**
- **What are some things you do during the day that God can help you do?**

 say
We need God, and God wants to help us. We can always ask God for help.

SONGS

Jesus Loves All of Us

Supplies: none

 say
Let's sing a song about Jesus right now! The fun thing about this song is that the song is in lots of different languages. Sing "Jesus Loves Me." Have fun introducing your children to this familiar song sung in different languages.

Jesus loves me! This I know,

For the Bible tells me so.

Little ones to him belong.

They are weak, but he is strong.

Chorus in English:

Yes, Jesus loves me!

Yes, Jesus loves me!

Yes, Jesus loves me!

The Bible tells me so.

Chorus in Spanish:

Sí, Jesús me ama!

Sí, Jesús me ama!

Sí, Jesús me ama!

La biblia me dice tan.

Chorus in French:

Oui, Jésus m'aime!

Oui, Jésus m'aime!

Oui, Jésus m'aime!

La bible m'indique ainsi.

Chorus in German:

Ja Jesus liebt mich!

Ja Jesus liebt mich!

Ja Jesus liebt mich!

Die bibel sagt mir so.

Chorus in Italian:

Sì, Jesus mi ama!

Sì, Jesus mi ama!

Sì, Jesus mi ama!

La bibbia mi dice così.

GOD BLESSES ABRAM

Bible Basis:

 Genesis 12:1-8

Supplies:

Bible, backpack

Open your Bible to Genesis 12, and show children the words.

say ▶ **Today's Bible story tells us that we can trust God.**

A long time ago, a man named Abram lived in a nice place with his family. But one day, God told Abram to leave his home and go to a new place that God would show him. God said that he would bless Abram with many good things and that many other people would be blessed because of Abram. Abram knew that he could trust God to guide him.

ask ▶ **• If God told your family to move to a new place today, would you want to go? Why or why not?**

• If God told you that he'd bless you with many good things, then would you want to go? Why or why not?

• Have you ever moved to a new place? What was that like?

• If you had to move today, what would you want to take with you?

Pass the backpack around the circle, and have the kids tell you what they might put inside for a trip.

say ▶ **We'd pack a lot of things for a trip! Well, Abram packed his bags and took his wife, Sarai; his nephew Lot; and the people who worked for him. Abram trusted God to guide his family as they moved away. Let's pretend that we're walking with Abram, trusting God to lead us.**

Lead the children on a short journey through your church, bringing the backpack with you. Along the way, collect several items from each room to remind the children of their journey. For example, you could get a pencil and a piece of paper from the office, a book from the library, or a Bible from a classroom. Put the items in the backpack. Then lead the kids back to your classroom, and have them sit in a circle.

say ▶ **During the journey, God showed Abram a special land. God said that he'd give the special land to Abram's children someday. Abram wanted to remember that God talked to him and led him, so he built an altar. An altar is something that reminds a person of an awesome and wonderful thing God has done. In Abram's day,**

people usually built altars out of rocks. But we're going to use other things.

Take out the items from the backpack, and have the children combine the items on the floor.

say ▶ This altar reminds us of our trip through the church, and it reminds us that God has blessed us.

ask ▶ • How do you think Abram felt during his trip to a new land?

• How can you remember to trust God just as Abram did?

say ▶ Although moving to a new place can be scary, it can also be exciting. God blesses us so much! We never have to be afraid because we can trust God to guide us, just as God guided Abram.

BiBLe eXPeRienceS

Special Surprises

Supplies: map of classroom; surprises such as stickers, small toys, box of crayons, and so on

Before class, prepare a map of the classroom, with simple words or pictures to locate various areas in your room. The map should have a starting point, several stopping points along the way, and a destination. For example, the map might show the doorway as the starting point. Then it might show a dashed line to the blocks, a dashed line from the blocks to the bookcase, and a final dashed line from the bookcase to a table. At each stopping point, hide special surprises such as stickers, small toys, or a box of crayons for children to share.

Help children follow the map through the classroom to find each special surprise. Explain that when God told Abram to leave his home, God didn't give Abram a map to follow, but Abram trusted God to show him the way.

CRaftS

Moving Day

Supplies: magazines, paper, washable markers, glue sticks, scissors

Set out age-appropriate magazines, paper, washable markers, glue sticks, and scissors. Have the kids write their names on their papers. Tell the kids that sometimes when people move, they need to pack things they want to take with them in a moving van. Have the children find pictures in the magazines or draw, color, and cut out items they'd take with them if they moved. Encourage kids to glue the pictures on their paper.

ask ▶ • How would you feel if you had to move?

• How do you think Abram felt as he packed before he moved?

• Why should we always trust God?

say ▸ When Abram moved, he trusted God. If you had to move, you'd need to trust God so that you wouldn't be scared. No matter what happens, we can trust God. God blesses us with good things, and he always guides us.

Trusting God on the Go

Supplies: file folders, staplers, crayons, stickers, squares of paper

Give each child a file folder. Help the children staple down both sides of the file folder. Write "[Child name]'s Suitcase" on each file folder, and help each child fill in his or her name. Encourage kids to use the crayons and stickers to decorate their "suitcases." Then hand out the squares of paper. Encourage the children to draw pictures of items they would pack for a long trip, and have them "pack" their suitcases. Encourage each child to draw on one of the squares a picture of one way he or she can trust God. Children might draw a night light to show that they can trust God in the dark or a picture of their school classroom to show that they can trust God at school. Remind children that we can always trust God, no matter where we are or what we're doing. Have each child pack the remaining square in his or her suitcase.

ask ▸ • Why did Abram have to trust God?

• When can you trust God?

say ▸ It's very important to remember that we can trust God all the time, no matter what!

Games

The Trusting Journey

Supplies: fabric ties or scarves

Group kids in pairs. In each pair, use a fabric tie or scarf to tie a leg of one child to a leg of the other. Tell the children that they are Abram and Sarai, and have them put their arms around each other's waists. Have the children say: "We can trust God."

Then have them walk in a rhythmic beat to a designated area. Give all the children an opportunity to play the game and say the phrase again.

ask ▸ • How did Abram, Sarai, and Lot trust God in our Bible story?

• When have you trusted God?

say ▸ Abram, Sarai, and Lot trusted God to take care of them during their trip to a new home. We can trust God just as they did.

PRAYERS

Heart of Trust

Supplies: none

PRAY **Dear God,**

Help me to trust in you (stretch arms in front with palms up, then point up)

In everything I do. (Stretch arms out wide.)

Keep my heart always true (form a heart shape using both thumbs and index fingers, and place over your heart)

So that I might trust in you. (Stretch arms in front with palms up, then point up.)

In Jesus' name, amen.

- -

Circle of Trust

Supplies: none

Have children stand in a circle and hold hands as they repeat this prayer after you.

PRAY **Dear God,**

Help us to always trust you.

Thank you for your love.

Thank you for your blessings.

No matter where we travel in life,

We know you'll be there.

In Jesus' name, amen.

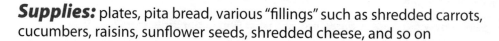

SNACKS

Pita Pocket Suitcases

Supplies: plates, pita bread, various "fillings" such as shredded carrots, cucumbers, raisins, sunflower seeds, shredded cheese, and so on

Have the children wash their hands before they prepare the snacks. Give each child a plate and half of a pita pocket. Show children that the pita pocket looks kind of like a suitcase. Tell children that they are going to "pack" their suitcases with the food items they choose. While they are packing their pita pockets, remind children that Abram and his family had to pack all their things so they could move to a new place. Abram and his family trusted God to take care of them in this new place.

When children have finished making the snack, invite one child to pray for the food.

After kids have finished their snack,

ask
- **Have you ever had to pack up your things and move to a new place? How did you feel?**

- **Do you think it was hard for Abram to move to a new place? Why or why not?**

- **How can you trust God as Abram did?**

say **Change can be very scary. When we move to a new house or town, or when we go to a new school or baby sitter, we aren't sure what it's going to be like. One thing we know for sure is that we can trust God, just as Abram trusted God in our Bible story.**

A Happy Home

Supplies: graham crackers, Hershey's Kisses or Hugs

Give each child two graham crackers. Show children how to lean the crackers together to make tents. Give each child three Hershey's Kisses or Hugs candies to represent Abram, Sarai, and Lot. Encourage kids to use their snack to replay the Bible story.

ask
- **How do you think Abram, Lot, and Sarai felt when they finally reached the end of their journey?**

- **What can you trust God to provide for you?**

say **Abram, Sarai, and Lot were so happy to be in the land of Canaan— their new home—that the Bible says they thanked God for bringing them there. We can trust God, just as Abram, Sarai, and Lot trusted God.**

SONGS

"Abram's Journey" Rhyme

Supplies: none

 say **Abram went a walkin'** (stand and walk in place)

'Cause God told him to go. (Point up to God, then into the distance.)

He trusted God with all his heart (hug self)

So very long ago. (With thumbs up, bring both hands over shoulders so thumbs point to the back.)

God Makes a Covenant With Abram

Bible Basis:

Genesis 15:1-18

Abram's Promise

Supplies:

Bible, tape; 1 sheet of black construction paper and 1 piece of white chalk per child

Before class, tape the construction paper to a classroom wall, allowing enough space for kids to work, and set the chalk nearby for use during the Bible story. Mark Genesis 15 in your Bible.

Open your Bible to Genesis 15, and show children the words.

say ▸ **Today's Bible story teaches us that God has good plans for us. The Bible says that Abram and Sarai were getting very old. They had wrinkled skin and gray hair. They were old enough to be grandmas and grandpas, but God had not given them children yet. Poor Abram. He had waited his whole life, hoping and praying for a little baby to hold and tickle, take on walks, and tell stories to.**

ask ▸ **· When did you have to wait a long time for something?**

say ▸ **Abram sighed.** Have the class sigh deeply with you. **"Well, God, I know you promised to give me lots of children, but I'm getting too old now. Did you forget me?"** Have the children show you their saddest faces. **Abram went into his tent to go to sleep.** Have the children go into pretend tents and lie down. Whenever "the Lord" talks in the rest of the story, use a deep voice.

All of a sudden, Abram heard a voice. It was the Lord! "Abram, don't be afraid. I have good plans for you."

Abram said, "Lord, I have everything I need. I have a strong tent, a good wife, lots of animals, and plenty of food to eat. The only thing I really want is a child."

The Lord answered, "Abram, I have good plans for you. I will give you your very own child! Come outside. I want to show you something special in the nighttime sky." So Abram came out of his tent to look at the sky. Have the children leave their "tents." Lead children to the pieces of black construction paper taped to the wall. Give each child a piece of white chalk to make lots and lots of dots on the black "sky." Then encourage the children to lie down and look at the stars.

God said to Abram, "Look at the heavens and count the stars." Abram looked up and saw thousands of stars in the sky. God said, "Just as you see thousands of stars in the sky, you will have thousands of children, more than you can count."

ask • How do you think Abram felt when God told him he would have that many children?

say When God showed Abram the stars, God was telling him that there would be thousands of people in his family. There would be grandmas, grandpas, aunts, uncles, and cousins—as many people as there are stars in the sky! Abram was so glad that God had good plans for him. God has good plans for us, too.

ask • How would you feel having that many people in your family?

• How can you trust God with your family?

say God has always had good plans for people. One of the good plans God had for people was to send Jesus to earth to die for our sins and forgive us. If we believe in Jesus and have a friendship with Jesus, we can live in heaven forever. Now that's a great plan!

BiBLe eXPeRieNCeS

When I Grow Up

Supplies: Bible, glow-in-the-dark stars, paper, pencils or crayons, dress-up clothes (optional)

Before class stick several glow-in-the-dark stars on your ceiling or on another high point in your room.

Have kids form a circle and sit down. Open your Bible to Genesis 15, and show children the words. Then turn off the lights in the classroom, and have children lie down on the floor. (If some children are afraid, you may want to leave the door open or leave a small light on.) Point out the stars on the ceiling.

say Abram had trusted God and followed God to a new land. Abram loved God and was very happy in the new land. But there was one thing that was still making Abram sad—Abram didn't have any children!

ask • Have you ever been sad? What made you sad?

• What made you feel better?

say One night God told Abram to go outside and look at the stars in the sky. God told Abram to count the stars. Abram probably thought that was kind of silly. Who can count the stars? There are way too many stars to count! But God told Abram that someday his family would have as many people in it as there are stars in the sky. Wow, that's a really big family! Turn on the lights, and give each child a piece of paper and a pencil (or crayons). Encourage children to draw a picture of their family and to tell a partner about their family.

God has given all of us wonderful families that love and care for us. God promised Abram that he would also have a family. This was part of God's good plan for Abram's life. God has good plans for all of us!

God cares for us and wants us to have a wonderful life and do wonderful things.

ask · **What are some things you'd like to do?**

· **What do you think you want to be when you grow up?**

· **What are some good plans God might have for your life?**

say **Let's play a game now to show each other some of the good plans God might have for our lives.** Have kids stand up one at a time and act out what they want to be when they grow up. If you have dress-up clothes, let children use them to complete their charade.

We don't know exactly what God's plans are for us, but we do know that God has good plans for each one of us, just as God had a good plan for Abram! Let's pray together right now and ask God to help us trust his plans.

pray **Dear God, we know that you have wonderful plans for us. Help us to trust your plans and to follow you. In Jesus' name, amen.**

Crafts

A Star-Studded Sky

Supplies: 1 piece of black construction paper and 20 star stickers per child, colorful chalk, hairspray

Give each child a piece of black construction paper and about 20 star stickers. Remind kids that, in today's Bible story, God promised Abram that someday there would be as many people in his family as there are stars in the sky. That's a lot of people!

ask · **What are some of the good plans that God had for Abram?**

say **God had good plans for Abram, and God has good plans for us, too! Let's think about some good plans that God might have for us.** Encourage kids to suggest a good plan that God might have for their life, such as becoming a firefighter, riding on an airplane, or going to college. Tell kids to use the chalk on their black paper to draw themselves doing the good thing they think God might have planned for their life.

ask · **How do you know that God has good plans for you?**

When kids have finished drawing, have them put the star stickers on the black paper around the picture they drew.

say **These stars can remind us that God has good plans for us, just as God had a good plan for Abram's family to have as many people as there are stars in the sky.**

You may want to spray the chalk pictures with hairspray to keep them from rubbing off.

Games

Family Stars

Supplies: chalk

Take your class outdoors, and use chalk to draw a big star on the pavement. Ask kids to stand around the star.

 say **Abram's family became very big. The people in his family were like the stars. We'll pretend that this big star is like your family. When I name someone in your family, you can say that person's name and jump into the star. Then we'll all jump out and try it again.**

For example, say, "Aunt or auntie!" The kids name an aunt, maybe Auntie Bonnie, and jump inside the star. Have the children jump out of the star, then call out a new title, such as cousin, grandma, brother, sister, or mom.

How I Wonder

Supplies: bedsheet

Have the children form two teams and sit very close to their team members. Tell one team that they are the stars in the night. Tell the other team to be Abram, and have those children close their eyes until you've covered the stars team with a sheet. Tap one child under the sheet. Have that child silently stand up, being careful to keep the other team members covered.

When the stars are ready, have Abram's team say, "Twinkle, twinkle, little star, how we wonder who you are. You are [child's name]." Give the Abram team three chances to guess who the star might be. Then pull back the sheet to reveal the real star. Have the teams reverse roles so each child can be the star at least once. Remind children that God has good plans for us.

Prayers

Action Prayer

Supplies: none

Gather the children in a circle. Repeat the prayer for each child in the circle.

PRay **Thank you, God, for who you are.** (Point up.)

Thanks for [child's name. He or she]**'s a star.** (Point to child.)

My God has good plans for me. (Point to self.)

I'm in God's big family. (Hold hands in the circle.)

In Jesus' name, amen.

Snacks

Popcorn Stars

Supplies: popped popcorn, resealable plastic bag, unpopped kernels, napkins

Before class, pop enough popcorn for each child to have a handful. Fill a small resealable plastic bag with unpopped kernels.

Give each child a handful of popcorn. Invite one child to pray and thank God for the snack before you begin. Suggest that the children pretend the popped kernels are stars, and encourage them to count how many "stars" they can eat.

As children eat, sing "My God Has Good Plans for Me" to the tune of "Mary Had a Little Lamb." Encourage children to sing along when they finish eating.

> **My God has good plans for me,**
>
> **Plans for me, plans for me.**
>
> **My God has good plans for me**
>
> **Because he loves me so.**

 · What are some good plans that God might have for your life?

Pass around a resealable plastic bag containing unpopped kernels so the children can enjoy feeling it.

say ▸ **God has good plans for the seed kernels to pop and make popcorn, just as God has good plans for us.**

Songs

Trust the Lord

Supplies: none

Use this song to teach children to trust God just as Abraham did. Sing it to the tune of "Frere Jacques."

> **Trust the Lord, trust the Lord,**
>
> **Every day, every day.**
>
> **Turn to him and pray.**
>
> **Trust him and obey.**
>
> **Every day, every day.**

Isaac Is Coming

Bible Basis:

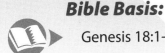

Genesis 18:1-19; 21:1-7

Supplies:

Bible, guest "Sarah" in a Bible-time costume and a pillow for her to put under her costume (outside classroom) to show she is "pregnant"

Open your Bible to Genesis 18, and show children the words.

say ▸ **Today's Bible story teaches us that God does amazing things.**

We have a special visitor coming today. Let's see if she's here yet.
Open the classroom door and invite "Sarah" in.

Come in, Sarah. Welcome. (Speak to the class.) **Friends, you remember Sarah from our Bible stories. Her name used to be Sarai, and her husband's name was Abram. Well, God changed their names because he wanted them to remember that God does amazing things.**

Sarah, tell us about the promise God has given you and Abraham.

Sarah: Hello, friends. How are you today? (Addressing one boy) I've always wanted a little boy like you. Abraham and I have never been able to have children. (Directs specific greetings and comments to each child, hugging or touching each one.) But no! (Crying a little) I never got a child! I've seen that God does amazing things, but not for me. Everybody else gets children, but not me. (Sniffling and crying some more) Now I'm way too old. Can you guess how old I am? I'm old enough to be somebody's great-grandma, but I've never even been a mom! (Crying louder) I'll never have a baby. I'm way too old, and people can't have babies when they're 90 years old. (Cries softly.)

Well, anyway, let me remember what I came here for. (Pauses.)

Oh, yes. Earlier today, my husband, Abraham, was in our tent under the huge trees. All of a sudden, he jumped up and went running off. I yelled at him, "Abraham! Don't you know an old man like you shouldn't be running around?" But he didn't hear me. I peeked out from behind the flap of the tent and saw him talking to three men. I wondered who they were. They must have been important!

Abraham came running back and was so excited! He wanted me to make a meal for the three men with our best milk and cheese. "Does this tent look like a restaurant?" I asked. Abraham then told me that he thought these men were from God. At our house? God does amazing things!

(Addressing kids) Well, don't just sit there looking at me. Come help me. Why should I do all the work around here? Can't you see how old I am?

(Children pretend to stir the dough with Sarah.)

Now we have to milk the camel. Have you ever gotten milk from a camel? I hate to milk that cranky, old camel. Once she even spit in my eye! Anyway, help me out. My old hands hurt. *(Gesturing to show hurting hands)* Give me your milk. We'll serve it to those men out there. *(Pretends to gather the milk from the children.)*

It sure is nice to have you wonderful boys and girls helping me today. *(Pauses. Acts surprised, then excited.)* Oh, they're coming over. What are they saying? Put your hand to your ear. I can't hear. Shush! Did you hear that? *(Touches hand to ear, as if listening. Then starts to snicker. Laughs louder until laughing hilariously.)*

Did you hear that? You simply won't believe what those men told Abraham. They said I was going to have a b-b-baby! An old lady like me? *(Bumbles out of the room laughing. Puts a pillow under her costume or clothes and waits a few minutes before returning to the classroom.)*

After Sarah leaves the room,

ask · **Why was Sarah laughing?**

Sarah: *(Returning)* Guess what, friends? Those men were right! *(Showing off the big belly)* Look! Yes, me! I'm going to have a baby. Wow! God does amazing things!

There's a little baby in there. I guess God really can do amazing things. A baby for an old lady like me! I've got to go tell everyone. Goodbye, friends. *(Leaves the room laughing and repeating "God does amazing things!")*

After Sarah leaves, **say** **God does amazing things!**

ask · **What amazing thing did God do for Sarah?**

· **What amazing things has God done for you?**

say **One of the most amazing things God has ever done was send his Son, Jesus, to earth. Jesus lived on earth and then died to forgive all our sins. That's amazing! God says that if we get to know Jesus and have a friendship with Jesus, we can live in heaven forever! God really does do amazing things!**

BiBLe eXPeRieNCeS

Baby Care Center

Supplies: Create a baby care center. Provide enough baby dolls so each child can play with one. Also provide accessories, such as baby wipes, bottles, rattles, blankets, and pacifiers.

Explain to the children that babies can't do anything for themselves; their parents have to do everything for them. Ask your preschoolers what they know about baby care. Have each child practice caring for a baby, including giving the baby a bottle, burping the baby, and wrapping the baby securely in a blanket. (Many preschoolers will be very familiar with baby care.)

ask • How did you take care of your babies?

• How does God take care of you?

say God gives joy. One way God gives us joy is by taking good care of us, just as you were taking good care of your baby dolls.

Special Names

Supplies: baby name book, paper, crayons

Show the baby name book to children. Tell kids that the book helps parents decide what to name their baby. Give kids a piece of paper and some crayons, and help children write their name on the paper. Look up each child's name in the book, and tell him or her what the name means. If you can't find a child's name in the book, then look up a name that sounds similar, as the names may have similar roots. Encourage kids to draw a picture of what their name means.

CRaftS

Miracles Possible

Supplies: blank paper, pencils, markers, baby lotion

Have kids write their names on their papers. Encourage children to use the markers to draw pictures of things that seem impossible to them, such as tying their shoes or riding a two-wheeled bicycle. Then have each child dip a finger into the lotion and rub the lotion onto a corner of their paper. Tell the children that the smell of baby lotion can help them remember that God made it possible for Sarah and Abraham to have a baby. Remind the children that God can do amazing things—even impossible things! Nothing is impossible with God.

ask • What impossible problem did you draw on your page?

• How does the Bible story give you hope about your problem?

say Smell the baby lotion and remember how God gave a baby to Sarah and Abraham. What seemed impossible was really possible! God does amazing things. Trust God to help you with your problems.

Handprints

Supplies: finger paint, white paper, wet wipes

> **say** ▸ **The day you were born was a very happy day for your parents. They were full of joy. God gives joy to parents when their babies are born. At the hospital, the nurses made prints of your feet and your fingers. Today we are going to make handprints for your parents to say thank you to them for taking such good care of you, just like Abraham and Sarah took good care of their baby.**

Help the children dip their hands into the finger paint and then make handprints on the white paper. Use wet wipes to wash children's hands. Set the pictures aside to dry.

> **ask** ▸ **• Why do you think your parents were so full of joy when you were born?**

> **say** ▸ **The day that Abraham and Sarah's baby was born was a joyful day for them. The day you were born was a joyful day for your parents. God gives joy to parents. This week you can also bring joy to your parents by giving them these special handprints that we made.**

Games

Isaac's Shower

Supplies: gift box containing several baby items

> **say** ▸ **Often when a baby is born, people have a party to "shower" the baby's parents with gifts. Let's pretend that we're at a baby shower for Abraham and Sarah's baby. I'll ask one of you to close your eyes and pull something out of the box. Then you can feel the item and try to guess what it is. When you guess correctly, the other children will all shout, "Boy, oh, boy! God gives joy!" Ready?**

Choose a child to go first. Have the child close his or her eyes, reach into the box, pull out an item, and try to guess what it is by touch. Remind the other kids not to say what it is. When the child guesses correctly, have all of the children shout for joy. Let each child have a chance to pull an item out of the box.

> **ask** ▸ **• Why do babies bring such joy to families?**
>
> **• What gift would you have given their baby if you had been with Abraham and Sarah?**

> **say** ▸ **God gives joy. God gave Abraham and Sarah a baby boy. God gives us our families to love us, and God gave us his own Son, Jesus! Everyone who loves Jesus will live forever in heaven!**

PRayeRS

Amazing God Prayer

Supplies: none

Have the children think of amazing things that God has done, such as making rainbows or making plants grow. Then help your children say the following prayer and complete the sentence.

PRay ▶ **Dear God,**

You are so amazing! Thank you for the amazing things that you do, such as…[have the children mention their ideas]. **Thank you for doing impossible things for us, just as you did for Abraham and Sarah.**

In Jesus' name, amen.

Action Prayer

Supplies: none

Take this opportunity to thank God for each child in your class individually. Use the following as an example:

Dear Lord,

Thank you so much for [child's name]. **Thank you for bringing** [him/her] **into our class and giving** [him/her] **to us as a special friend. Thank you for** [his/her] [special trait]. **I know** [he/she] **brings you lots of joy. In Jesus' name, amen.**

snacks

Amazing Mixture

Supplies: instant pudding mix (enough to serve your class), milk, measuring cup, airtight container with a lid to "shake" the pudding in, bowls, spoons

Have children wash their hands and sit down at the table. Remind the children that God does amazing things. Ask kids if they would like to help do something amazing. Read the instructions on the pudding box, and have one child pour the correct amount of milk into the measuring cup. Allow another child to pour the milk into the container, then another child can pour the pudding mix into the container. Place the lid on the container, and then ask the children if they think that the milk and mix will turn into pudding. Have the children take turns shaking the pudding mixture for approximately five minutes until it becomes thick.

Once it has thickened, pour it into bowls, and have one child pray for the snack.

ask · Did you believe me when I told you that we were going to turn the mixture into pudding? Why or why not?

· What are some amazing things that God does?

say Making pudding out of milk and some powdered mix was pretty amazing, but in our story today, God did something really amazing—he gave Abraham and Sarah a baby. God did amazing things for Abraham, and God does amazing things for you and me.

A Meal for Angels

Supplies: small rolls, slices of cheese, milk, paper plates and cups, blanket (if going outside for a picnic)

If possible, take the class to a grassy area outside for a picnic. Provide a blanket for the children to sit on. Remind kids that Abraham entertained his guests under the big trees. Serve the children small rolls, slices of mild cheese, and "camel's" milk. Before the snack, have each child thank God for the food and for one amazing thing God has done in the child's life or in the Bible.

ask · What is your favorite amazing story in the Bible?

· What amazing things has God done for you or your family?

say God does amazing things for us, just as he did amazing things for Abraham and Sarah!

Songs

Sarah Had a Baby Boy

Supplies: none

Sing "Sarah Had a Baby Boy" to the tune of "Mary Had a Little Lamb" to continue the celebration of Isaac's birth.

Sarah had a (hold hands on stomach)

Baby boy, baby boy, baby boy. (Cradle and rock arms.)

Sarah had a (hold hands on stomach)

Baby boy. (Cradle and rock arms.)

He brought his family joy. (Point to your happy face.)

ask · How did God give Sarah and Abraham joy?

· How does God give you joy?

say God loves us very much, and God gives us joy.

a Wife is Found for Isaac

Bible Basis:

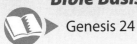

Genesis 24

Supplies:

Bible, "beautiful" bracelets, paper cups (one per child), pitcher of water, large bowl

Open your Bible to Genesis 24, and show the children the words.

say ▸ **Today's Bible story teaches us that we can seek God's direction.**

ask ▸ **• What does *direction* mean?**

say ▸ *Direction* **means choosing which way to go. Abraham told his servant to find a wife for his son, Isaac. Abraham wanted Isaac to marry a girl from his hometown that was far away, and he made his servant promise that he would find the right girl for Isaac. So the servant left with special gifts for this special girl. He took beautiful bracelets!** Show the bracelets.

As the servant got close to the city where Abraham told him he would find the girl, he stopped and prayed. Have the children kneel and pretend to be praying like the servant. **He asked God for wisdom and direction to choose the right girl for Isaac.**

ask ▸ **• Why did the servant ask God for help?**

• Think of a time you had to make a choice between two different toys or playing with two different friends. Was it hard to choose?

• Why do you think it's important to ask God for help when we have to make choices?

say ▸ **We can seek God's direction. Jesus also asked for direction from God when he was here on earth. Jesus often went away from the crowds to pray and ask God for help. He even taught his disciples how to pray and told them to "seek and you will find" (Luke 11:9). We, too, can seek and will find God's direction for our lives.**

The servant asked God to have the right girl come to the well to give water to him and to his 10 camels. Set out the pitcher of water and large bowl.

Before Abraham's servant finished praying, Rebekah came to get water from the well. Give children each a cup, and encourage them to pretend to pull water from the well as they dip their cups into the pitcher of water. **Not only did she give the servant some water without even being asked, but she also asked to give his 10 camels water, too, just as the servant had prayed!** Have the children pour their water into the bowl, pretending to share with the camels. As they pour the water, encourage them to say, "We can seek God's direction."

The servant went to Rebekah's house and asked her parents if she could marry Isaac and live far away. Rebekah and her parents agreed to let her go and marry Isaac. So the servant gave Rebekah the beautiful bracelets (hold up the bracelets), **and they left to go back to where Abraham and Isaac lived.**

ask · **How do you think the servant felt when God answered his prayer and sent Rebekah?**

· **What things can we talk to God about?**

say **God gave direction to Abraham's servant and wants to give us direction, too. All we have to do is seek God's direction.**

BiBLe eXPeRiences

Keep Praying

Supplies: paper plates, a variety of ways kids can travel: boots or shoes, a toy airplane, a toy train, a toy truck, and a "rocket ship" (Put a cardboard paper tube on a piece of yarn stretched across the class, so kids can zoom it back and forth as if it were a monorail—be sure to place it at the children's waist level so they won't choke if they accidentally walk into it.)

Set out the variety of ways kids can "travel." Tell kids that the servant prayed all through his adventure. Before kids "travel" and play with the items, pray together. Then encourage them during their play to stop and pray from time to time.

PRay **Dear Lord,**

Before we go along our way,

Lord, you hear us as we pray.

In Jesus' name, amen.

ask · **What did the servant do before the trip? During the trip?**

· **What can you do before your mom or dad drives the car?**

say **The servant prayed! Let's learn to pray to God in everything we do. God wants us to pray always. When we pray, we can ask for God's direction.**

Wedding Quilts

Supplies: quilt with a special story behind it—either yours or someone else's, construction paper, squares of white paper (cut so that each child has six squares that will fit on their one piece of construction paper), crayons or markers, glue

Show the children the quilt that you brought in. Tell children why this quilt is so special.

say ▶ **Many times at weddings the bride and groom receive a quilt as one of their gifts. Often quilts are made to tell a story.** Allow each child to choose a piece of construction paper. Give them each six squares of white paper. Encourage children to draw one picture on each square that will help tell the story of Isaac and Rebekah. Some things children could draw would be camels, a jar, Rebekah, Isaac, Abraham, the servant, or jewelry. As the children work, review the story. When they've finished drawing pictures, encourage children to glue the six squares to the construction paper.

ask ▶ • **How do you think Isaac and Rebekah would have felt to receive your beautiful quilts as wedding presents?**

• **Can you tell me about a special quilt or blanket that you have?**

say ▶ **It was a very special day for Isaac and Rebekah when they got married. God had a special plan for them, and they knew that they could seek his direction. We can seek God's direction for our lives, too!**

CRafts

Merry Maracas

Supplies: plastic pop bottles with tops (one per student), funnel, rice, glue, stickers

Give each child a pop bottle. Help each child place the funnel into the top and then pour a scoop of rice into the bottle. Line the bottle cap with glue and screw it on tightly. Let the children decorate their maracas with stickers. Have the children shake their maracas as they sing this song to the tune of "The Farmer in the Dell."

> **God shows us his way,**
>
> **We ask God every day.**
>
> **God helps us know just where to go;**
>
> **God shows us the way.**

ask ▶ • **Why do you think the servant felt like celebrating in our story today?**

• **Where can we go to learn God's direction and wisdom?**

say ▶ **In our story today, God gave wisdom and direction for the servant to find a bride for Isaac. We can seek God's direction, and he will answer us, too.**

Beautiful Gifts

Supplies: 10-inch piece of yarn per student; tube-shaped pasta, such as rigatoni; tape

Before class, cut a piece of yarn about 10 inches long for each child. Tie a piece of tube-shaped pasta to one end, and reinforce the other end with a piece of tape for easier stringing.

Give children each a piece of yarn, and direct them to the table where you have pasta set out for stringing. Tell the children that in today's Bible story a man brings beautiful gifts for a special lady. After children string the pasta, help them tie the ends together to make bracelets.

For a more colorful bracelet, dye the pasta the day before class. Pasta can be dyed a variety of colors using a mix of ¼ cup rubbing alcohol and food coloring to about 4 cups of pasta. Stir the pasta into the mixture until it's completely covered. Then spread it thinly onto newspaper to dry. The alcohol evaporates within an hour, and the colored pasta is safe for children.

PRAYERS

Walk and Talk Prayer

Supplies: none

Have children repeat each line of this prayer after you:

> **Dear God** (place a pointer finger forward and walk that way)**,**
>
> **Thank you for giving us direction**
>
> **As we walk in life.**
>
> **In Jesus' name, amen.** (Stop walking, fold hands together, and bow head.)

Snacks

Wedding Cake

Supplies: cupcake, plates, white icing, food coloring, bowls to mix colored icing, spoons, plastic bags to use for decorating (put colored frosting in, cut a small corner off, and decorate), wet wipes

Have kids sit down and use a wet wipe to wash their hands. Give each child a cupcake on a plate. Encourage children to work together to use the food coloring to tint some of the small bowls of white icing. The children should be very careful when using the food coloring since it will permanently stain anything it gets on. Make sure to leave some of the icing untinted to use as the base layer of icing on their cupcake. Help the children put the colored icing into the decorating bags. Have each child put white icing on his or her cupcake then use one of the decorating bags to make fancy decorations. As the children work, **ask** them the following question:

- **Can you tell me about a time you went to a wedding and ate wedding cake?**

say **Wedding cake is a special part of a couple's wedding. It is a way that everyone who comes to the wedding can celebrate.**

ask • How do you think Isaac and Rebekah celebrated their wedding day?

• What special foods do you think they might have eaten at their wedding?

say It's fun to think about how Isaac and Rebekah may have celebrated their wedding day. It is exciting to know that God had a special plan for their lives. God has a special plan for your life as well. We can seek God's direction, too. Let's pray and then eat our special wedding cakes.

Have one child pray, and then let the kids enjoy their snacks.

Giving Wisdom

Supplies: Bible, fortune cookies (can be found in Asian markets and local grocery stores that stock various ethnic foods)

Have the children wash their hands or use wet wipes. Give children each a fortune cookie, and let them break the cookies open. Go around the room reading the fortunes aloud to the children. Hold up the Bible. Talk to the kids about how people try to be wise and give advice, but only God can give true wisdom and direction. Encourage kids to have their parents read the Bible to them so they can know God's wisdom. Pray and thank God for wisdom. Then let the children enjoy their cookies.

SONGS

"God's Help" Rhyme

Supplies: none

As you teach the children this active rhyme, remind them that God wants to help us and we can seek God's direction. To start this rhyme, have children get down into a squatting position on the floor.

God helps me see what is right. (Place hands above eyes.)

God helps me hear him day and night. (Hold both hands behind ears.)

God helps me say what he wants me to say. (Place hands around mouth.)

God helps me grow both night and day! (Stand up slowly.)

GOD KEEPS BABY MOSES SAFE

Bible Basis:

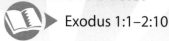

Exodus 1:1–2:10

Supplies:

baby doll in a basket, toy (or puppet) fish

Open your Bible to Exodus 1, and show children the words.

say ▶ **Today's Bible story tells us that God protects us.** Hold up the fish. **This is Frieda the Fish. She is going to tell us a story about how God protected a special baby. Frieda isn't really mentioned in the Bible; she's just going to tell us the Bible story as if she were there!**

Choose two children to be the soldiers in the story and one person to be Miriam. As Frieda (the toy fish) speaks, move her back and forth as if she were a puppet.

Frieda: **Hello, kids! I'm Frieda the Fish. My home is here in the Nile River in Egypt. I love living here! I can play and swim. It's sooo much fun being a fish! Right now, it doesn't seem to be as much fun being a person, though. A new leader has forgotten all about Joseph and how he helped them. The mean Pharaoh makes God's people, the Israelites, work way too hard! He doesn't pay them or give them a choice about working. God's people are very sad being Pharaoh's slaves.**

Shh! I hear someone coming. Crouch down as tiny as you can so nobody can see you!

Show kids how to crouch down in a little ball on the floor as if hiding. Have the two children pretend to be Egyptian soldiers and walk by the hiding children, pretending not to see them.

Soldier 1: Pharaoh wants to get rid of all of the Israelite baby boys.

Soldier 2: What a terrible job we have! Let's get it over with.

Have the soldiers walk away.

Frieda: **How mean they are! You can lift your heads now. They're gone. One day a baby boy was born to one Israelite family. They were sooo afraid when they heard what Pharaoh wanted to do. They tried to hide the baby for a while, but babies can't help crying sometimes, and they knew they couldn't hide him from the mean Egyptians much longer. So the baby's mom and sister made a special basket, put the baby in it, and then set it in the water! Shhh!**

Place the baby doll in the basket. Remind children to continue hiding. Have Miriam walk past the hiding children and pretend to secretly watch her brother float along the river.

Do you know what? God protected the family and the baby! His sister was hiding in the tall grass watching the basket to make sure the baby was safe. Do you know what happened then? Pharaoh's daughter saw the basket and had it brought to her. Have Pharaoh's daughter take the basket out of the water and look surprised.

She was surprised when she saw the baby inside! He was crying, and she felt sorry for him. Have you ever been sad and someone helped you? Have children turn to the people next to them and tell whether they have ever felt sad, as baby Moses did.

Pharaoh's daughter wanted to take care of the baby so he'd stop crying. The baby's sister went up to Pharaoh's daughter and said she could find someone to help her take care of the baby. Guess who that would be? The baby's very own mother. So the baby's sister went and got her mother to take care of him! The Pharaoh's daughter named the baby Moses because she "drew him out of the water."

Wow! No soldier ever hurt baby Moses. God protected him with a basket, a loving family, and Pharaoh's daughter. What a day! You can see a lot hanging out with a fish! Remember, kids, God protects us, too. Bye!

say ▶ Moses' family was afraid for him and didn't know how to save him from the soldiers, but they knew God would protect him. Let's cover baby Moses with a blanket like his sister and mom did. As we do, let's remember that even when we are afraid and don't know what to do, God protects us. Let the children take turns covering and hiding the baby Moses with a blanket. Encourage the children to say "God protects us" each time.

ask ▶ • How did God protect Moses?

• When has God protected you?

• How do you feel knowing God protects you?

say ▶ God protected Moses with a basket, his loving family, and Pharaoh's daughter. God protects us, too. He gives us homes, families, friends, and our wonderful church! When Jesus was here on earth he protected those around him, even his enemies. As Jesus was being dragged away by the soldiers, his friend Peter tried to attack them and stop them. Even though the soldiers were going to hurt Jesus, he still ordered Peter to put away his sword. Jesus was willing to even protect his enemies, and he will protect you each day.

BiBLe eXPeRIenCeS

Safe and Sound

Supplies: small basket with handles, string or yarn, one small "baby" toy

Cut a length of string about 7 feet long, and have two children hold each end tightly. Put the string through the handle of the basket. Place a toy inside to represent baby Moses. The basket will hang from the string or yarn while the children take turns guiding "Moses" down the "river" of string.

Have the children sit in two rows facing each other. One row will guide the basket down the string, while the other row of children will pretend to be hungry crocodiles by clapping their hands with outstretched arms. Have the "crocodiles" sit far enough away from the basket so they can't reach it but can make loud snapping noises with their hands. One child can hold the string at one end, pretending to be Moses' mother. Another child can hold the string at the other end, pretending to be the Pharaoh's daughter. The children will guide Moses safely from one end to the other and back again.

> **ask** • How did Moses stay safe in the river?
>
> • Can you tell me about times God keeps you safe?

> **say** God is like an invisible hand helping us, guiding us, and protecting us—all because he loves us. It's nice to know that God loves and protects us!

CRafts

A Basket for Moses

Supplies: brown and green paper cut into small squares, water, glue, cups, newspaper, paintbrushes, paper bowls, wax paper

Before class, cut brown and green paper into small squares. Mix an equal amount of glue and water in a cup. Lay newspaper over the tables, and have paintbrushes available for the children to brush the glue onto paper bowls. Quickly make a basket to show the children.

Show children the table where they can make a basket for baby Moses. Turn over a foam or paper bowl, and have the children paint it with a thin layer of the glue and water mixture. Then show children how to lay the colored-paper squares on the glued bowl. When they've covered the outside of the bowl with the squares, have children coat the outside with a final layer of the thinned glue mixture to give the "basket" a shiny gloss when it's dry. Use a paper towel to absorb any excess glue on the basket. Set the baskets aside to dry on wax paper to keep them from sticking.

Helpful Friends

Supplies: paper, crayons

As children arrive, lead them to a table where you've set out paper and crayons. Tell children that today they'll learn that God protects us. One of the ways he protects us is by giving us people who help. Let children draw pictures for local firefighters or police officers as thanks for the protection they provide us. During the week, mail the pictures to the firehouse or police station as an affirmation for all these people do.

- -

Bedside Baby

Supplies: basket with baby wrapped in a blanket to represent Moses, craft foam or cardstock, blue crayons, large cotton balls, 3x3-inch pieces of fabric, glue, cupcake liners

say **God protected Moses while he was in the river.** Hold up the basket with the doll in it. **God allowed Moses to float safely in the water until Pharaoh's daughter found him and took him home to live with her. Let's make a pretend baby in a basket to help us remember that God protects us, too.**

Give each child a piece of craft foam or cardstock and a blue crayon. Let each child scribble waves of water on one side of the craft foam.

Hand each child a large cotton ball and 3x3-inch piece of fabric. Ask the kids to pretend the soft cotton ball is Baby Moses, and invite them to wrap him up in a nice warm blanket. Help the kids place a drop of glue on the cloth to secure it in place.

Give everyone a paper cupcake liner, and ask the kids to place Baby Moses in the paper basket. Glue the cloth-covered cotton ball to the inside of the cupcake liner. Glue the cupcake liner to the craft foam square. When the craft is complete, allow the children to take turns pushing their paper baskets across a table (pretending that the table is the Nile River). As they do, encourage them to say: God protects us.

ask • **How did God protect baby Moses?**

• **How do you think Moses felt in his snuggly warm basket?**

• **How does it make you feel to know that God will protect you and keep you safe day and night?**

say **God protected Moses. God protects us, too. We can't see them, but God's arms are wrapped around us all day and all night. That doesn't mean we will never be hurt or sick. But even when sad things happen, God is with us. Let's give someone a hug and remember that God is with us all day long and that God protects us.**

Invite the kids to hug a friend, and whisper in their ear, "God protects us." Remind the children to take their Bedside Babies home, and put them where they will see them at night when they go to bed.

Games

God Is Our Help

Supplies: pictures of things that could scare children (examples: lightning, snakes, clowns, etc.)

> **say** When we're scared, God protects us. Let's play a game today to remind us that we don't need to be scared because we can trust God to protect us.

Have the children sit in a circle, and scatter the scary pictures face down in the middle of the circle. Have a child choose a picture, look at the picture, and say, "If I'm afraid of [scary thing on the picture], God will protect me." Then have the child return the picture face up to the pile. Have another child choose a picture and do the same. After all the kids have chosen a picture and said the Bible Point, have the group say collectively as you point to the pictures, "If I'm afraid of [snakes, clowns, lightning], I'll remember that God protects us."

> **ask** • What are you most afraid of?
>
> • What do you think big people are afraid of?
>
> • What should we remember to do when we feel afraid?

> **say** Even grown-ups are afraid sometimes, but we all need to remember that God protects us.

Down the River

Supplies: sturdy laundry basket or box, blanket

Let the kids take turns being Moses. Set out a sturdy laundry basket or a box, and have one child climb inside. Let the other kids cover him or her with a blanket or sheet. Please remember that not all children like to be covered up. Help the children push Moses down the river (across the room). The other kids can be Miriam hiding, parents praying, or Pharaoh's daughter.

Prayers

Helping Prayer

Supplies: baby doll wrapped in a blanket lying in a basket

Gather kids around the "baby Moses" in the basket.

> **say** Moses' family needed help to take care of their baby boy. God protected Moses and kept him safe in the basket until Pharaoh's daughter found him and raised him as her own son.

One at a time, have kids pick up the basket and say something they need help with, such as protection for their families as they go on vacation. Then join hands as you pray:

Dear God, thank you for your help. Thank you for watching over us always. We trust that you will protect us, just as you protected baby Moses. Have all the children join you in saying: **In Jesus' name, amen.**

snacks

Basket Boat

Supplies: paper plates, paper baking cups, coconut tinted green and blue with food coloring, jellybeans

Have children wash their hands. Distribute paper plates and paper baking cups to the children. Place one heaping tablespoonful each of the green- and blue-tinted coconut on each child's plate. Show kids how to use the blue coconut to create a river on the plate and use the green coconut to create the plants along the river. Give each child a jellybean to put into their paper baking cups to represent Moses in his basket. Allow kids to pretend to float Moses' basket on the river, or hide it among the plants along their river. Encourage the children to play and enjoy their snack.

 • **How do you think Moses' family felt while he was in the basket on the river?**

• **What should we do when we feel worried?**

• **When has God protected you?**

 When we feel worried we can talk to God. He loves you very much and watches over everything that happens to you. Just like Moses' family trusted God to keep him safe, we, too, can trust in God because God protects us.

SonGS

Moses Story Song

Supplies: baskets with baby dolls inside (one for every 2 children)

Have children sit in pairs. Provide children with baskets with baby dolls inside, and let them work in pairs during this song. Have children sit facing each other, with their legs spread apart and touching their partner's. Direct children to gently push the basket with baby Moses back and forth to each other as the song plays. Encourage them to sing along as they become familiar with the words.

Sing "Moses Story Song" to the tune of "Here We Go 'Round the Mulberry Bush." Repeat several times.

> **God protected Moses, Moses, Moses.**
>
> **God protected Moses,**
>
> **And kept him safe you see!**

God protects me every day, every day, every day.

God protects me every day,

And keeps me safe you see!

ask • How do you think Miriam felt as she watched her little brother float down the river?

• What can you do when you feel afraid?

say Whenever we feel afraid, we can pray to God and ask him to protect us. God uses lots of people to watch over us and keep us safe. God is always watching over us. Just as God helped Moses, God helps us, too.

- -

Hush, Little Moses

Supplies: none

Sing "Hush, Little Moses" to the tune of "Hush, Little Baby":

Hush, little Moses (cradle arms and rock a pretend baby)**,**

Don't be afraid. (Whisper, with fingers to lips.)

God will protect you (point up)

Where you are laid. (Palms up.)

Hush, little Moses (cradle arms and rock a pretend baby)**,**

Don't you cry. (Whisper, with fingers to lips.)

God will protect you (point up)

While you float by. (Make wave motions with hands.)

Hush, little Moses (cradle arms and rock a pretend baby)**,**

Don't make a peep. (Whisper, with fingers to lips.)

God will protect you (point up)

While you're asleep. (Fold hands to face and close eyes.)

Hush, little Moses (cradle arms and rock a pretend baby)**,**

Don't be alarmed. (Whisper, with fingers to lips.)

God will return you (stretch arms out, then pull them in)

To Mommy's arms. (Hug self.)

The Israelites Worship a Golden Calf

Bible Basis:

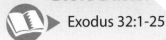 Exodus 32:1-25

The Golden Calf

Supplies:

Bible, modeling dough

Have the children sit around a table, or provide trays for them to use during this activity.

Open your Bible to Exodus 32:1-25, and show children the words.

say ▶ **Today's Bible story tells us that we should worship only God.**

Give each child a lump of modeling dough. As you talk, have children make jewelry such as rings and earrings with the dough.

say ▶ **Moses had gone up the mountain to talk with God. But he had been gone for so long that the Israelites didn't know what had happened to him. The people asked Moses' brother Aaron to make a new god for them.**

Have you ever made anything with your own hands that had as much power as God? Well, neither had Aaron or any of the other Israelites. But Aaron told the Israelites to bring him all their gold jewelry. Have the children pile all the "jewelry" together. As you tell the next part of the story, mold the dough into the shape of a cow.

Aaron melted the gold jewelry. Then he formed it into the shape of a calf, which is a baby cow. The Israelites threw a big party for the golden calf, and they worshipped it instead of God. Hold up the calf.

ask ▶ • **Can a pretend cow love us and help us like God can? Why or why not?**

• **How do you think God felt when he saw the people worshipping the golden calf?**

say ▶ **God was angry. He let Moses go down the mountain to talk to the Israelites. When Moses saw what they had done, he was very angry. God had said, worship only God. But the people were acting like the pretend cow was better than God! Moses put the golden calf into a fire until it burned up.** Let the children take turns smashing the calf until it's flat. Make sure every child gets a turn to help.

Moses taught the people to worship only God.

ask · Why did the Israelites make a golden calf?

· Why was it wrong to worship the calf?

· Why should we worship only God?

say God made us. God made the world. God loves us and cares for us like no one else can. No one is more important than God. Worship only God!

BiBLe eXPeRiences

Crayon Worship Drawings

Supplies: newspaper, foam plates, cooking oil, cotton balls, hole punch, 1 white paper plate per child, yarn, scissors, marker, crayons, paper towels, CD player, worship music CD

Before class, line a table with newspaper. Place cooking oil and cotton balls on separate foam plates and put off to the side. Punch a hole at the top of a white paper plate, and string a piece of yarn through for hanging. Prepare one of these paper plates for each child. Write each child's name on the edge of one of the plates, and write the words "I worship God" on each one.

Give each child one of the paper plates you prepared before class. Set out crayons and cue your CD to your children's favorite worship music.

say God wants us to worship only him. We're going to make some beautiful drawings that you can hang in your bedroom windows. As you make your picture, worship God and tell him you love him and will worship only him.

With worship music playing in the background, encourage your children to sing and draw freely, pressing hard with the different colors of crayons on one side of the paper plates. Encourage them to fill in as much of the white areas as possible with the colors.

After several minutes of coloring, set out the foam plates of oil and cotton balls. Have each child turn his or her paper plate over, dip a cotton ball in the oil, and rub it generously all over the opposite side of the plate until the crayon shines through. Give each child a paper towel to rub off the excess oil. Then encourage kids to hold their plates up to the light. Point out how the light shines through their drawings, just as God's love shines through us when we worship only God.

ask · What are some ways you like to worship God?

say We can worship only God through everything we do each day. There are lots of different ways to worship God. We can worship God when we sing, run and play, dance, or make things for others. Jesus worshipped God by listening to him, telling others about God, and by loving the people around him. When we know and love Jesus, we can ask him to help us worship only God, too.

Alphabet Worship

Supplies: none

Ask kids to form a circle.

say ▸ **The Bible says we should worship God alone. Worshipping God is easy—there are so many different reasons to worship God! Let's think of some of those reasons now. Let's go around the circle and name the letters of the alphabet. For every letter, we'll name a reason to worship God.**

Have kids take turns around the circle, with each child naming a letter of the alphabet and a reason to worship God that begins with that letter.

CRafts

Room Only for God

Supplies: heart drawings (make one and photocopy the others for the children), red crayon for each child, pen, scissors, stiff paper, glue sticks

Before class, draw an 8-inch heart on a piece of blank paper and photocopy the others for the children. Cut out several cross shapes from stiff paper.

Distribute the heart drawings and write children's names on them.

Show the children how to use glue sticks to glue a cross shape you prepared inside the heart on the page. Give each child a red crayon. Have the children each color the heart in completely, coloring over the cross as well. Caution the children to color lightly so they won't move the cross from its place.

say ▸ **We don't know what God looks like, so we often use a cross to show we are thinking of God. When we love God, it's as if God lives right inside our hearts. Right now, the hearts on your papers are empty. Let's change that and show that we worship only God.**

Show the children how to carefully peel the crosses off the hearts. When children have finished, they'll have red hearts with white crosses inside.

ask ▸ • **Why should we worship only God?**

• **How can we show God that he alone is inside our hearts?**

say ▸ **We worship only God because he made us, he loves us, and he cares for us like no one else can! God deserves all our worship, love, and thanks.**

Games

Worship God

Supplies: none

Play a game like Simon Says. Have the leader stand up and say, "Worship God," as he or she leads the other children in doing one thing to worship God, such as sing, twirl, or hop. Tell kids that if the leader doesn't say, "Worship God" before he or she does the actions, then they shouldn't follow the actions. If a child follows the actions when the words aren't said, that child becomes the next leader. Remind children that there are many ways to worship, but we should worship God alone.

- -

Big, Big Cow

Supplies: masking tape, blocks

Use masking tape to make an outline of a simple cow shape on the floor, and set out blocks. Have children fill in the cow shape with the blocks. Talk about the Bible story as kids work, and remind them that we should worship only God.

Prayers

Action Worship Prayer

Supplies: none

Have children stand in a circle, and explain that they're to say "We worship only you" after you say each line of the following prayer.

 God, you made everything. (We worship only you.)

God, you are greater than anyone or anything. (We worship only you.)

God, you care for us. (We worship only you.)

God, you are never wrong. (We worship only you.)

God, you give us what we need. (We worship only you.)

Thank you, God. (We worship only you.)

In Jesus' name, amen.

snacks

Golden-Calf Snack

 **allergy alert**

Supplies: crispy-rice treat or graham cracker for each child

Have the children wash their hands (or use wet wipes) and then sit down to prepare their snack. Give each child a crispy-rice treat or a graham cracker. Let the children use their teeth to nibble "golden calves" shapes out of the bars. Even though children may not be able to perfectly create cow shapes from the treats, they'll have fun enjoying their snack while reviewing the Bible story. Have children say, "Worship only God!" and then destroy the calves by eating them.

ask
- **Why was God angry with the Israelites?**
- **Why did Moses destroy the golden calf?**

say Moses destroyed the golden calf because the people were worshipping it. God tells us that we should worship only God. Let's thank God for being our king and for providing our snack. Invite a child to pray for the snack.

 songs

Worship God Only

Supplies: none

say The Bible says, "Have no other gods before me." Let's say it together. Lead the children in repeating the verse with you: "Have no other gods before me."

Have two children stand and face each other with their hands together over their heads as in the game London Bridge. Direct the other children to form a line and take turns walking under the "bridge" during the song.

Lead the children in singing "Worship God Only" to the tune of "Pop! Goes the Weasel."

> **"Have no other gods before me."**
>
> **This is what God tells us.**
>
> **God wants to be first in our lives.**
>
> **Worship God only!**

At the end of each stanza, have the children playing the bridge drop their arms to choose a friend. Then allow children to switch roles.

Afterward, have children sit down.

say God wants us to choose him just as you chose friends during our game. God tells us to love him more than anything. We must worship only God.

GOD SENDS PLAGUES on EGYPT

Bible Basis:

Exodus 7:8–10:29

Powerful Persuasion

Supplies:

Bible

Have kids form a circle and sit down. Open your Bible to Exodus 7–10, and show children the words.

 say ▶ **Pharaoh kept God's people, the Israelites, in Egypt for a very long time. He made them build beautiful palaces and tall pyramids and wouldn't let them leave. He thought he was the strongest king ever, but there was someone even stronger—God!** Lead children in shouting: **Nothing matches God's power!**

The mean Pharaoh made God's people slaves and worked them harder and harder all the time. Every day the people cried to God to set them free. Then one day God said, "That's enough of that mean Pharaoh! I'll send Moses to set you free."

Moses prayed to God for help. Encourage children to fold their hands and pray, "Dear God, help me set your people free."

So God turned all of Egypt's water red. (Run fingers back and forth like water.)

It looked as if the water was dead. (Flip hands over so they're palms up.)

After God turned the water red, Moses went to Pharaoh and asked, "Will you let my people go?" But mean Pharaoh still wouldn't change his mind. Have kids shout, "No way!" as they shake their index finger.

Moses prayed to God for help. Encourage children to fold their hands and pray, "Dear God, help me set your people free."

So God sent a bunch of frogs to cover all the land. (Hop like a frog.)

There were so many, you couldn't even see the sand! (Keep hopping.)

Moses went to Pharaoh and asked, "Will you let my people go now?" But even the frogs didn't change his mind. Have kids shout, "No way!" as they shake their index finger.

Moses prayed to God for help. Encourage children to fold their hands and pray, "Dear God, help me set your people free."

So God sent little gnats and flies (twinkle fingers like bugs)

That got in people's hair, nose, and eyes. (Touch hair, nose, and eyes.)

Moses went to Pharaoh and asked, "Will you let my people go now?" But even with all those flies, Pharaoh didn't change his mind. Have kids shout, "No way!" as they shake their index finger.

Moses prayed to God for help. Encourage children to fold their hands and pray, "Dear God, help me set your people free."

God gave the people sores and made the animals sick. (Rub arms and belly.)

He sent hail and locusts to kill the plants—there was nothing left to pick! (Look around and shrug shoulders.)

Moses went to Pharaoh and asked, "Will you let my people go now?" But even with all that had happened, Pharaoh wouldn't change his mind. Have kids shout, "No way!" as they shake their index finger.

Moses prayed to God for help. Encourage children to fold their hands and pray, "Dear God, help me set your people free."

So God made the daytime into night (cover eyes)

And gave all the people quite a fright! (Put hands over mouth.)

God showed Pharaoh that nothing matches God's power!

ask • **How do you know God is powerful?**

• **How can you thank God for his power?**

BiBLe StoRY eXPeRienCes

Attractive Power

Supplies: large horseshoe magnets, metal objects

> NeVeR use small magnets WiTH younG CHiLDRen. Not onLy aRe tHey a CHoKinG HaZaRD, But if SWaLLoWeD, magnets can attRact eaCH otHeR inSiDe tHe BoDy anD cauSe seRious HaRm oR DeatH.

Place metal objects such as paper clips, staples, metal washers, and screws on the table, along with several large horseshoe magnets. Form pairs, and have one child use a magnet to pick up a metal object. Then have the second child try to take the object off of the magnet using another magnet.

ask ▸ • How did it feel when you picked up things with your magnet?

• How can God use his power to help you when you're afraid?

say ▸ God's power is like this magnet. He can pick up your fears and take them away. Nothing matches God's power.

Just as you are bigger than what you made, God is bigger and stronger than everything he made. Nothing can match God's power.

ask ▸ • Do you think the moon is bigger than God? Have children shout: "Nothing matches God's power!"

• Is thunder stronger than God? Have children shout: "Nothing matches God's power!"

say ▸ Our God is loving and strong, and nothing matches God's power!

CRafts

A Trip to Plan

Supplies: blank white paper, pencils, crayons

Option: Instead of having the children draw and color on their white paper, have old magazines available for the children to cut or tear out items they would bring on a trip.

Give each child a piece of paper and write kids' names on the papers. Have the children use pencils to draw things they would bring on a trip. Then have them color the items with crayons.

say ▸ Sometimes new things scare us, like moving to a new place or going on a long trip. But we don't have to be afraid because our God is strong!

ask ▸ • Have you ever gone on a trip? Where?

• What would you take with you?

say ▸ Sometimes when things change, we feel afraid, but all we have to do is tell God about it. He's right here beside us. He's more powerful than anything we're afraid of and he'll help us to not be afraid.

- -

Bouncy Bugs

Supplies: Bible, colored yarn, safety scissors, florists' wire, chenille wire, wiggly eyes

Briefly review the story of the 10 plagues, especially the part about the locusts. Have volunteers read aloud Exodus 10:3-20. Then read aloud Psalm 147:5. Tell kids that the plagues showed how powerful God is and that nothing matches God's power.

Give each child at least 6 feet of yarn. Have each child hold one hand horizontally so the thumb is on top and the palm is facing in. Show kids how to wrap the yarn around their hands, keeping their fingers together. (The more yarn kids use, the puffier their bugs will be.) When kids reach the end of their yarn, help them carefully pull the wound yarn off of their hands and pinch it in the middle to form figure eights. Then hand out 5-inch sections of yarn, and show students how to tie them around the middle of their bundles. Have kids cut off the leftover strands.

Distribute 9-inch lengths of florists' wire, and help kids wrap one end of the wire around their knots a few times. When kids have secured one end of the florists' wire to the yarn, have them cut the looped ends of their figure eights and fluff up the loose strands of yarn. Allow kids to decorate the bugs using wiggly eyes and chenille wire. The bugs will bounce on their stems!

Make a Mountain

Supplies: enough modeling dough for every child

Give each child a small portion of modeling dough. Ask the children to mold it into the shape of something big like a mountain, the sun, or the moon. When the children are finished, have each child tell what they've made.

ask • How did you feel when you made something big?

• How did you think God felt when he sent the plagues to Egypt?

say God is stronger than anything!

PRAYERS

Action Prayer

Supplies: none

Have the kids repeat this prayer after you or say a spontaneous prayer of their own.

pray Dear God,

Thank you for protecting me

When I am afraid.

Your power is all around to see

In everything you've made.

In Jesus' name, amen.

God's Never-Ending Power

Supplies: Bible, fan

Talk with kids about the different sources of energy we use to power our televisions, cars, radios, bicycles, and so on. Then talk about how different the power of wind is from all the others—it doesn't cost any money, and it never runs out.

Read aloud Psalm 147:5. Have kids close their eyes and think about God's power. As they sit with their eyes closed, tell them to ask God to give them power in their lives.

Then turn on your fan, and slowly blow it across each child's face as he or she prays. Leave the fan on, and set it to the side. Allow kids to sit in front of the fan and pray again if they choose.

Snacks

Lovely Locusts

Supplies: celery, softened cream cheese, crackers, plastic knives, small paper plates

Before class, cut the celery into 2-inch lengths.

Give each child a length of celery. Show kids how to spread the cream cheese in the celery "trough." Then demonstrate how to stick two crackers in the cream cheese as locust wings.

Thank God for the snack, then talk about the Bible story as kids enjoy their treats.

Songs

God Told Moses

Supplies: none

Have your children stand up and do the motions for the verses. Sing "God Told Moses" to the tune of "Did You Ever See a Lassie?"

> **God told Moses, "Take my people** (rock back and forth holding hands with a partner)
> **From Pharaoh—he's evil!"**
> **God told Moses, "Take my people**
> **From Pharaoh right now!"**
>
> **So Moses told Pharaoh** (one partner points away)**,**
> **"The Israelites must go."**
> **But old Pharaoh, he said,**
> **"Oh, no! They're staying with me."** (Second partner points down.)
>
> **God sent frogs and gnats and locusts** (act like frogs and flies)
> **And flies and diseases.**
> **Finally Pharaoh changed his mind**
> **When his firstborn son died** (skip in a circle)**.**
> **"Take God's people—please go!"**
> **So the Israelites were free**
> **To go worship the Lord.**

GOD SENDS QUAIL AND MANNA

Bible Basis:

Exodus 16:1-26

A Divine Dinner

Supplies:

Bible, large blanket, package of marshmallows, plates, assorted lunchmeats

ALLERGY ALERT

Before class, place assorted lunchmeats on two plates.

Have kids form a circle and sit down. Open your Bible to Exodus 16, and show children the words.

say ▶ **God had helped Moses and the people escape from Egypt, and now they were no longer slaves. When they left Egypt, they began to walk in the desert. They walked and walked and walked.** Encourage kids to march together in a circle for a few minutes. Then stop and begin to complain.

I'm so tired. We've been walking forever. Wipe your brow and act very tired. I'm hungry, too. Does anyone have any food? There's no food here! We're going to starve to death. This isn't any fun. We were better off in Egypt. At least in Egypt we had food! Encourage kids to sit back down.

The Israelites were angry with God and with Moses because there was no food. They complained and complained and complained. They whined and whined and whined. Then one day God finally said, "Enough!" God told the Israelites that he would provide for them.

Spread a large blanket on the floor, and direct kids to sit on the blanket. Then open a package of marshmallows, and empty the marshmallows over kids' heads. Encourage each child to pick up one marshmallow and eat it.

say ▶ **Every morning God sent bread to the Israelites. The bread was white and tasted sweet. God told the Israelites to pick up just enough bread—not too much—for each person in their family.**

Hold up two plates of assorted lunchmeats and "fly" the two plates down to the blanket. Encourage kids to snack on the lunchmeats.

say ▶ **Every evening God sent birds so the Israelites would have meat to eat. God sent the bread and birds to the Israelites so they wouldn't**

be hungry and so they'd remember that God provides everything we need.

When you're finished telling the story, lead children in this simple action rhyme:

God's people were tired and hungry; they'd walked and walked and walked. (Rub tummy and march in place.)

"We had more food in Egypt," they grumbled and whined and talked. (Point over your shoulder, and then cross arms over your chest.)

They yelled at God; they complained and whined. (Shake your finger, and stick your bottom lip out in a pout.)

Then God sent bread and meat on which they dined. (Twinkle hands down from above to imitate falling rain, and then pretend to eat.)

"Don't worry or fret, I'll provide for you," God said. (Shake your head, and then hug yourself.)

And God provides for us, too, from morning till bed. (Point to yourself, spread your fingers open wide like a sun, and then put hands under your head to look as if you're sleeping.)

 • **How did God help the Israelites when they were hungry?**

• **How can you trust God to provide for you?**

CRafts

Heaven in My Home

Supplies: house drawings (draw an outline of a house on a piece of a paper and photocopy one for each child), pen, magazines, glue sticks

Place glue sticks and magazines filled with pictures on a table. Distribute the house drawings, and write children's names on them. Remind children that just as God gave the Israelites food, he gives us what we need, too. Instruct children to look through the magazines for pictures of good things God gives them, such as clothes, families, and food. Show kids how to tear out the pictures and glue them to their papers.

 • **What good things does God give us that are inside our homes?**

• **What good things does God give us that are outside our homes?**

• **What could we do to say "thank you" to God?**

say ▶ **God gives us what we need. Just look at all the things God gives you inside and outside your homes! God will always take care of us.**

Bird Feeders

Supplies: yarn or chenille wire, bread slice for each child, paper plates, plastic knives, honey, bird seed, sandwich-size resealable plastic bags

Before class, poke pieces of yarn or chenille wire through the tops of bread slices. Tie or twist the ends of each to form a loop hanger. You'll need one piece of bread with a hanger for each child.

Set the bread aside to dry out for a day or two, or put it in a warm oven to speed up the process. (If the bread is too dry, it'll crumble when the kids spread honey on it.)

say ▶ **God gave the Israelites the food they needed in the desert. He gave them quail, which were small birds, and manna, which was like bread. Let's make something to feed creatures smaller than us— birds—just as God fed his people manna.**

Set out a few paper plates with birdseed so the children can reach them. Give each child a paper plate and a piece of the bread with a hanger on it. Have kids spread honey on their bread with the plastic knives. Then show your children how to press the bread, honey side down, into the birdseed until the seeds stick to the honey. Then have them put their bird feeders into plastic bags to take home.

say ▶ **God gives us what we need, just as he did for the Israelites when he gave them quail and manna. When you have your mom or dad help you hang up your bird feeder, you will be giving the birds what they need—just as God gives us what we need. God knows that we need Jesus more than anything else. God sent Jesus to earth so that we could have a friendship with him. Let's think about what other things God gives us and thank him for loving us and sending Jesus.**

Games

Sock Match

Supplies: 5 pairs of socks in different colors and sizes

Collect about five pairs of socks in different colors and sizes. (Be sure the size difference is very obvious, and limit the pairs of socks so preschoolers won't feel overwhelmed.) Place one sock from each pair somewhere in the room where preschoolers can find it easily. Place the other socks in a pile on a table.

ask ▶ • **How do you think the Israelites felt when God gave them what they needed?**

• **How do you feel when you think of the things God gives you?**

• **What are some other ways we can show God we are thankful?**

say ▶ **God gives us what we need. Each sock on the table needs its matching sock. Choose a sock, and look in the room for the matching sock. This game can remind us to look every day for the things God gives us so we can thank him. God will always care for us. We can show God how happy we are that he loves us by praising him for his good and loving gifts. When you find a matching sock, hold the socks up in the air and shout "Praise God!"**

PRAYERS

Action Prayer

Supplies: none

Have children repeat each line of the following prayer. Ask each child to choose one of the lines and act it out.

PRAY Thank you, God, for eyes to see.

Thank you, God, for family.

Thank you, God, for ears to hear.

Thank you, God, for clothes to wear.

Thank you, God, for food to eat.

Thank you, God, for friends to meet.

Thank you, God, for all you bring.

Thank you, God, for everything.

In Jesus' name, amen.

SNACKS

Desert Snack

Supplies: for each child: 1 resealable plastic bag, 1 graham cracker, a few raisins, 1 plastic spoon

Have the children wash their hands (or clean their hands using wet wipes) and then sit down to prepare their snack. Give each child a resealable plastic bag with a graham cracker sealed inside. Explain to children that a desert is a hot, dry place with very little water and lots of sand. Let children crush the crackers into crumbs and pretend that the crumbs are the sands of the desert. Add a few raisins to each bag, and reseal the bag so the child can shake it. Then distribute plastic spoons so children can search for food just as the Israelites did.

ask • What kinds of things does God give you to eat?

• How can we thank God for giving us such good food?

say The Israelites were angry because they forgot that God gives us what we need. Even so, God gave them good food. Instead of being angry like the Israelites, let's thank God for caring for us and providing our snack. Invite a child to pray for the snack.

Me and My Manna

Supplies: popped popcorn, a clean bedsheet or a piece of plastic sheeting, and enough small paper bags for each child to have one

say ▶ **Today we are going to find out what it was like for the Israelites to wander around in the sandy desert.** Have children follow your lead as you take them through the desert. **Drag your feet through the hot sand. Climb up that next tall dune. Oops! You went the wrong way! Turn around and go back. Imagine that you had been wandering for 45 days and your tummy was growling. Start to grumble about how hungry you are as you keep walking and walking. Now stop grumbling because it's getting dark and you're too tired to even talk! Lay down with your eyes closed. Keep your eyes closed until I tell you it's morning.** Leave an area open so you can spread out the sheet or plastic with a layer of popcorn spread over it while the children have their eyes closed.

The Lord heard the grumbling of his people, and he sent a miracle in the morning. When the grumbly people woke up, there was "manna" scattered all over the ground. They gathered just enough to eat that day. Give each of the children a bag. Have them each fill up a bag and then sit down to eat their "manna" snack.

Songs

God Is So Good

Supplies: none

Sing "God Is So Good." After the children have learned the words, have them share some of the ways God is so good to them. Create new verses by replacing the words "is so good" with "gives us." Then have children name things God gives them.

> **God is so good.**
>
> **God is so good.**
>
> **God is so good.**
>
> **He's so good to me.**
>
> 1. God gives us [food].
>
> 2. God gives us [love].

After you sing the song, have children thank God for being so good to them.

God Gives Moses the Ten Commandments

Bible Basis:

Exodus 19:16–20:21

Supplies:

Bible, a male toy figure, "boulders" made out of large brown grocery sacks filled with crumpled newspaper, a flat rock, piece of chalk, small cotton balls

Open your Bible to Exodus 19:16–20:21 and show the children the words.

say Today's Bible story tells us what we need to do to show that we love God.

Bring over the boulders you or the children made beforehand and let kids build a mountain. Have the children form a circle around the mountain when it is finished.

say **One day as the Israelites were camped under this huge mountain called Mount Sinai, they began to feel the ground moving.** Have the children hold hands and rock from side to side like an earthquake. **They could hear trumpets sounding and thunder rumbling.** Have the children clap hands and pound on the floor. And they could see lightning, fire, and smoke coming from the very top of the mountain. Point to the top of your mountain.

ask • **How would you feel if you were standing at the bottom of this loud, shaking mountain?**

say Moses told the people not to be afraid; God was calling Moses to come to the top of the mountain. So the people stepped away from the mountain, and Moses obeyed God and met him at the top of the mountain. Have the children take a small scoot back from their mountain. Walk the toy figure up the mountain and set it there.

God loved Moses very much, and he wanted to give Moses good rules to follow. While Moses was listening to God on Mount Sinai, God began to carve into stone ten important rules, called the Ten Commandments, for all the people to follow and obey. God wanted the Israelites to have the Ten Commandments because God loved them and wanted them to know how they could love him back. Take out the flat rock and scribble some writing on the rock with the piece of chalk.

God's number one rule says, "I am the only real God. Make me more important than everything else." That means God is the greatest, the most powerful, and the best.

ask • What's something that you think God is the best at?

say We say we love God when we tell him he's the best.

God's second rule tells us to worship only God and not to make statues of other gods. We show we love God when we worship only him.

ask • How can we worship God?

say God's third rule tells us to say God's name nicely.

ask • How can you say someone's name nicely?

say You might call adults Mr. or Mrs. and use their last names instead of using their first names. We show we love God when we say his name using a nice meaning like God or Father.

God's fourth rule tells us to rest on the seventh day and remember God.

ask • What are some ways you remember people?

say We remember people when we think about them or when someone reads to us about them. We show we love God each time we stop and think about how good he is to us.

ask • How can we show God we love him?

• What's one thing you can do this week to show how much you love God?

say We can come to church and love God more than anyone or anything else in the whole world. When Jesus was here on earth, he showed his love for God by always listening and obeying God even when it was hard. When we know Jesus, we can ask him to help us show God that we love him.

God's fifth good rule says, "Obey your mom and dad." By obeying our moms and dads, we treat our parents kindly and that makes God happy.

ask • How did you obey your mom or dad this week?

say God's sixth good rule says, "Don't hurt anyone."

ask • How do you feel when someone hurts you?

• How should we treat others?

say God's seventh good rule says, "Be true to the person you marry."

God's eighth good rule says, "Don't take anything that's not yours."

ask • Have you ever taken something that wasn't yours? What happened?

say God's ninth good rule says, "Always tell the truth." When we're honest and tell the truth we make God and our friends happy because God says to treat others kindly.

God's tenth good rule says, "Don't wish for something that's not yours." When our friend gets something new and we don't try to take it away, we make God happy because God says to treat others kindly. God's rules teach us to be kind to others. When we are kind, God is happy.

ask > • Which of the Ten Commandments do you remember?

> • What is one kind thing you can do for someone today?

say > When we follow God's good rules, we make God happy! When Jesus was on earth, he made God happy by being kind to others, too. He never made fun of anyone, and he always had time to spend with people. When Jesus is our friend, we can ask him to help us be a kind friend, just like he was.

BiBLe eXPeRienCes

Following God's Rules

Supplies: modeling dough, rolling pins, pencils

Place modeling dough on the table along with some rolling pins and pencils. Give children each a handful of modeling dough and have them roll out the dough. Have kids create their own tablets to draw God's good rules on. Show children how to push their pencils into the dough to create pictures of some of God's rules.

ask > • How do you think God felt when he wrote his good rules on the stone tablets for us?

> • What's one way we can show our love to God every day?

say > One of the most important rules is that we love God. Let's show God we love him by making good choices to follow his rules.

Dress and Obey

Supplies: dress-up clothes

Explain that we can show that we love God by obeying God's rules. Have children dress up and act out obeying rules. Encourage children to form a circle and call out, "God says to [pray]." Have children follow your instructions. Other examples include pretending to help a friend, pretending to get dressed for church, or pretending to give hugs to show love.

ask > • How could the Israelites show love to God?

> • How can you show love to God?

say > Moses told the people that we should love God. We can show we love God by obeying him.

Crafts

Cloud Mobile

Supplies: blue and white construction paper, scissors, pencils, quilt batting or cotton balls, glue, blue or white yarn, stapler, hangers (one per child)

say ▶ **Mount Sinai was the name of the mountain Moses climbed. He came down from this mountain with the Ten Commandments God gave him. The Bible tells us there was a thick cloud over Mount Sinai. Today we'll make a hanging mobile to remind us of those thick clouds that covered the mountain.**

Show the children how to draw clouds and cut them out. Each child should have three to five clouds. Tear off pieces of quilt batting or cotton balls, and let kids glue them to both sides of their clouds.

Give each child one piece of yarn for each cloud. Help kids tie a knot in one end of the yarn. Then help them staple the knotted end of the yarn to the edge of the clouds. Next, tie the other end of the yarn along the hanger, allowing the clouds to hang at different lengths.

say ▶ **When you look at your cloud mobile, remember that one of the rules God gave Moses was to love God. Just as the Israelites loved God, we love God, too!**

Fingerprint Friends

Supplies: blank paper, washable stamp pad, wet wipes, colored pencils

Distribute the paper to the children. Set out the stamp pad, along with wet wipes and colored pencils.

say ▶ **God says to treat others kindly. We can be kind to everyone we see! Let's create some people we can be kind to.**

Show children how to make fingerprints on their pages. Have the children turn the fingerprints into people they can be kind to by adding facial features and bodies to the fingerprint "heads."

ask ▶ **• Who can you be kind to?**

• What kind things can you do?

say ▶ **We can be kind to lots of people! God says to treat others kindly. We can learn how to treat others kindly by remembering the ways Jesus treated people when he was here on earth. Jesus loved and cared for his disciples and the people around him. When we know Jesus, we can ask him to help us love and treat everyone around us kindly, too.**

Games

Building Mount Sinai

Supplies: connecting blocks, such as LEGO bricks

Place connecting blocks on a table and have the children work in small groups to build a mountain to represent Mount Sinai where God gave Moses the Ten Commandments.

ask • **How do you think Moses felt when he came down the mountain after being with God?**

• **What are some ways we can treat God and others kindly?**

say **God gave us many good rules to follow. God wants us to love him and to love others just as we like to be loved. God says to treat others kindly and think of them before we think of ourselves. That's one way we can make God number one in our lives.**

Prayers

Ten Handy Rules

Supplies: none

Have kids stand in a circle and repeat this prayer after you. Then teach the motions and have the kids say the prayer again.

pray **Thank you, God, for 10 good rules** (raise up both hands with all 10 fingers outstretched)**;**

They are like 10 precious jewels. (Turn around once, waving both hands from side to side.)

I love you, Lord! (Reach up and pretend to give God a hug.)

In Jesus' name, amen.

Snacks

Tablets of Grahams

Supplies: paper plates, graham crackers, marshmallow crème, craft sticks

Have the kids wash their hands before making the snacks. Pass out paper plates, graham crackers, marshmallow crème, and craft sticks. Have kids pretend to write rules on their graham crackers by dipping their craft sticks into the crème and spreading it on the crackers. When they have finished, have the children snap their crackers to remind them that we break (or disobey) God's rules all the time, but God still loves us. Remind children that God gives us good rules to follow and good things to eat, all because he loves us.

• **What's one good rule God gave Moses?**

• **What good rule helps you show love to God?**

 When we obey God's Ten Commandments we show that we love God.

Hearts-Full-of-Love Snack

Supplies: loaf of sliced bread, heart shaped cookie cutters, craft sticks, jam

Have the children wash their hands (or clean them with wet wipes) and then sit down to prepare their snack. Have children use a heart-shaped cookie cutter to cut heart shapes out of bread. Then set out craft sticks for children to use to spread jam on the bread to create heart-shaped sandwiches.

 • **Who did Moses tell the Israelites to love?**

• **What are different ways you can show you love God?**

 Let's thank God for giving us special rules and for providing our snack. Invite a child to pray for the snack.

Sharing Snack

Supplies: cups, plates, napkins, crackers, cheese (cut into squares), juice

Have the children wash their hands (or use wet wipes) and then sit down to prepare the snack. Have kids form two groups of equal size. Ask the first group to set out enough cups, plates, and napkins for everyone. Ask the second group to make enough cracker-and-cheese sandwiches for everyone. Pour juice and then have members of each group share what they prepared with the members of the other group. Point out that when we share, we're listening to God. God says to treat others kindly.

 • **How does it feel when someone shares with you?**

• **Who do you like to share with? Why?**

 God likes us to share and God says to treat others kindly. Let's thank God for giving us special rules and for providing our snack. Invite a child to pray for the snack.

Moses Sends Spies Into the Promised Land

STORY 13

Bible Basis:

Numbers 13:1–14:23

Supplies:

Bible

Open your Bible to Numbers 13:1–14:23 and show the children the words.

say ▸ **Today's Bible story tells us to stand up for God.**

Choose two children to be Joshua and Caleb. Tell the rest of the kids that they will be the other spies.

say ▸ **I'm going to tell our Bible story today, and I'll need your help to do it. Listen very closely as we pretend to be the spies Moses sent out. God told Moses to send 12 spies to check out the land called Canaan. Canaan was the land God had brought the Israelites to live in. Let's all pretend we're going to spy on the land. Lie down on your tummies and slide across the floor like a spy.** You might want to join the children and lead them on their stomachs around the room. Then have children return and form a circle.

Spies, look at this beautiful land. There are lots of yummy fruits like grapes and there are also vegetables! We never had any of these good foods when we were in the desert. I see other things, too, like milk and honey. We haven't eaten those in a long time!

ask ▸ **· How big do you think the grapes were?** Encourage the kids to show you with their hands.

say ▸ **We don't know for sure how big the grapes were, but the Bible says that two men carried one bunch of grapes on a long pole. That's big!**

Tell the children to get into groups of three, and choose one child in each group to be the grapes. Have the grapes stand in between the other two kids in their group, leaning on their shoulders while they "carry" the grapes a short distance. When all the kids have had a chance to be the grapes, tell children to return to the circle.

say ▸ **Look at the big people who live here—they're giants, and they look very strong. Do you see them?** Have kids pretend to see the giants.

Spies, let's go back and tell Moses that the land looks great but we're afraid of the giants who live here.

ask ▸ **· Would you be afraid of people who were as tall as our ceiling? Why or why not?**

say ▸ **Every one of the spies is afraid of the giants except for you two.** Look at the two children who are pretending to be Caleb and Joshua.

ask ▸ • **How come you're not afraid?** Let the two children make up their own brave answers.

say ▸ **All of the other spies say that we can't attack those people because they're bigger and stronger than we are. But you aren't afraid. You're so brave.** Have Joshua and Caleb stand up and say, "We will stand up for God! He will help us fight the giants, and we will win!"

ask ▸ • **Why do you think Joshua and Caleb weren't afraid of the giants?**

• **Why do you think they were so sure God would help them?**

say ▸ **God can make us brave and strong when we stand up for him as Joshua and Caleb did. God wants us to tell the truth even when others don't believe us. God was happy that Joshua and Caleb stood up for him, so later on God let them live in Canaan. When Jesus was here on earth, he stood up for God, too! He told people the truth and showed them how to follow God. When you have Jesus for a friend, he can help you stand up for God.**

BiBLe eXPeRieNCeS

A Giant Feast

Supplies: pictures of different fruits and vegetables, modeling dough

Show the children pictures of different fruits and vegetables, and then place the pictures on the table. Give the children modeling dough, and let them create clusters of grapes and the fruits or vegetables they see in the pictures. Remind the children that one of the best things about the land of Canaan was the big fruits and vegetables God wanted the people to have.

ask ▸ • **Why were Joshua and Caleb so excited to go to the land of Canaan?**

• **How can we stand up for God like Joshua and Caleb did?**

say ▸ **God helped Caleb and Joshua be strong and brave, and not be afraid to go into the new land. God helps us be strong and brave. We can stand up for God, too!**

CRafts

Spying for God

Supplies: paper, crayons or markers, shallow bowls, tempera paint, unsharpened pencils

Distribute the paper and have kids write their names on their pages. Give the children shallow bowls of purple tempera paint and unsharpened pencils. Let kids each dip the flat end of a pencil into the paint, then have kids stamp the pencils onto the papers to create the cluster of grapes hanging from the pole. Remind the children that the fruit Joshua and Caleb found in the land of Canaan was so big they could hardly carry it.

ask • **Why do you think God wanted the spies to go and check out the land?**

• **How do you think the spies felt when they saw all the big, beautiful fruit?**

• **How can we stand up for God even when we're afraid?**

say Even when we're afraid, we can stand up for God. When all the other spies were afraid, Joshua and Caleb told the Israelites that God would help them. They believed God wanted them to live in the land of Canaan and enjoy all of the beautiful fruits God made for them.

Who'll Stand Up?

Supplies: cut out a simple paper doll for each student, crayons or markers

say In our Bible story we learned that Joshua and Caleb were willing to stand up for God when all the other Israelites were not brave enough to stand up for God. The Israelites did not trust that God would take care of them. Joshua and Caleb trusted God and stood up for God.

Give each child a paper doll, and set out crayons or markers. Have the children color one side of the paper doll to look like a young boy, like Joshua and Caleb. Then have each child turn the paper doll over and color that side to resemble him- or herself.

When the children are finished, help them fold their dolls at the waist, placing the dolls on the table as if they are sitting. Start with the "young boy" side.

ask • **Who'll stand up for God?**

Encourage each child to stand his or her paper doll and respond, "Joshua will stand up for God." Then have the child "sit" the paper doll again.

ask • **Who'll stand up for God?**

Encourage each child to stand his or her paper doll and respond, "Caleb will stand up for God." Then have the child "sit" the paper doll again, this time on the self-portrait side.

ask • **Who'll stand up for God?**

Encourage each child to stand the paper doll and respond, "[Child's name] will stand up for God."

ask • **How did Joshua and Caleb stand up for God?**

• **How can you help someone else stand up for God?**

say God likes us to stand up for him. Find someone in this room, and pretend you don't know that person. Introduce yourself to that person, shake that person's hand, and then tell him or her these words: "God wants you to stand up for him."

PRAYERS

Stand Up for God

Supplies: none

Have the children sing the following prayer and jump up when they say the words "stand up." Sing "Stand Up for God" to the tune of "I'm in the Lord's Army."

PRAY **Dear God, help me stand up for you** (stand up, then sit down)**,**

Stand up for you (stand up, then sit down)**,**

Stand up for you. (Stand up, then sit down.)

Dear God, help me stand up for you. (Stand up, then sit down.)

I will tell about you. Amen!

I will tell about you. Amen!

I will tell about you. Amen!

Dear God, help me stand up for you. (Stand up, then sit down.)

I will tell about you. Amen!

Snacks

Standing Firm Snacks

Supplies: flavored gelatin, pretzel sticks, paper plates

Have the kids wash their hands, and then let one of the children thank God for the snacks. Place a square of flavored gelatin and 12 pretzel sticks on a plate for each child. Have kids stand up their pretzel sticks in their gelatin squares. Then have them count their pretzel sticks. Remind kids that Moses sent out 12 spies to check out Canaan, the Promised Land.

ask • **What was one thing that the spies said about Canaan?**

• **What would you have said about Canaan if you had been one of the spies?**

say **All of the 12 spies came back and told Moses what they saw. But only Caleb and Joshua believed God would keep them safe from the giants. God wants us to trust him and stand up for God, just as Caleb and Joshua did.**

Balaam's Donkey Talks

Story 14

Bible Basis:

Numbers 22

The Talking Donkey

Supplies:

Bible, cardstock, scissors, markers

Use cardstock and markers to make simple finger puppets of a man and a donkey. You'll need only one of each.

Open your Bible to Numbers 22, and show the children the words.

say Today's Bible story tells us to pay attention to God.

ask • What does it mean to pay attention?

• Can you show me how you listen carefully?

say When we listen and watch carefully, we're paying attention. Let's hear what happened to a man in the Bible who didn't pay attention to God.

As you tell the story, let the children take turns using the finger puppets to act out the story.

say Balaam was a man who didn't pay attention to God. A bad king wanted Balaam to come see him and pray that bad things would happen to the Israelites. God told Balaam not to pray for bad things. But Balaam didn't listen.

ask • Why do you think Balaam didn't obey God?

• How do you think God felt when Balaam didn't obey him?

• What do you think Balaam should have done?

say Balaam got on his donkey and rode to see the king. God was angry with Balaam, and he sent an angel to talk to him. Balaam didn't hear the angel, but his donkey did. The donkey walked into a field and lay down. Balaam was angry, and he hit the donkey with a stick. Then God let the donkey talk.

The donkey said, "Why are you beating me? Have I ever treated you this way?"

Balaam said, "I'm angry at you because you are making me look like a fool."

Then Balaam saw the angel and fell to the ground. The angel said,

"Don't beat your donkey

And make it a fool.

Pay attention to God,

And obey God's rule."

Teach your children the words to the rhyme, and have them repeat the rhyme with you several times.

say ▶ **So Balaam went to the king, but he prayed for good things for the Israelites.**

ask ▶ **• How do you think God felt when Balaam obeyed him?**

• How do you think God feels when we obey him?

• What are some ways we can pay attention to God?

say ▶ **We can see that God did great things to help Balaam pay attention to him. God sent Jesus to help us pay attention to him. When we have Jesus for a friend, we can spend time with him and Jesus will teach us more about how to pay attention to God each day.**

CRafts

Donkey Talk

Supplies: donkey ears cut from brown construction paper, tape, markers, brown lunch bags

say ▶ **Let's make donkey puppets you can use to help act out the story of Balaam.**

Show children how to tape their donkey ears to the top of a paper bag. Let the children add eyes and a nose to the front of the bag to make the donkey. Don't worry if the faces don't look "donkey-like."

When the puppets are done, encourage children to use their puppets to act out the story of Balaam and his donkey.

ask ▶ **• Why do you think it was hard for Balaam to pay attention to God?**

• Why should we pay attention to God?

say ▶ **Just like Balaam, we need to pay attention to God.**

Games

Listen Up!

Supplies: donkey poster (create a simple poster with a donkey drawn on it), blindfolds, donkey ears (cut from brown construction paper)

Hang the donkey poster on the wall (or lean it up against the wall if it's mounted on cardboard) with the bottom of the poster touching the floor so kids can reach the donkey's head. Have kids form pairs, and let pairs take turns playing Touch the Ears to the Donkey. Explain that kids will try to touch the ears to the appropriate spot on the donkey's head. One child in each pair will be blindfolded and will hold the donkey ears while the other child verbally guides his or her partner. Then partners will switch roles.

Encourage kids to cheer others on as they wait for their turns. When everyone has had a turn, have kids sit with their partners to answer the following questions. After each question, invite children to share their answers with the rest of the class.

ask • **What was it like trying to pay attention to your partner while everyone was cheering?**

• **When is it hard for you to pay attention in real life?**

say It's important for us to pay attention to God. When we pay attention to God, we learn more and more about him. And that's good!

PRayeRS

Thankful Prayer

Supplies: paper, crayons

Give children paper and crayons, and let kids each draw a picture of something they are thankful to God for. A child might draw a picture of puppies, for example. When children have finished, have them hold their pictures as you teach them this prayer:

> **Dear God,**
>
> **Thank you for all you've done,**
>
> **Thank you for sending your Son.**
>
> **Help me to be good and true,**
>
> **As I pay attention to you.**
>
> **In Jesus' name, amen.**

snacks

Donkey Food Snacks

Supplies: trail mix (no peanuts if you have allergies in your class), paper towel

Place some trail mix on a paper towel for each child, and place the snacks on the floor. Have your class pretend to be donkeys and eat only with their mouths. Then gather kids together in a circle.

ask • **What was it like when you were pretending to be a donkey?**

• **How do you think the donkey in our story felt when he saw the angel?**

• **How would you feel if you saw an angel of the Lord? What would you say or do?**

Balaam learned to pay attention to God. We can learn to pay attention to God, too.

Happy-Face Snack

Supplies: small paper plates, craft sticks, small bagels (half for each child), cream cheese, raisins, banana slices (two per child)

Have the children wash their hands (or use wet wipes) and then sit down to prepare the snack.

For each child, you'll need a small paper plate, a large craft stick, half of a small bagel, softened cream cheese, raisins, and banana slices. Have children use craft sticks to spread their bagel halves with cream cheese, and have them use raisins to make "smiles" on their bagels. Tell children not to put eyes on their bagels yet.

 Balaam didn't use his eyes. He didn't see the angel. Balaam didn't pay attention.

ask • **What happened to make Balaam pay attention to God?**

• **How do you think God feels when we pay attention to him?**

Show children how to place two banana slices on their bagels as eyes.

say **We can pay attention to God by watching with our eyes. Let's thank God for providing our snack, and ask him to help us pay attention to him.** Invite a child to pray for the snack.

JOSHUA BECOMES LEADER OF ISRAEL

Bible Basis:

 Joshua 1:1-11

Strong and Courageous

Supplies:

Bible

Open your Bible to Joshua 1:1-11, and show children the words.

say ▸ **Today's Bible story tells us that God helps us.**

Moses had been leading the Israelites through the desert for a very long time when he died. After he died, God told a man named Joshua, "My people need someone to help them know the right thing to do. So you, Joshua, will be their leader. I will be with you wherever you go."

But Joshua was afraid. So God told him, "Be strong and courageous!" Can you say that with me? Have children stand up, flex their muscles, and repeat the phrase. Then have kids sit down again.

God said to Joshua, "You are going to lead my people into the land I will give them. I will be with you wherever you go." But Joshua was still afraid. What do you think God said to him? Let's stand and say it together. Have children stand up, flex their muscles, and say, "Be strong and courageous!" Then have kids sit down again.

God told Joshua, "Always remember to follow the rules I gave to Moses, and I will help you."

But Joshua was still afraid. What do you think God said to him? Let's stand and say it together. Have children stand up, flex their muscles, and say, "Be strong and courageous!" Then have kids sit down again.

God told Joshua, "I'll help you, so don't be afraid or sad." And do you know what? Joshua wasn't afraid anymore! He led the people into the land God had given them because he believed that God helps us. With God's help, Joshua was strong and courageous. Have children stand up, flex their muscles, and say, "Be strong and courageous!" Then have kids sit down again.

ask ▸ **• What made Joshua feel brave about the big job he had to do?**

• How can you remember that God helps us the next time you feel scared?

say When you're afraid or sad, you can remember that just as God helped Joshua, God helps us.

CRafts

God With Me

Supplies: mirror pages (draw a handheld mirror on a piece of paper and photocopy it for the children), 1 aluminum-foil square per child, glue sticks

Distribute photocopied mirror pages to the children and write their names on the pages. Place aluminum-foil squares and glue sticks in the center of the table. Have kids glue aluminum-foil squares in the center of the mirror.

ask • Who do you see when you look into this "mirror"?

• How does it feel to know that God helps us?

say No matter where you go or what you do, God is with you! It's as if God is always holding you in his hands. God helps us to be strong and courageous.

Brave Hearts

Supplies: red construction paper, scissors, hole punch, 2-foot piece of yarn per child, dry colored pasta to thread

Before class, cut out several heart shapes from red construction paper (one for each child). Use a hole punch to make a small hole at the top-middle of each heart. Cut a 2-foot piece of yarn for each child.

Give each child a construction-paper heart you prepared before the lesson and a piece of yarn.

say When people are in the army, they can earn medals for being brave. Let's make medals to remind us how God helped Joshua to be brave.

Show the children how to thread one end of the yarn through the paper heart. Have kids thread pieces of dry colored pasta on their pieces of yarn. Tie the ends of the yarn together to close each necklace.

ask • Why did Joshua need help being a brave soldier?

• When do you need help from God?

say God helps us, too, just as he helped Joshua. We're going to give these medals to some special people in our church. We can thank the men and women who served as soldiers and sailors in our country. God helped them be brave. We can thank them by giving them these medals.

Arrange for you or your children to present the medals to veterans in your church.

Games

Fear Bubbles

Supplies: bubble wand and bubble solution

> **say** Sometime when we're afraid, we just need to remember that God can help us with all our fears.

Explain that you'll blow some bubbles. Kids can each call out something they're afraid of, and then pop a bubble. Each time they pop a bubble, kids can say something like, "I don't have to be afraid of [scary item] because God is with me." Begin blowing bubbles. Continue blowing bubbles until children run out of fears to name.

Prayers

Action Prayer

Supplies: one piece of gold chenille wire

Before class, form the chenille wire into a circle and twist the ends together to make a crown.

Have children stand in a circle. Explain that they'll pass the chenille crown around the circle. The child holding the crown will pray, "Dear God, please help me to be strong and courageous," and then pass the crown to the next child to pray. When everyone has had a chance to pray, close with the following:

> **Pray** Dear God, please help us to be strong and courageous, just as you helped Joshua. Thank you for being with us wherever we go. We love you. In Jesus' name, amen.

Snacks

Stuck-Together Snack

Supplies: for each child: 1 large marshmallow, 8-10 chocolate chips, napkins

Have the children wash their hands (or use wet wipes) and then sit down to prepare the snack. Give each child a napkin, eight to 10 chocolate chips, and a large marshmallow. Show kids how to lick the ends of their marshmallows and then use their sticky marshmallows to pick up the chocolate chips. Explain that just as the chocolate chips stick to the marshmallows, God sticks with us wherever we go.

> **ask** • When has God helped you in the past?
>
> • How would you like God to help you now?

> **say** Let's thank God for sticking with us and for helping us be strong and courageous. And let's thank him for our snack, too! Invite a child to pray for the snack.

"God Is With Me"

Supplies: washable marker

Have children stand in a circle. Teach children to sing "God Is With Me" to the tune of "Jesus Loves Me." While they sing, use a washable marker to draw a cross on each child's hand.

SING ▶ **My God loves me, this I know.**

He'll be with me where I go.

No matter what the time of day,

God is in my heart to stay.

Yes, God is with me.

Yes, God is with me.

Yes, God is with me.

He's in my heart to stay.

After the song, explain that a cross is something we use to remember God's Son, Jesus. God sent Jesus to forgive our sins and be our best friend forever. Tell children that the crosses will be on their hands today to remind them that God helps us.

God Called Joshua

Supplies: none

Sing "God Called Joshua" to the tune of "Hush, Little Baby":

God called Joshua for his plan. (Touch mouth.)

But Joshua said, "I don't think I can." (Shake head "no.")

God said, "Joshua, don't be afraid. (Make a scared face.)

I'll help you be strong and brave." (Make muscles arms.)

God called Joshua for his plan. (Touch mouth.)

God knew he was the right man. (Nod head "yes.")

God said, "Joshua, don't be afraid. (Make a scared face.)

I'll be with you every day." (Make a happy face.)

GOD GIVES GIDEON VICTORY

Bible Basis:

Judges 6:1-16; 7:1-24

True Trust

Supplies:

Bible, a block

Open your Bible to Judges 6 and 7, and show the children the words.

say ▶ **Today's Bible story tells us that we can trust God. Let's use this block to learn a little about trust.** Hold a block in your outstretched hand.

ask ▶ • **What will happen if I drop this block? How do you know?**

Drop the block and watch it fall. Ask children what will happen if you drop the block behind your back, at your side, from a few inches off the ground, and from high above the ground. Allow different children to demonstrate what happens in each instance. Set the block out of sight.

ask ▶ • **How did you know that the block wouldn't fly away when it was dropped?**

• **Did you trust that the block would fall? Why?**

say ▶ **You trusted that the block would always fall…because that's what blocks do! Well, in today's Bible story, a man named Gideon learned to trust that God would help him, because that's what God always does!**

God's people lived in a beautiful place, but some mean people came and took over the land. So God's people had to live in caves. Let's all crouch down as if we're living in a tiny, dark, cold cave. Lead children in crouching down and shivering. **God sent an angel to talk to a man named Gideon. The angel told Gideon that God was going to use him to save God's people and get their land back. Gideon did not trust the angel or God. Gideon was not strong or powerful, so he didn't think he could do what God asked. But the angel told Gideon, "Do not fear, God is with you." Let's say that to a partner: "Do not fear, God is with you." So Gideon trusted God and did what God said to do.**

One night, God told Gideon to take only a few men with him and make a circle around the camp of the mean people. Let's make a circle like Gideon's men. Help children form a circle. **Each man had a**

trumpet in his hand. Gideon's men also carried large torches so they could see in the night. God made the fire in the torches burn really high and really bright to scare the Midianites. The Midianites saw all those torches and heard the loud noise of the trumpets and it confused those mean people so much that they fought with each other and ran away. Have children walk or run their fingers away on the floor. **God won and his people got their homes and land back. They didn't have to hide in caves anymore! Stand and stretch up tall! God did just as he said he would. Gideon could trust God.**

ask ▸ • **What did you like about the story of Gideon?**

• **What did God do for Gideon?**

say ▸ **Just like you trusted that the block would always fall to the floor, Gideon learned that he could always trust God to do what is right. Gideon trusted God, and God sent the mean people away for good. We can trust God to be with us when we're afraid.**

BiBLe eXPeRieNCeS

Victory March

Supplies: paper, several flashlights

Roll several sheets of paper into megaphones for the kids to use as "trumpets." Give each child either a "trumpet" or a flashlight. Lead the children in a march around the room. Encourage them to blow on their "trumpets" and to hold up their flashlight "torches" as high as they can. Tell the kids that in today's Bible story they learn how God used trumpets and torches to give the Israelites victory over a big, mean army.

Cave Play

Supplies: classroom tables and chairs, blankets

Using tables, chairs, and blankets, have the children build the Israelite's homes and caves. Have the children act out how the Israelites had to leave their homes and hide in the caves. Let children joyfully return to their "homes." Children may pretend to be Gideon and the angel. Have the angel say to Gideon, "Do not fear, God is with you."

ask ▸ • **How would you feel if you didn't have a bed to sleep in?**

• **How do you think Gideon felt when God asked him to do something hard?**

• **When should we trust God?**

say ▸ **Gideon trusted God. He did what God said and helped the Israelite people get their land and homes back.**

CRafts

Trumpets of Trust

Supplies: one large foam cup per child (carefully cut out the bottoms of the cups), chenille wire, tape, stickers, markers, glitter glue

say ▶ **When God told Gideon to gather his men in a circle around the mean people and blow the trumpets, Gideon obeyed. He trusted God. Let's make our own Trumpets of Trust to remind us that we can trust God, too!**

Give each child a prepared cup and a large chenille wire. Show children how to fold the wire in half. Then help them tape the ends of the wire to one side of the cup as a handle. Set out stickers, markers, and glitter glue for children to decorate their trumpets. Help children apply the Bible story to their lives.

ask ▶ • **When is a time you were afraid and needed to trust God?**

say ▶ **The next time you're afraid, remember how Gideon trusted God and how God helped Gideon. God can help you, too! That's good news! Let's celebrate because we can trust God whenever we're afraid!**

Lead children in a parade as they pretend to play their trumpets. Remind children to take their trumpets home to help them remember the Bible story.

PRayeRs

Trust God

Supplies: washable marker

Have each child think of a time when he or she might have been afraid. Pray the beginning of this prayer aloud. When you get to the blank, have each child take a turn saying what he or she might have been afraid of. As each child speaks, have the person to his or her right draw a cross on the speaker's hand as a reminder that "God is with you."

PRay ▶ **Dear God, thank you that we don't have to be afraid of** [name of fear]**.**

Then finish the prayer by saying: **Thank you for being with us when we're afraid. In Jesus' name, amen.**

Tasty Trumpets

Supplies: trumpet-shaped corn snacks, bowl, apple juice, bowl of sugar, cotton swabs

Have the children wash their hands (or use wet wipes) and then sit down to prepare their snack. Set out trumpet-shaped corn snacks, a bowl of apple juice, and a bowl of sugar. Demonstrate how to use a cotton swab to "paint" juice on each trumpet, then roll it in sugar to make it glittery. As children make their shiny trumpets, remind them that Gideon's men blew their trumpets just as God told them to do.

Invite one child to give thanks to God for the snack. Children may pretend to blow their trumpets and then eat them.

ask
- **How do you think the Israelites felt when they were about to blow their trumpets?**
- **Have you ever been afraid? What did you do?**

say **When God told Gideon to fight the mean people, Gideon was scared. But he learned that we can trust God. Next time you're afraid, remember God is with you!**

GOD GIVES SAMSON a SPECIAL GIFT

Bible Basis:

Judges 15:9-16

The Strongest Man in the World

Supplies:

Bible

Open your Bible to Judges 15:9-16; 16:4-30, and show the children the words.

say ▸ **God gave a man named Samson a secret strength that made him stronger than anyone else in the land.**

ask ▸ **• Who is the strongest person you know?**

▸ **• What do you think makes people strong?**

say ▸ **Samson was an Israelite who promised to serve God from the time he was very little. Once thing he promised God was that he would never cut his hair. He must have had very long hair by the time he was a grown man. Let's find out if any of you have shorter or longer hair than Samson.**

Let children who want to come stand by you and line up in order of hair length. Starting with the person who has the shortest hair,

ask ▸ **• Do you think Samson's hair was shorter or longer?** Continue doing the same with each of the children in line. Thank the children for helping you, then let them return to their seats.

say ▸ **Samson was just an ordinary man, maybe like your dads, but God gave him a special gift of strength so that he could serve God in a big way. Everyone wanted to know what made him strong, but Samson wouldn't tell. The Israelites' enemies especially wanted to know what made Samson so strong because they wanted to stop him. They were always trying to think up ways to trick him into telling them.**

One time Samson's enemies told him they would kill him if he didn't tell them the secret of his strength, but Samson wouldn't tell. They even tried to tie him up, but Samson wouldn't tell. He just broke the ropes, laughed, and ran away.

Samson's girlfriend, Delilah, tried to trick him into telling her the secret of his mighty strength. Many times Delilah tied up Samson, and every time Samson broke the ropes.

Help the children form trios for this fun game. Have two of the partners form a bridge with their arms, and let the third child stand in the center, pretending to be Samson. Tell the two partners to "lock" their arms around "Samson" so he can't get away. At the end of the following song, tell Samson that he or she can break out of the "locked" arms. Sing the following song to the tune of "London Bridge." (You'll only be singing the verse part.) Repeat the game twice, giving the other kids a chance to be Samson.

SING ▸ **What's the secret of your strength,**

Of your strength, of your strength?

What's the secret of your strength?

Tell me now!

Say ▸ **Delilah begged and pleaded and cried, but Samson wouldn't tell her the secret of his mighty strength. Let's beg and plead.** Have the children to pretend to beg, getting down on their knees with praying hands and saying, "Pleeeeease!" **Let's all cry and beg.** Encourage them to whine and cry as they continue on their knees saying, "Pleeeeease!"

She was going to find out the secret of Samson's strength no matter what!

Finally, one night when Delilah was begging and pleading with Samson to tell her the secret of his strength again, Samson finally gave up. "Stop! Enough! I'll tell you, already! The secret is my long hair. If I cut my hair, my strength will be gone."

ask ▸ **• That night, what do you think Delilah did?**

Say ▸ **Delilah told her friends (who were also Samson's enemies) to come stand on the other side of the door and wait for her to yell. Then they could come in and get Samson. So that night, Delilah tied up Samson again and this time cut his hair while he was asleep. When she yelled, Samson's enemies came running in.**

ask ▸ **• Do you think Samson broke the ropes and got away this time? Why or why not?**

• How do you think Samson felt when he couldn't get away?

Say ▸ **Samson had lost his strength. He couldn't get away no matter how hard he struggled. Samson was as weak as any other man that lived there in the town. Samson's enemies hurt him and tied him up. It was very sad.**

Samson was sorry that he had trusted Delilah and broken his promise to God. He asked God to forgive him and use him again to win the victory over his enemies.

ask ▸ **• What do you think God did?**

Say ▸ **God forgave Samson and gave him back his mighty strength, and Samson won a victory for all of Israel that day.**

ask ▸ **• What are some good gifts God has given you?**

Say ▸ **God gives us good gifts to use to serve him in mighty ways.**

BiBLe eXPeRieNces

Good Gifts

Supplies: brightly colored wrapping paper, dust rag, broom, dust pan, other cleaning supplies or treats

Before class, secure permission to enter the sanctuary to do some cleaning. Wrap the following items in brightly colored wrapping paper: a dust rag, a broom, a dust pan, a package of instant hot cocoa, and other cleaning supplies or treats. You'll need one "gift" for each child.

Let children take turns opening a gift. Once all of the gifts have been opened, let each child carry his or her gift to the sanctuary. Encourage the children to use their gifts to clean the area. Write a thank you note to the pastor, and allow each child to sign it (you will need to help the kids write their names). Leave the note for the pastor, and return to your classroom.

 • **What gifts did you get?**

• **How did you use your gift to serve the pastor and our church?**

• **What kinds of good gifts does God give?**

• **How can you use those gifts to serve others?**

say God gave Samson the gift of great strength. We don't get to choose which gifts God gives us. But we do get to pick how we will use those gifts to serve others. Let's use our gifts this week to serve God!

CRafts

Barbell Bonanza

Supplies: cardboard paper towel tubes (1 per child), newsprint, squares of colored cellophane (2 per child), tape

 God gave Samson the gift of being strong. Sometimes really strong people lift weights to keep their muscles big and strong. Let's make some barbell weights to remind us how God gave Samson the gift of strength.

Give each child a cardboard tube. Set out newsprint, squares of colored cellophane, and tape. Demonstrate how to wad newsprint into a large ball and cover the ball with cellophane by draping the cellophane over the paper wad. Gather the edges of the cellophane together under the paper wad, then twist and tape them so it looks like an inflated balloon. You'll need two cellophane balls for each child.

Demonstrate how to insert the taped end of a cellophane ball into each end of a cardboard tube, and tape the balls in place to make a barbell. After each child has made a barbell, gather everyone together in a circle. Show children how to lift their barbells as if exercising to a count as you teach them this simple rhyme:

God gives good gifts

To you and me.

God gives good gifts,

Just look and see!

ask • **Of all the good gifts God has given you, what's your favorite?**

Encourage children to take their barbells home with them to remind them that they can use their gifts to serve God and others, just as Samson did.

Games

Good Gifts

Supplies: none

Gather children in a circle and play this game called "If you've ever received…" Tell the children to sit on the floor and you'll stand in front of them. You will say a gift that they might have received, and someone who has received the gift will do the action that you describe to them. For example, you might say: "If you've ever received a toy car, do five jumping jacks!" or "If you've ever received a ball, stand on one foot!" Try to name common gifts that the children might have received, and also try to name gifts that are not gender-specific. Remind the children that God gives us good gifts we can use to serve him.

Prayers

Gifts to Serve

Supplies: none

Have kids kneel in a circle. Help children repeat each line and do the motions as they say this finger-play prayer:

Dear God, (Right hand, open, drawn down the face as sign for God.)

Thank you for your gifts so good. (Lift both hands up to heaven.)

Help me serve you as I should. (Slowly take arms down and out, palms up.)

I'll be happy as I share, (Index fingers on cheeks as you smile.)

So those around will know you care. (Hug self.)

In Jesus' name, amen.

snacks

Servant Snack

Supplies: pretzels, round oat cereal, miniature marshmallows, and small resealable plastic bags

Have the children wash their hands (or use wet wipes) and then sit down to prepare their snack. Set out pretzels, circle oat cereal, miniature marshmallows, and small resealable plastic bags. Let each child take a handful of each ingredient and place it in a bag. Seal the bags and let children shake them to mix the ingredients. Then instruct children to each give their bag to another child.

ask • **How did you just serve others?**

• **How can you serve your family this week?**

say **God gave Samson the gift of being very strong. Let's thank God for giving us good gifts, too, and for providing our snack.** Invite one child to pray for the snack, then allow children to enjoy the treats.

songs

Let Us Praise God

Supplies: none

Sing "Let Us Praise God" to the tune of "She'll Be Coming Round the Mountain." Encourage the kids to join you in repeating the verses. After children have learned the song, you may want to substitute actions such as "stomp our feet," "shout out loud," or "lift our hands" for the phrase "clap our hands." As you sing, remind the children that God gave Samson the gift of great strength, and God gives us good gifts, too. We can use our gifts to praise God.

sing **Let us clap our hands and praise, God right now.** (Clap hands.)

Let us clap our hands and praise, God right now. (Clap hands.)

Let us clap our hands and praise God. (Clap hands.)

Let us clap our hands and praise God. (Clap hands.)

Let us clap our hands and praise God right now. (Clap hands.)

GOD ANSWERS HANNAH'S PRAYER

Bible Basis:

1 Samuel 1:1-28

Hannah's Prayer

Supplies:

Bible, baby doll or folded towel

A Simple Prayer

Have kids form a circle and sit down. Open your Bible to 1 Samuel 2, and show children the words. Have children form trios to act out the following simple drama. Designate a child in each group to be Hannah, a child to be Eli, and a child to be Elkanah (pronounced "el-KAY-nuh"). Then read the story and have children follow your directions.

say ▶ **There once was a man named Elkanah and a woman named Hannah. Elkanah loved his wife Hannah. But they had no children, and Hannah wanted a baby very badly. Elkanah and Hannah went to the temple to worship.** Have the children portraying Elkanah and Hannah hold hands and skip or jump to the front of the room.

Elkanah and Hannah prayed. Instruct Elkanah to kneel and fold his hands in prayer, and ask Hannah to stand, fold her hands in prayer, and move her lips as though praying.

Eli, the priest, saw Hannah's great faith as she prayed to the Lord. Hannah told him (have Hannah repeat after you), **"I would like to have a baby."** Then Eli said to Hannah (have Eli repeat after you), **"May God give you what you wish."**

Hannah was very happy. Have Hannah jump for joy and clap hands. **She had faith that the Lord would answer her prayer. Elkanah and Hannah went back home.** Allow Elkanah and Hannah to hold hands and skip away.

Soon Hannah and Elkanah had a baby boy. Have Elkanah pick up a baby doll or a folded towel and hand it to Hannah. **Hannah and Elkanah were very happy.**

Instruct Hannah and Elkanah to say together: "His name is Samuel." Then say: **Hannah and Eli gave their son to God so that one day, Samuel would grow up and serve God.**

After you tell the story, have kids sing the following song to the tune of "The Mulberry Bush." Encourage kids to hold hands and move in a circle as they sing.

A lady named Hannah wanted a child,

Wanted a child,

Wanted a child.

A lady named Hannah wanted a child.

So she prayed to God.

God said, "Yes, you will have a child,

Have a child,

Have a child."

God said, "Yes, you will have a child."

His name was Samuel.

Hannah took Samuel to the church,

To the church,

To the church.

Hannah took Samuel to the church.

She took him to the temple.

Hannah showed how she loved God,

She loved God, she loved God.

Hannah showed how she loved God.

She gave her son to God.

BiBLe eXPeRieNCes

Hannah in the Temple

Supplies: building blocks, several small dolls or action figures

Place large cardboard or wooden blocks on the floor. Have children work together to create a building where people could worship God. Set out small dolls or action figures, and encourage children to use them to act out the story of Hannah in the temple.

ask
- **How did Hannah feel when she went to the temple?**
- **How did God turn Hannah's sad face to a smile?**
- **How could you help a sad friend today?**

say
Long ago, God asked people to build a temple, or church, where they could come to learn about and talk to God. Hannah turned to God when she was sad. Hannah went to the temple to pray. Later she brought her son Samuel to learn about God. You can turn to God when you're sad, too.

CRAFTS

Rock-a-Bye Baby

Supplies: 1 white plastic spoon per child, 1 small wooden craft stick per child, 1 chenille wire per child, fine-tipped markers

Review the Bible story as you help children make a spoon mother with her baby. Give each child a plastic spoon, and say that the spoon represents Hannah. Have children use markers to draw a smiling face on the concave bowl of the spoon. Explain that Hannah is very happy because God answered her prayers and gave her a baby.

Next, give each child a small wooden craft stick and say that it represents Hannah's baby, Samuel. Let children draw a face for Samuel. Finally, help them twist a chenille wire around the upper handle of the spoon to make Hannah's arms. Wrap the arms around the craft stick, so Hannah is holding her baby.

ask ▸ • When is a time you felt sad?

• What did Hannah do when she was sad? What can you do when you're sad?

say ▸ Hannah turned to God when she was sad, and God helped her. You can turn to God when you're sad, too. God cares how you feel. And God will always make you feel better. Take your spoon mother and baby home with you so you can tell your family the story of Hannah and her baby.

Games

Where's Samuel?

Supplies: baby doll

Before the children arrive, hide a baby doll somewhere in the room. Tell the kids that you've hidden something very special; you've hidden baby "Samuel" somewhere. Encourage them to explore, looking for and calling for baby Samuel. When they find him, hide the doll again. Play several times. Tell the children that in today's Bible story, Hannah prayed to God for a baby, and God answered her prayers.

PRAYERS

Prayer Necklaces

ALLERGY ALERT

Supplies: colored loop cereal, red licorice whips

Have kids string colored loop cereal on red licorice whips. Help kids tie the ends of the licorice whips together and then put on the prayer necklaces.

Encourage kids to eat a piece of cereal as each prayer request or praise is shared during class prayer time, or encourage kids to take home their prayer necklaces and pray at home. Remind them to turn to God with their feelings.

Say Just as Hannah did, you can turn to God when you're sad. These necklaces can help you remember to turn to God with your feelings.

Action Prayer

Supplies: none

Say Hannah was sad because she wanted a baby—but her arms were empty. Hold your arms as if you're holding a baby. While you hold your arms this way, we'll take turns telling something that makes us sad.

Go around the circle and let each person say something that makes him or her sad.

Say Let's give these sad things to God.

Have children raise their hands, as if lifting the sad things to God. Lead children in this prayer.

Pray Dear God, thank you that we can turn to you when we're sad. Please take all of these sad things and turn them into happy things. In Jesus' name, amen.

Snacks

Surprise Snack

Supplies: graham crackers, bag, plastic knives, frosting, sprinkles, chocolate chips, marshmallows, 1 plate per child

Before class, place canned white frosting, plastic knives, sprinkles, chocolate chips, and marshmallows in a bag. Set the bag out of sight until it's time to bring it out.

Have the children wash their hands (or use wet wipes).

Say We're going to have an exciting snack!

Give each child a graham cracker on a plate.

Ask • Does this snack look exciting? Why or why not?

• What would make this snack more exciting?

Bring out the bag of "goodies," and allow children to frost and decorate their graham crackers.

Say God surprised Hannah and made her life more exciting by giving her a baby just as I surprised you with our snack. Let's thank God for surprising us and helping us feel happy when we're feeling sad. And let's thank God for this snack, too! Invite one child to thank God for the snack.

SONGS

Lord, We Want to Praise You

Supplies: none

Sing "Lord, We Want to Praise You" to the tune of "Sing a Song of Sixpence." Encourage the children to join you in repeating the verses. Remind them that we should praise God because he turns our sadness into gladness!

Lord, we want to praise you (lift hands overhead)

For you love us so. (Cross arms over chest.)

Lord, we want to praise you (lift hands overhead)

For you love us so. (Cross arms over chest.)

We will clap our hands (clap hands in time to music)

And raise our voices, too! (Cup hands around mouth.)

This is how we show our love (cross arms over chest)

And sing our praise to you! (Lift hands overhead.)

I Hope in God

Supplies: none

Sing "I Hope in God" to the tune of "The Ants Go Marching." Encourage the kids to join you in repeating the song and the hand motions.

I hope in God, I trust in God. (Raise right hand, then left.)

Hooray, hooray! (Jump up on each word.)

I hope in God, I trust in God. (Raise right hand, then left.)

Hooray, hooray! (Jump up on each word.)

God will never let me go. (Shake head and hug self.)

He has great plans for me, I know. (Tap temple with index finger.)

And so I can hope and trust (Raise right hand, then left.)

In God. (Point up.)

Hooray, hooray! (Jump on each word.)

GOD SPEAKS to SAMUEL

STORY 19

Bible Basis:

1 Samuel 3:1-21

God Speaks, Samuel Listens

Supplies:

Bible, tape, crepe paper streamers, blankets

Open your Bible to 1 Samuel 3:1-21, and show the children the words.

say **Today's Bible story tells us to listen to God like Samuel did.**

When Samuel was a boy, his mother took him to live somewhere very special. Can you guess where Samuel lived? Give the children a chance to guess. **Samuel didn't live in a house or an apartment or a tree or a trailer. He lived in God's house! It was like our church, and they called it the temple. You're going to pretend to be Samuel, the boy who served God.**

Samuel wore a special vest. Only people that served in the temple were allowed to wear it. Put an "ephod" on each child. Crisscross a streamer over each child's chest and tape it in back. **This shows that you are a servant of the Lord.**

In those days, God didn't speak to people very often. But one night, something amazing happened! Eli the priest was sleeping in his usual place. I'll pretend to be Eli, sleeping over here. Lie down on the blanket. **You will all pretend to be Samuel, sleeping over there.** Have all the children lie down, pretending to be Samuel. It's a good idea to have children lie down in the same direction. This way no one gets kicked in the head while pretending to sleep!

Samuel was lying down when the Lord called him, "Samuel, Samuel!" Samuel jumped up and ran over to Eli. He shook Eli, saying, "Here I am. You called me." Have the children act this out.

Eli said, "I did not call; go back and lie down." So Samuel went back and lay down. Send the children back to their places, where they'll lie down.

Again the Lord called, "Samuel! Samuel!" Samuel got up, went to Eli, and said, "Here I am. You called me." Let the children come and "wake" you.

"My son," Eli said, "I did not call; go back and lie down." Send the children back to lie down. **The Lord called Samuel a third time.** Let the children "wake" you again. **This time Eli realized that it was the Lord calling the boy. So Eli told Samuel, "Go and lie down, and if God calls you, listen to God. Say, 'Speak, God, for your servant is listening.'" So Samuel went and lay down in his place.** Send the children back to lie down. **He listened for God's voice.**

The Lord came and stood there, calling, "Samuel! Samuel!" Then Samuel said, "Speak, God, for your servant is listening." Have the children repeat this phrase together.

And the Lord spoke to Samuel. God told him that he was upset because Eli didn't stop his own sons from being bad. Samuel listened to God. In the morning Samuel told Eli everything that God had said. The Lord was with Samuel as he grew up, and people believed that what Samuel said was truly from God. Samuel helped people put their hope in God.

Have the children join you and then sit in a circle.

ask • Who spoke to Samuel at night?

• If God talked to you, what would you do?

say God knows that children are important. Sometimes children listen to God better than big people! Samuel did the right thing when he answered, "Speak, God, for your servant is listening." And then he listened to God!

BiBLe eXPeRienceS

Samuel Listens to God

Supplies: 2 clean soup cans, awl, string, duct tape

Before class, make a play telephone by poking a hole in the bottom of each can, threading the string through the holes, and tying each end of the string in a knot. Cover the cans' edges with duct tape to avoid cuts.

Show children the play phone of two soup cans connected by string.

say I need a volunteer to take one end of our play phone and stand as far away from me as possible, with the string tight. Wait for the child to get into position, and then say: **Place the can to your ear, and repeat what I'm about to say into this end of the phone.** As softly as possible, say into the can: **God loves you.** Do this several times, each time speaking a little louder until your message is finally heard. Then ask the child to return to the group.

Let each child have a turn listening with the "telephone." Vary what you say each time, using phrases such as, "God cares for you," "Jesus loves you," and "God is good."

say Sometimes we have to repeat what we say so others can hear and understand. When Samuel was a boy, God talked with him and told him many important things.

ask · How does God speak to us?

· What are some things God tells us to do?

say God spoke to Samuel at night and called his name. God speaks to us through worship, Christian friends, prayer, songs, and the Bible. Let's listen to God and tell others about him, too.

Games

Listen to the Leader

Supplies: none

Choose one child to whisper to another child an action such as, "Touch your nose and stand on one foot." The child who received the directions will start doing the action, and then the rest of the class should follow. Make sure each child gets a chance to whisper directions as well as to receive directions. Tell the kids that in today's Bible story, Samuel listened when God spoke to him.

Prayers

Help Me Listen

Supplies: none

Teach children this simple prayer. Talk about the importance of listening to God and being used by God.

> **God, help me listen when you call.**
>
> **For even though I'm very small,**
>
> **You can use my hands and feet**
>
> **To show your love to those I meet.**
>
> **In Jesus' name, amen.**

Snacks

Apple Ears

Supplies: small paper plates, round cracker, two raisins, and two apple wedges for each child

Give each child a paper plate, a round cracker, two raisins, and two apple wedges. Show the children how to make cracker faces with raisin eyes and apple ears. As children, enjoy their snacks, talk about how Samuel listened to God when God spoke to him.

SONGS

I Love God

Supplies: none

Sing "I Love God" to the tune of "The Mulberry Bush." Encourage the kids to join you in repeating the song and the hand motions. Remind the children that since we love God, we should listen to him, just as Samuel did.

> **Oh, I love God with all my might** (cross arms over chest)**,**
>
> **All my might, all my might.**
>
> **I'll listen to God day and night.** (Cup hands around ears.)
>
> **I love God!** (Raise arms overhead in praise.)

Are You Sleeping?

Supplies: none

Sing "Are You Sleeping?" to the tune of "Frere Jacques."

> **Are you sleeping?** (Lie down and pretend to sleep.)
>
> **Are you sleeping,**
>
> **Samuel?** (Continue to pretend to sleep.)
>
> **Samuel?**
>
> **Wake up, it is true.** (Open eyes.)
>
> **God is calling you.** (Hold hand to ear.)
>
> **Samuel.** (Stand up and turn around in place.)
>
> **Samuel.** (Turn around in place.)

Listen to God

Supplies: none

As you teach your children this finger play, remind them to listen to God, just as Samuel did.

> **Listen to God. What do you hear?** (Place hand behind ear and lean.)
>
> **Listen to God. Use your ears.** (Point up.)
>
> **Listen to God, like Samuel did.** (Place head on hands.)
>
> **Listen to God. God speaks to kids.** (Point to others.)

Solomon Asks for Wisdom

Bible Basis:

 1 Kings 2:1-4; 3:3-28

A Sad Story

Supplies:

Bible

Have kids form a circle and sit down on the floor. Open your Bible to 1 Kings 3, and show children the words. Children will enjoy acting out this rhyming story. Lead kids in doing the motions as you read the following Bible story.

Say **Solomon was the king** (make a circle with hands, and place them on head)

And ruled with God in mind (tap side of head)**,**

Obeyed God's rules and laws (point up)**,**

Was fair and good and kind.

Once, while Solomon slept (rest head on hands)**,**

God asked him in a dream,

"Solomon, what do you want? (Hold hands up and shrug shoulders.)

I'll give you anything." (Bring hands forward with palms up.)

Solomon asked for wisdom (tap side of head)**,**

To be smart and oh, so wise.

He asked to be a good king (make a circle with hands, and place them on head)

And always know what's right. (Show thumbs up.)

God was pleased with Solomon (smile big and point to mouth)

For his unselfish plea. (Bring hands forward, palms up.)

God said, "You'll get your wisdom. (Tap side of head.)

And much more than that, you'll see." (Spread hands out, palms up.)

Solomon ruled God's people (make a circle with hands, and place them on head)

And showed them what was right. (Show thumbs up.)

He taught them to do good

And be pleasing in God's sight. (Point up.)

The people were amazed (show a surprised look)

At what Solomon would do. (Point up.)

They knew he was of God;

They knew it through and through. (Show thumbs up.)

Obey God's rules and laws (point up)**,**

And you'll be richly blessed.

Obey God's rules and laws (point up)—

That was Solomon's test.

ask ▸ • **What good choice did Solomon make?**

• **How can you make good choices that please God?**

say ▸ **God will help us make good choices that please God. Hooray for God!**

crafts

Wise King Puppets

Supplies: pink or tan construction paper, purple construction paper, 3 large craft sticks per child, sequins, yarn, crayons, glue, tape

Before class, cut three 1-inch circles for each child from pink or tan construction paper. Also cut three 1-inch triangles for each child from purple construction paper.

Set out the construction paper circles and triangles you cut before class, three large craft sticks per child, sequins, yarn, crayons, glue, and tape.

Give each child three large craft sticks, three construction paper circles, and three triangles. Instruct them to tape each circle to a craft stick. Show the children how to glue the triangles across the top of one circle to form a crown. Encourage the children to glue sequins on the crown. Then have them draw a face on the circle. Give them several pieces of yarn to glue to the bottom of the circle for the king's beard.

ask ▸ • **What kind of person wears a crown?**

say ▸ **Sometimes people come to kings and ask very hard questions. They expect the king to know the right answers. King Solomon wanted to be wise in the choices and decisions he made, so he asked God for help.** Have the children draw faces on the other two circles to represent the women in the story who came to King Solomon. Use pieces of yarn to make hair. Encourage the children to use their stick puppets to retell the story.

ask ▸ • **What are some hard choices you've had to make?**

• **How does it feel when you make the right choice?**

say ▸ **We can ask God for wisdom, just like King Solomon did. God will teach us and help us be wise!**

Games

Crown Around

Supplies: paper crown

Before class, make a paper crown from colored construction paper.

Have the kids sit down in a circle. Pass the crown from person to person as you say the rhyme from the first part of class:

 say ▸ **God teaches us to do what's right**

In the morning, noon, and night!

When the rhyme ends, have the person holding the crown say one thing he or she has learned in class today. Children might say things such as, "King Solomon was wise," "God teaches us," "It's good to know right from wrong," or "God taught Solomon." After the person shares, lead children in saying "God teaches us." Repeat the rhyme while preschoolers pass the crown. Continue until all the children have had a chance to hold the crown and say something they've learned.

ask ▸ • **Who taught Solomon to make wise choices?**

• **Who teaches us to make wise choices?**

say ▸ **God taught King Solomon, and God teaches us. God uses Bible stories and other Christians to teach us, too!**

Snacks

Solomon Snack

Supplies: 2 large marshmallows, 5 pretzel sticks, and one napkin per child

Have the children wash their hands (or use wet wipes) and then sit down to prepare the snack. Set out napkins, pretzel sticks, and marshmallows. Tell the children that you'll teach them how to make a Solomon snack. Form the head and body by sticking two marshmallows together with a pretzel stick. Attach arms and legs by sticking four pretzel sticks into the bottom marshmallow. Have children work in pairs and help each other make the Solomon snacks.

say ▸ **God teaches us good things, just as he taught Solomon how to be wise. God helps us learn from other Christians and from stories in the Bible, too. Let's thank God for teaching us and for providing our snack.** Invite one child to pray for the snack.

SONGS

Ask God for Wisdom

Supplies: none

Sing "Ask God for Wisdom" To the tune of "Pop Goes the Weasel." Remind kids that Solomon asked God for wisdom, and God gave it to him!

God will teach us if we just ask (fold hands and bow head in prayer)

The things we need to know (point to side of head)

Make good choices every day. (Stretch arms out wide.)

Ask God for wisdom! (Jump up with hands stretched up in the air.)

Be Wise

Supplies: none

As you teach children this active rhyme, remind them that Solomon obeyed God and followed his rules. God told Solomon he would reward him with wisdom, riches, and a long life if he would walk in his ways, obey God, and do what's right.

God teaches us to do what's right (point up, then give thumbs up)

In the morning (stretch arms as if waking up),

Noon (make a circle with arms above head),

And night. (Lay head on hands.)

Solomon Writes Many Proverbs

Bible Basis:

1 Kings 3:16-28; 4:29-34; Proverbs 1:1-7

Who Belongs to This Baby?

Supplies:

Bible, toys

Before class, gather enough toys for half the children in your class.

Have kids form a circle and sit on the floor. Open your Bible to 1 Kings 3, and show children the words.

say **Solomon asked God for wisdom to rule wisely, and God gave him lots of wisdom—as well as lots of riches and nice things. One day King Solomon had to use the wisdom God had given him to solve a problem.** Set out several toys, but only enough for about half of the kids.

Oh! I only have enough toys for half of you.

ask **· How do you feel if you got a toy?**

· How do you feel if you didn't get a toy?

Help kids solve the problem by sharing the toys or by passing the toys back and forth.

say **Two women came to King Solomon. They were arguing. The women had one baby with them, and both of the women said the baby was theirs.**

ask **· How is this problem like the one that we just had with our toys?**

· How would you solve this problem if you were Solomon?

say **Solomon asked to have his sword brought to him, and then he said, "I'll solve this problem. Each of you can have half of the baby."**

ask **· Do you think that was a good idea? Why or why not?**

· How would you feel if we just cut these toys in half so each of you could have half of a toy?

say **One of the women stopped Solomon and said to go ahead and give the baby to the other woman instead of hurting him. The other woman said to go ahead and cut the baby in half. Solomon wouldn't really have cut the baby in half; he just wanted to find out who the real mother of the baby was.**

ask ▸ • Who do you think was the real mother?

say ▸ Solomon knew that the real mother was the woman who didn't want the baby to be hurt. So he gave the baby to the real mother. When all the people heard about how Solomon had solved that problem, they were very excited about his wisdom. Lead children in clapping and applauding for Solomon's wisdom.

Solomon was wise because God gave him wisdom. Solomon wrote much of his wisdom down in the Bible for us to read. We can get wisdom when we read the Bible. The Bible can teach us many things and help us to be wise. The Bible gives us wisdom.

ask ▸ • How did Solomon use his wisdom?

• How can you get wisdom?

• When can you use wisdom?

crafts

Thumbthing Wise

Supplies: blank drawing paper, colored pencils, wet wipes, washable ink pad

Give each child a piece of drawing paper. Write the children's names on their papers. Set out the ink pad, wet wipes, and colored pencils.

Have each child press a thumb on the ink pad, then onto the page. Have them use wet wipes to wipe the ink from their thumbs, then let children use colored pencils to turn each thumbprint into something Solomon was wise about. Remind children that Solomon knew a lot about plants, animals, birds, and fish. Allow children to make as many thumbprint creations as they want.

ask ▸ • Who made King Solomon so wise?

say ▸ King Solomon knew God, and God made him wise. Just like King Solomon, we can know God and become wise, too. The Bible is one way that we can learn about God and become wise; the Bible shows us how to live.

Wise Solomon

Supplies: modeling dough

Give the children modeling dough, and allow them to create things that King Solomon was wise about, such as plants, animals, birds, and fish. Then let children make the shapes of things they know about. Children might make shapes of people, animals, or toys.

ask ▸ • What did King Solomon know a lot about?

• Why was King Solomon so wise?

say ▶ King Solomon knew God and became wise about so many things—plants, animals, birds, and fish. One way we can know God and become wise is by using the Bible; the Bible shows us how to live. We can also learn more about God by coming to church, praying, and listening to our parents and teachers as they tell us about God.

Wisdom Encyclopedias

Supplies: 1 piece of colored construction paper, 3 or 4 sheets of blank white paper, 12-inch piece of ribbon or yarn, and several decorating accessories and tools per child; glue; hole punch

Before class, make a stack of paper for each child. The stack should have one piece of colored construction paper and three or four sheets of blank white paper. On top of each stack lay a 12-inch piece of ribbon or yarn. Set out a hole punch; glue; and decorating accessories such as jewels, sequins, feathers, stickers of animals and plants; old magazines; markers; and colored pencils.

Lead each child to one of the stacks of paper. Show the children how to fold each piece of paper in half. Instruct them to put the pieces of white paper inside each other as the pages of the encyclopedia, and to put all the white paper inside the colored construction paper as the cover. Use the hole punch to make two holes in each child's book. Make the holes about two or three inches apart in the middle of the folds. Show the children how to string the ribbon or yarn through the holes and tie it in a bow on the outside to hold the book together.

Encourage the children to decorate the pages of the book with things they know about. They could tear out pictures from magazines and glue them in, draw pictures of animals or the sky, or use the decorating accessories to create their own scenes.

ask ▶ • What are some things you know now that you didn't know when you were a baby?

• What are some more things you would like to know about?

say ▶ God gave Solomon wisdom to know about all sorts of things in the world. He is giving you wisdom, too! Your personal encyclopedias are full of the many things God is teaching you, just as the Bible is full of the many things that God taught Solomon. God wants us to use the Bible because it shows us how to live.

PRAYERS

Action Prayer

Supplies: Bible

Have kids sit in a circle for prayer.

say ▶ God gave Solomon wisdom. God gives us wisdom, too. One way he does that is through the Bible. The Bible shows us how to live. That's because the Bible is filled with special words from God. When we

follow and obey God's words in the Bible, we know that we'll please God and live as his children. Pass the Bible around the circle. Instruct the children to say the following rhyme as they hold the Bible.

The Bible shows us how to live.

Thank you God, for the wisdom it gives.

After each child has participated, lead the children in the following prayer.

 Dear God, thank you for giving us the Bible to show us how to live. We're glad that we can read your words and learn more about you. In Jesus' name, amen.

snacks

Bible-Shaped Snacks

Supplies: Bible, napkins, plastic spoons, vanilla frosting, 2 graham cracker squares per child

Have the children wash their hands (or use wet wipes) and then sit down to prepare the snack. Set out napkins, plastic spoons, graham crackers, and containers of vanilla frosting. Each child will need two full graham cracker squares. Show children how to use a spoon to scoop out some vanilla frosting, then spread it on a graham cracker. Have children place a second graham cracker on top of the frosting. Hold up a Bible.

 These graham cracker sandwiches are shaped kind of like a Bible. God gave Solomon wisdom, and God gives us wisdom, too. The Bible is one way that God gives us wisdom. The graham cracker sandwiches are filled with good things! The Bible is filled with good things to know about God. The Bible shows us how to live. Let's thank God for our good snack and for the Bible that's filled with good things. Invite one child to pray for the snack.

songs

Ask Our God

Supplies: none

Sing the following song to the tune of "If You're Happy and You Know It." Remind kids that God gave Solomon wisdom when he asked.

> **When you need wisdom,**
> **Ask our God.**
> **When you need wisdom,**
> **Ask our God.**
> **He's always there, you know,**
> **And he helps us learn and grow,**
> **When you need wisdom,**
> **Ask our God.**

ELIJAH HELPS A WIDOW

Bible Basis:

1 Kings 17:7-24

Never Ending Care

Supplies:

Bible, small container of cooking oil, small container of flour, extra flour in a separate container, loaf of fresh bread covered by a cloth napkin, cups of water

ALLERGY ALERT

Have children form a circle and sit down. Open your Bible to 1 Kings 17:7-24, and show the children the words.

SAY **Today's Bible story tells us that God takes care of us.**

Our story is about a prophet named Elijah, a woman, and her son. A prophet tells others what God wants them to know.

God told Elijah to go to another city and meet someone who'd take care of him. When Elijah got to the city, he was very thirsty and tired. The weather was hot and dry because it hadn't rained for a long time. Elijah met a lady and asked her for a drink of water. When have you been really thirsty like Elijah?

Let children each tell a partner about a time they've been really thirsty.

SAY **It doesn't feel good to be thirsty, so I'll care for you and give you a drink.** Pass out the cups of water, and give children a drink. Point out how cool the water feels as it goes down their throats. Have children say "aah!"

Elijah also asked the lady for some bread. She said that she had only a little oil (hold up a container of oil) **and a little flour** (hold up a container of flour) **left to make bread for herself and her son. The woman was sad—she thought that after they ate what was left, they'd have nothing else and they might die. Elijah promised that if she made him some bread first, God would take care of her.**

So the woman mixed the oil and flour. Place a drop of oil on each child's finger so children can feel the texture. Next, let each child take a tiny pinch of flour to see what it feels like. **The woman made some delicious bread for Elijah.** Pass around the covered bread, and let children smell it.

When the woman gave Elijah the bread made from the last of her oil and flour, she thought she'd just given Elijah all her food. She

thought she'd probably be hungry for a long time. But she trusted God to take care of them, so she shared the food. Tear off one piece of bread and hold it up. **As Elijah promised, God took care of the woman and her son. The next time she went to make bread, there was more oil and flour! God kept adding more oil and flour to her jars. Let's add a little more flour to this jar. In fact, God never let her oil and flour run out, so she could make bread for a long time! Let's eat this yummy bread and remember that God takes care of you, too!**

Tear off a chunk of bread to serve to each child.

 • **How did God take care of the woman, her son, and Elijah?**

• **How does God take care of you?**

 God took care of the woman, her son, and Elijah by giving them lots of oil and flour to make bread. Jesus also trusted God to always take care of him. Jesus didn't have lots of money or food or even a home. But Jesus always trusted that God would provide those things for him. Jesus told us not to worry, but to trust God to give us what we need. God takes care of us by giving us all we need— food, family, and people who love us.

Crafts

God Really Cares!

Supplies: paper, glue, wheat crackers, small container of oil, small container of flour, eye dropper

Give each child a piece of paper. Set out glue, wheat crackers, oil, and flour.

 • **What did the woman need oil and flour for?**

 The woman used oil and flour to make bread for Elijah.

Use a dropper to place a tiny drop of oil on each paper. Let children rub the oil into the paper. Then have each child dip his or her finger in the flour and smooth it on the page. Finally, have each child glue a wheat cracker on the page to show the bread the woman baked for Elijah.

 God took care of the lady and her son by making sure their oil and flour didn't run out. They had enough bread for a long time! Aren't you glad God takes care of us, too?

- -

Count Your Blessings Jar

Supplies: baby food jars, family-oriented magazines, cotton swabs or paintbrushes, paints, felt squares (approximately 3-inch squares), ribbon

 In today's Bible story we learned how God took care of Elijah and the widow. They didn't need to worry, God took care of them, and

God takes care of us, too! The ways God provides for us can be called "blessings." We are going to make a "Count Your Blessings" jar. First, let's find some pictures of things we are thankful for.

Provide family-oriented magazines with pictures children can easily identify. Encourage the children to tear out one or two pictures of something for which they are thankful. Save the pictures to place in the baby-food jars later.

Give each child a jar, and instruct the children to use cotton swabs or paintbrushes to paint a design on their jars. Help the children cover their lids with squares of felt. Tie the felt on with ribbon. Encourage the children to place their pictures inside the jars.

say ▶ **When you are worried about something, pull out a blessing and thank God for caring for you!**

PRayeRS

"Don't Worry" Prayer

Supplies: none

Have children form a circle on the floor.

say ▶ **We all get sad and worried about things.** Have the children share something that they each worry about (a thunderstorm, a new school, the loss of a pet). **The Bible tells us "don't worry." That's because God takes care of us. Let's pray about these worries and thank God for taking care of us.**

Let children take turns praying, "God, thank you for taking care of me when I'm worried." When each child has had a turn, pray:

In Jesus' name, amen.

God Heals Naaman

Bible Basis:

 2 Kings 5:1-16

Supplies:

Bible, white frosting, plastic knife, dishpan, water, several hand towels

 **ALLERGY ALERT**

Pretend that the classroom doorway is the door to Elisha's home. Gather the kids on the side of the room opposite the door.

Open your Bible to 2 Kings 5, and show children the words.

say ▸ **Today's Bible story tells us that God wants us to be humble.**

Our story today is about Naaman, a man who was a great leader of many soldiers. Why don't you all stand and pretend that you're Naaman's soldiers? Pause to let kids stand in a straight line.

Naaman was a great leader, but he was very proud. Naaman always wanted to be first in everything. Stand straight and tall as you walk proudly to the front of the line. Lead the kids in marching around the room, then let the children sit down.

God wants us to be humble. God wants us to remember that he's the great one, not us. Well, even though Naaman was a great leader, he had two problems. One (hold up one finger)**, he didn't know God; and two** (hold up two fingers)**, he was sick with a disease called leprosy. Leprosy is a disease that causes sores all over a person's skin. Let's pretend that there are sores on our arms.** Put a few smudges of frosting on each child's arms. Put some on your arms, too. (If you'd rather not use frosting, sunscreen works well, too.)

ask ▸ **· Have you ever been sick? What was it like?**

say ▸ **Naaman's wife had a young servant girl who loved God. When the girl heard that Naaman was sick, she told Naaman's wife about the prophet Elisha who could cure Naaman. So Naaman went to Israel hoping that he would be healed.**

Proud Naaman traveled to Israel with his horses and chariots. Chariots are like fancy wagons. Naaman thought he could use his great riches to buy healing for his body. Let's pretend to be proud, rich Naaman and go to Israel with all of our fine horses and chariots. Ask the kids to walk tall and proud or to pretend to ride horses. Lead them to the doorway of your classroom.

ask ▸ · What do you have that you really like?

say ▸ God blesses us with nice things, but God wants us to be humble and thankful, not proud. Naaman was proud that he had beautiful horses and chariots and lots of money.

Finally Naaman arrived at Elisha's house. Pause for the children to knock. **But Elisha didn't come to the door. He sent a messenger to tell Naaman to wash himself seven times in the Jordan River to be healed. Naaman couldn't believe that Elisha hadn't come to the door to give him that message himself! Surely Elisha would come out to see such an important man as Naaman! Well, this made Naaman mad. "How dare Elisha not come out of his house to greet me!" he thought. "What a joke! Why would I want to wash seven times in the muddy waters of the Jordan River?"** Have the children stomp back toward the other side of the room.

ask ▸ · When have you been told to do something that you didn't want to do? How did you act?

say ▸ Naaman's humble servants came to Naaman and told him that if Elisha had asked him to do something great, Naaman would have done it. So why wouldn't Naaman try a simple thing like washing in the Jordan River? Naaman decided to do what Elisha had told him to, and he washed seven times in the muddy water. Let's pretend to go to the river with Naaman and wash our arms.

Have the kids walk to the dishpan. Encourage them to slowly count to seven as they wash and dip their arms in the water seven times. The children may notice that not much happens to the frosting on their arms for the first few times. When kids reach the seventh time, have them shout the number seven and wash all of the frosting off. Then let the children dry their arms and hug each other. Celebrate that everyone is clean!

say ▸ When Naaman obeyed Elisha, who was speaking for God, Naaman got better! The leprosy was gone! Naaman realized that he shouldn't have been so proud of himself and that he should have trusted God. Naaman thought, "God is greater than I am!" Have everyone repeat the sentence. **Humble Naaman went back to Elisha and told him that he believed in God. God wants us to be humble, too.**

ask ▸ · How did Naaman act at the beginning of the story?

· How did Naaman act after God healed him?

· What can we do to show that God is greater than we are?

say ▸ Naaman didn't want to wash in the Jordan River, because the river was muddy and Naaman was too proud to do something so yucky. But God wanted Naaman to be humble and obey. When Naaman obeyed God and washed in the river, God healed Naaman's sickness.

ask ▸ · Can you think of ways to be humble?

say ▸ **God doesn't want us to be proud and think that we're better than everyone else. God wants us to know how important he is, and not to act like we're the important ones. God is greater than everyone. God wants us to be humble.**

One way we can be humble is to follow Jesus' example and serve our friends. When Jesus was on earth, he washed the feet of all of his disciples. Jesus was a king; he wasn't supposed to wash the feet of people—that's a job for servants! But Jesus loved his disciples and he wanted to serve them. Jesus humbled himself and served his friends out of love. We can serve and love our friends just as Jesus did.

BiBLe eXPeRienceS

A Dip in the River

Supplies: plastic tub, towel, water, plastic figures (people)

Before class, set up a water station by placing a plastic tub on a towel and partially filling the tub with water. Set out plastic figures next to the tub. Encourage kids to dip and swim the plastic figures in the "river."

As kids are playing, help kids remember that in today's Bible story, a sick man dipped himself in a river to get well.

Leper Hands

Supplies: black construction paper (one per child), paint brush, pie tin full of washable white poster paint, wet wipes or paper towels

Before class, set out the construction paper, paint brush, paint, and wet wipes or paper towels. Write each child's name on a piece of construction paper. Paint the palms of the child's hands with white poster paint, and have the child place his or her hands on the construction paper. Use wet wipes or paper towels to wipe off the child's hands. Tell kids that today's Bible story is about a man who had a sickness called leprosy, which turned his hands white and made the skin peel and hurt.

CRaftS

Obedient Naaman

Supplies: white chalk, wet wipes, paper (not white) with an outline of a man on it (representing Naaman)

Set out white chalk and wet wipes. Distribute the paper, and have the kids write their names on them. Have the children form pairs, and tell the partners to help each other retell the Bible story. Let the children use the chalk to color "leprosy spots" on

Naaman's arms. At the end of the story, when Naaman obeys and washes in the river, have the kids use wet wipes to remove the chalk spots.

ask ▸ • Why didn't Naaman want to obey Elisha?

• What made Naaman humble at the end of the story?

• How can you be humble?

say ▸ At first, Naaman was proud and thought that he was a great and important man. Later Naaman learned that God was more important. Naaman was healed when he became humble and obeyed God! God wants us to be humble and obey him, just as Naaman did.

Seeing Spots

Supplies: white paper with a gingerbread figure drawn on it, fine-tipped washable markers, wax paper (cut into 8½x11-inch pieces), stapler

say ▸ In today's Bible story, God healed a man named Naaman. Naaman was sick and had spots all over his body, but God healed him. Let's make something to help us remember this story.

Give each child a sheet of paper with the gingerbread figure drawn on it. Explain that the figure represents Naaman. Set out fine-tipped washable markers and let kids color clothes, hair, and facial features on their figures.

When kids have finished coloring their Naaman figures, go around the room and staple a sheet of wax paper on top of each child's Naaman page. Staple the papers together only at the top, so kids can lift the sheet of wax paper.

Point out that kids can look through the wax paper and see the Naaman figure underneath. Have kids use a permanent marker to trace the outline on the wax paper page, and then draw spots all over the wax paper figure.

ask ▸ • Why didn't Naaman want to dip himself in the Jordan River at first?

• What happened when Naaman followed God's directions?

say ▸ At first, Naaman wasn't humble. He thought he was too good to dip himself in the yucky Jordan River. But when Naaman finally became humble and followed God's directions, God healed him! Let's use our papers to see what that was like!

Lead kids in counting to seven, just as Naaman dipped himself in the river seven times. Then have kids lift the wax paper up to see Naaman's spots disappear! Encourage kids to use their papers to tell their families the Bible story. Remind them that God wanted Naaman to be humble, and God wants us to be humble, too.

Games

Proud Run

Supplies: none

say ▶ **When people think more of themselves than others, we say they are "stuck up" and have their noses in the air. They think of only themselves and don't notice others around them! Have the kids stand and stick their noses in the air. But God wants us to be humble and notice others around us.** Have the children look around at all of the other kids in the room.

Then direct the kids to line up on one side of the room. When you say "Go," have the children stick their noses in the air and walk quickly, but carefully, across the room and back. Then let the children race a second time while they look forward—with no noses in the air!

ask ▶ • **Which way was easier for you to go across the room?**

• **Who is the greatest of all?**

say ▶ **It was much easier to run when you didn't have your nose in the air, wasn't it? God wants us to be humble and not to think of just ourselves! Let's remember to think of others before ourselves. And let's remember that God is the greatest of all!**

Seven Dips

Supplies: blue sheet, CD player, children's music CD

Lay out a blue sheet on the floor. Have the children stand in a circle around the sheet. Tell the children that the sheet will be the river.

Cue the CD to play an upbeat children's song. As you play the song, have children walk around the "river." When the music stops, they are to jump onto the sheet seven times, pretending to be Naaman dipping himself in the Jordan River. Help kids count out loud each time they jump into the river until they have done it seven times.

ask ▶ • **How did you feel as you were dipping in our "river"?**

• **After each dip in the water, what do you think Naaman was feeling?**

• **How do you think God felt as Naaman obeyed him and dipped in the water?**

say ▶ **Elisha told Naaman to dip himself in the river seven times, just as you dipped in our river seven times. Even though Naaman didn't want to, he humbled himself and obeyed God and Elisha. Naaman was healed because he learned how to be humble. God wants us to be humble.**

PRAYERS

River Prayer

Supplies: blue sheet

Lay out a blue sheet on the floor to make a pretend river.

Remind kids that God healed and helped Naaman when he finally obeyed God. Gather the children around the "river." As you say each line in the following prayer, have the children step into the river together and repeat the line after you:

> **Dear God,**
>
> **Thank you for loving me.**
>
> **Please help me be humble.**
>
> **Help me obey you.**
>
> **Thank you for taking care of me.**
>
> **I love you, God.**
>
> **In Jesus' name, amen.**

snacks

Time for a Dip

Supplies: chocolate pudding cups, seven bear- or elf-shaped cookies, plastic spoons

Have children wash their hands.

say ▶ **In today's Bible story, we learned how Naaman finally humbled himself and obeyed God by dipping in the Jordan River seven times.**

Before we make a snack to remind us of today's story, let's be humble and say a prayer to God. Have children close their eyes and bow their heads.

pray ▶ **Dear God, thank you for always knowing what's best for us. Thank you for being patient with us. Thank you for loving us. Help us to be humble. In Jesus' name, amen.**

Give each child a cup of chocolate pudding. Explain that the pudding represents the muddy Jordan River from the Bible story. Then give each child seven bear- or elf-shaped cookies. Tell kids that the cookies represent Naaman. Explain that before kids eat each cookie, you'll lead them in dipping the cookie in the pudding seven times. Count to seven for each cookie.

After kids enjoy their treats, **ask** ▶ the following questions:

> • **What happened when Naaman finally humbled himself and did what God told him?**

- **What does it mean to be humble?**
- **Why do you think God wants us to be humble?**

 God wanted Naaman to be humble and not think he was too good for what God wanted him to do. God wants us to be humble, too. God knows what's best for us, just as he knew what was best for Naaman. Let's try to remember this week to be humble and do what God wants us to do.

Eating Humble Pie

Supplies: bowl of wafer crumbs, bowl of butterscotch pudding, paper cups, plastic spoons, bear-shaped cookies

Have the children wash their hands or use wet wipes before beginning. Set out the bowl of wafer crumbs and the bowl of butterscotch pudding. You'll need a paper cup, a spoon, and a bear-shaped cookie for each child. Invite the children to thank God for their snack and to ask God to help them be humble just as Naaman was humble.

Give each child a paper cup. Encourage children to put several spoonfuls of wafer crumbs and several spoonfuls of pudding in their cups. Then have kids mix the crumbs and pudding together to make "mud." Remind them that God had Elisha tell Naaman to dip himself in the muddy river seven times so he could be healed. Give each child a bear-shaped cookie, and encourage children to pretend the cookies are Naaman. Have them dip their cookies in the mud seven times.

 Naaman didn't want to swim in the yucky river, but he wanted God to heal him. He learned that God wants us to be humble and do whatever God tells us to do.

SONGS

Be Humble

Supplies: none

As you teach the children this active rhyme, remind them that when we obey God, we are being humble.

> **When God tells me to stop, I stop!** (Shout out the last "stop" and hold out your hand to signal "stop.")
>
> **When God says go, I go!** (Shout out the last "go" and march in place.)
>
> **I'll be humble and obey his Word** (hold out your hands like an open book)
>
> **Because I love him so!** (Cross your arms across your chest.)

JeHoSHaPHaT TRUSTS GoD FoR ViCToRY

Bible Basis:

2 Chronicles 20:1-30

Sing Your Worries Away

Supplies:

Bible, paper crown, poster board, markers or crayons, CD player, children's praise music CD

Open your Bible to 2 Chronicles 20:1-30, and show the children the words.

say ▸ **Today's Bible story tells us that God helps us.**

Jehoshaphat was a very good king of the Israelites. Put on the paper crown. **One day someone told him that a huge army was coming to fight the Israelites. Jehoshaphat was worried and scared, because he knew that he didn't have many people to fight back! Let's pretend you're the Israelites and I'm Jehoshaphat. There aren't very many of us to fight a big army!**

ask ▸ **• What do you think King Jehoshaphat should do?**

say ▸ **Jehoshaphat knew what to do. He decided to pray and give God his worries. He asked all the people to pray to God.** Lead children in kneeling and folding hands as if praying.

ask ▸ **• What are some things that you pray for?**

Hand out markers or crayons, and encourage the children to draw one thing they pray for onto the poster.

say ▸ **Well, God told the people not to worry, because he'd help them. The people were so thankful that God was going to help them, they sang songs and worshipped him.**

The next day, the Israelites left to meet the big army that wanted to fight. As they marched, the Israelites sang and praised God.

Lead children in marching around the room, singing a familiar praise song with the CD.

say ▸ **While Jehoshaphat and the people were singing, the men in the mean army began fighting themselves! The soldiers got confused. They fought each other and lost! By the time the Israelites got to the army, there were no soldiers left! God's people were so happy that they praised God.** Have children jump up and down and say, "Praise God!" Then instruct the children to draw one thing they praise God for beside their earlier picture of a prayer request.

ask ▸ • How did God help King Jehoshaphat and his people?

• What can we do the next time we're worried?

say ▸ When Jehoshaphat and his people were worried, they prayed and sang and asked God to help them. And God helped them. Jesus also prayed to God when he was worried. All through his life, Jesus would pray to God to help him and take care of him. God answered Jesus' prayers, and he will answer our prayers, too. Any time you're worried, you can pray and sing. God will help you, too!

Crafts

Pray Today

Supplies: paper plates (one per child), crayons or markers, brad paper fasteners, paper arrows to represent the hands on a clock (one long, one short per child)

Explain that children will be making clocks to help them remember that God helps us all the time, just as he helped Jehoshaphat. Give each child a paper plate, and instruct children to draw the numbers 1 through 12 around the face of the "clock."

Poke a brad through the blunt end of each arrow you made before class, and help attach it to the center of the plate. Show children how to spin the arrow to point to different times.

Direct the children to sit in a circle with their clocks. Go around the circle, and let each child hold up his or her clock and say, "I trust God to help me when I'm [name of activity or place]. I'll remember to pray today!" After all of the children have had a turn, lead kids in a prayer thanking God for helping us.

ask ▸ • What did Jehoshaphat do when he was worried?

• When are times you're worried?

• What can you do the next time you get scared or worried?

say ▸ Jehoshaphat prayed when he was worried, and you can pray, too. God helped Jehoshaphat, and God will always help you! In fact, there's never a time that God won't be ready to help. At any time of the day or night, God is ready to help us.

Games

Lend a Hand

Supplies: a sheet

Set out a sheet, and choose one child to sit on one end of the sheet. Ask if the child can move across the room without using his or her hands or legs. Then let the rest of the children hold the other end of the sheet and work together to pull the child across the room. Then choose another person to have a ride on the sheet. Continue until everyone has had a ride.

• How did your friends help you get across the room?

• What was it like to help someone ride on the sheet?

 You all worked hard to help your friends. It's good to have helpful friends we trust, and it's good to serve a God who loves us and helps us! God helped Jehoshaphat, and God will always helps us!

snacks

Put 'Em Together

Supplies: mini bagels (cut in half), jelly, plastic knives, napkins

Have the children wash their hands (or use wet wipes) and then sit down to prepare their snack. Give each child two mini-bagel halves, jelly, a plastic knife, and a napkin. Help children spread jelly on their mini-bagels, then let preschoolers hold one half of a bagel in each hand.

 Our hands hold something good! When we put our hands together, we'll make a yummy snack we can eat. Have children carefully put their hands together and make a mini-bagel sandwich. Instruct children to set the sandwiches down on their napkins. **When we put our hands together we can also pray and ask God to help us. Jehoshaphat prayed, and God helped him. God will always help us, too! Let's put our hands together and pray for our yummy snack.** Ask a child to pray, then let everyone eat their treats.

songs

"Don't Worry" Rhyme

Supplies: none

As you teach your children this rhyme, remind them that they should give God their worries just as Jehoshaphat did.

Rhyme: **When you start to worry,** (Place hands on cheeks and look worried.)

Begin praying in a hurry! (Form praying hands.)

God will take your cares away. (Hide hands behind your back.)

So you can have a happy day. (Use index fingers to point to your smile.)

ESTHER SAVES GOD'S PEOPLE

Bible Basis:

 Esther 2–9

Esther Prepares for the King

Supplies:

Bible, baby doll, large cotton ball, perfume, silky fabric

Open your Bible to the book of Esther, and show children the words.

 say ▶ **Today's Bible story teaches us that God can use us to do good works for him.**

This is Esther. Show doll. **The king of Persia had captured Esther and the rest of God's people and had brought them to live in his country. One day the king of Persia decided that he wanted a new queen. He sent his servants throughout the country to gather all the pretty ladies who weren't married yet and bring them to the king's palace. There would be a big beauty contest, and the most beautiful woman would become queen.**

To prepare for the contest, the young ladies were given fancy clothes to wear. Let's dress Esther in some fancy clothes to get her ready to meet the king. Have each child glue a piece of silky fabric to Esther.

The ladies also took long baths and put on sweet-smelling perfume. Let's put perfume on Esther so that she smells good for the king. Spray a large cotton ball with perfume, and let kids pass around the cotton ball and dab the perfume onto Esther.

When all the girls were ready to meet the king, they were brought into the royal palace to stand in front of him. When Esther stood before the king, he liked her very much and chose her to be his new queen. God was planning on using Esther to do an important job for him.

Esther's cousin Mordecai told Queen Esther about a bad man named Haman who wanted to kill all of God's people, including Mordecai. Have children say, "Oh, no!" **Mordecai wanted Esther to tell the king about the plan. But in their country, it was against the rules for people to speak to the king if the king hadn't asked them first. Esther was afraid that the king would get mad at her if she asked to see him. So she told Mordecai to pray that the king would**

want to talk to her. Then she would go talk to the king. God was going to use Esther to do great things for him. Have children show "scared" expressions and then fold their hands and pretend to pray.

Esther and Mordecai prayed to God, and God helped Esther be brave when she went to talk to the king. She put on her fanciest clothes and went to see him. Lead the children in pretending to put on their nicest clothes.

The king was happy to see Queen Esther and invited her to come in. Esther asked the king and Haman to a dinner that she would make for them. Let's pretend to eat Esther's fancy dinner with the king and Haman.

After this special dinner, Queen Esther invited the king and Haman to another dinner party. At the second dinner, Esther told the king that Haman wanted to kill her and all the rest of God's people. This made the king angry because he loved Esther. The king decided that Haman would be punished instead of God's people. So Esther and God's people celebrated because God used Esther to save her people from death. Have children clap and cheer. **God used Esther to save her people, and God can use you to help others.**

ask • How do you think Esther felt when she went to see the king?

• How do you think she felt when the king let her and her people live?

say God gave Esther courage, and she was brave enough to go see the king. She also had courage to tell the king about what was going to happen to her. Because of Esther's courage, all of God's people were saved. God used Esther to save the Jewish people. God can use you to do brave things for him as well.

We can also read the stories about Jesus to see how God used Jesus to help him. God used Jesus to serve people and to help people get closer to God. God used Jesus to die on the cross so that all people who believe in him can live in heaven with Jesus and God forever! God can use you to help him, just as God used Esther and Jesus!

BiBLe eXPeRieNceS

Move to the Scepter

Supplies: "scepter" (use a toy wand or baton)

Have the kids think of ways that God can use them to do good works, such as hugging a neighbor, patting a back, and telling people that God loves them. Then give a child the "scepter," and have the child pretend to be a king or queen. Have him or her hold up the scepter and say one good work for the other kids to do, such as "hug as many children as you can," "pat other children on the back," or "say 'God loves you' to other children." As long as the scepter is up, the kids will continue to do that good work. When the child lowers the scepter, everyone stops. Then the child with the scepter will choose the next king or queen. The new leader will hold up the scepter and say another good work for all of the kids to do. If you have time, continue until all of the children have had the chance to be the king or queen and hold up the scepter.

ask · What good works did we just do?

· What good work did Esther do in the Bible story?

say God used Esther to save the Jewish people. We can do good things, too, by being kind to people. We can be friendly to new kids and invite friends to church to learn about God. God can use us to help him.

crafts

A Guiding Star

Supplies: small paper plates, scissors, stapler, ribbons (two pieces per child), crayons or washable markers, glitter glue, stickers

Ask children to cut a circle shape from the center of a small paper plate, then have the children staple two ribbons to the bottom of the circle. Tell the children to decorate the top of this award with star drawings, glitter glue, and stickers. Explain to the children that Esther had a family member guide her to do the right thing, just as they have parents to guide them. Have children present these awards to their parents as a thank you for being a "guiding star."

ask · What are some ways that your parents guide you?

· How can God use you to guide or help other people?

say In our story today, God used Esther to save her people. God uses your parents to help you and to guide you. God can use you to help others, too!

Blooming Beauties

Supplies: tissue paper (three pieces paper-clipped together per child), chenille wire

Give each child three pieces of tissue paper and a chenille wire. Show children how to fold the tissue paper back and forth like a fan. Make the folds about one-inch wide. Once the children have finished folding, encourage them to each find the center of their fan by folding it in half. Next, help each child wrap the chenille wire around the center of the tissue paper and twist the wire tight. Remove the paper clips from the tissue paper. Help kids pull apart the tissue paper to form beautiful flowers.

say In our story today, we met a woman named Esther who was very beautiful. The king married her because she looked beautiful on the outside. But Esther was beautiful on the outside and the inside. She loved God, and God used her to save her people.

ask · How did God use Esther in the Bible story?

· Why was Esther beautiful on the inside?

· What are some ways God can use you?

say ▸ Just as these flowers are beautiful, we can be beautiful by letting God use us to do good works. Take your flowers home, and put them somewhere that will remind you that you are beautiful on the outside and the inside, just like Esther. And God can use you, just as he used Esther.

PRAYERS

Royal Chair Prayer

Supplies: blanket, glittery garland

Cover a classroom chair with a blanket, and wrap glittery garlands around it. Give each child an opportunity to sit on the chair while other kids take turns praying for the child. Kids could pray, "Thanks, God, for using [name of child] to do your good works." After each child who wants to has had a chance to sit in the chair, close by having the kids fold their hands and bow their heads while you say the following prayer.

PRAY ▸ Dear God,

Thank you for creating Queen Esther to do good works and save the people.

Thank you for using each of us to help you and to tell others about you.

In Jesus' name, amen.

Good Works Plates

Supplies: paper plates

say ▸ God used Esther to do good works for him. We're going to pray and ask God to use us to do good works at home, such as helping set the table. As you pray, I'd like you to set a plate on the table to show one way you can do good works at home. Give each child a plate, and have children take turns setting their plates on the table as they say the following prayer.

PRAY ▸ Dear God, please use me to do good works. In Jesus' name, amen.

SNACKS

Food for a King and Queen

Supplies: plastic knives, plates, slices of cheese, crackers, scarves, play jewelry

Set out plastic knives, plates, slices of cheese, and crackers. Also set out scarves and play jewelry, and let the children pretend that they're kings and queens having a meal together. Tell the children that the name Esther means star and that they're going to have star snacks. Have the children wash their hands, then help the kids cut small squares of cheese. Demonstrate how to put one square on top of another, offset to look like a star. Let the children make several stars and put the stars on crackers, then encourage the children to do good works by serving one another. Say a prayer of thanksgiving, and let the children enjoy the snacks.

> **say** God created us to do good works, and you all were used by God to make special snacks for each other. You were all stars today, just as Queen Esther was a star in today's story! God can use you every day, just as he used Esther in the story.

Helping Others

Supplies: dish towels, clothespins, gelatin cups, plastic spoons

Have children wash their hands (or use wet wipes) and then find partners.

> **say** Today we learned about Esther and how God used her to save her people. God has created us to do good works for him. Let's do good works by helping feed each other.

Put a dish towel around the neck of one child in each group to serve as a bib, and fasten it in the back with a clothespin. Give the other partner in each group a bowl with a small amount of gelatin in it. Instruct the children with gelatin to feed the other children using spoons. Then have partners switch roles, giving them clean towels, spoons, and bowls of gelatin. When they're finished, have children wipe their hands and faces with wet wipes.

> **ask** • How did you feel when you were helping your partner eat?
>
> • What other ways can God use you to help others?

> **say** There are many ways you can help people. God can use you in many ways.

SONGS

"God Can Use Us" Rhyme

Supplies: none

As you teach the children this active rhyme, remind them that God can use them, just as he used Esther.

God can use us if we're tall. (Stand up tall and reach for the ceiling.)

God can use us if we're small (crouch low to the ground)**,**

If we're weak or have great might (show strong arm muscles)**,**

If we're brave or scared at night. (Cover your eyes.)

When we try and when we fall (sit down on the floor)**,**

God can use us one and all. (Spread your arms wide.)

JOB Remains Faithful in Suffering

Bible Basis:

 Job 1:1–2:10; 42:1-6, 10-17

God Helps Job

Supplies:

Bible, several plastic animals, several plastic people figures, adhesive bandage

Before class, set out several plastic animals and toy people figures. Designate one toy person to be Job.

Have kids form a circle and sit down. Open your Bible to Job 1, and show children the words.

say **Satan is a bad angel who tried to trick people to make them stop being friends with God. One day Satan decided he would trick Job into being mad at God by hurting Job. Satan thought that maybe Job would be so mad and sad that he would decide God wasn't any good anymore.**

Let's help Job stay true to God and remember that God helps us when we're hurting by shouting, "God helps us when we're hurting!" to Job at different times throughout the Bible story. Practice a few times with the children.

First, Satan tried to hurt Job by sending bad people to come and hurt his oxen and donkeys and the servants who took care of those animals. Take away a third of the plastic animals, and set them behind you so kids can't see them. **Job was sad, but he kept loving God, and God helped him feel better.** Encourage kids to shout, "God helps us when we're hurting!"

Next, Satan tried to hurt Job by sending a fire from the sky that hurt Job's sheep and his servants. Take away another third of the animals and a third of the toy people. **Job was sad, but he kept loving God, and God helped him feel better.** Encourage kids to shout, "God helps us when we're hurting!"

Next, Satan hurt Job by sending mean people to hurt all of Job's camels and servants. Take away the last of the animals and another third of the toy people. **Job was sad, but he kept loving God, and God helped him feel better.** Encourage kids to shout, "God helps us when we're hurting!"

Then Satan saw that he couldn't trick Job into hating God, so he knocked down a house where all of Job's children were eating. All of Job's children died. Take away the last of the toy people—be sure to leave the Job figure. **Job was sad, but he kept loving God, and God helped him feel better.** Encourage kids to shout, "God helps us when we're hurting!"

Satan tried one last time to trick Job into hating God. Satan gave Job painful sores and bumps all over his body. Put an adhesive bandage on the Job figure. **Job was sad, but he kept loving God, and God helped him feel better.** Encourage kids to shout, "God helps us when we're hurting!"

Even though Satan took away everything Job had and made Job sick, Job kept loving God. God saw that Job kept loving him, even when it was hard.

ask • **When have you felt sick or sad?**

• **How has God helped you feel better when you were hurting?**

say **God helped Job and made Job feel better. God gave Job gold, animals, servants, and best of all, 10 wonderful children for Job to love!** Put all of the plastic figures back in front of you. **God helped Job when he was hurting, and Job chose to keep loving God even when it was hard. God will help us when we're hurting, too. And we can always choose to love God!**

Crafts

Favorite Animals

Supplies: blank paper, crayons, scissors

Have children draw, color, and cut out pictures of their favorite animals. Tell kids that Job had lots of animals, but then he lost all the animals.

ask • **Why are these animals your favorite?**

• **How would you feel if you lost them?**

• **How do you feel when you lose things that are important to you?**

• **What can you do when you feel that way?**

Tell kids that God gave Job new animals, and took care of Job. Say that God will take care of us, too.

Games

Help Me!

Supplies: none

Divide kids into pairs. Once all the kids have partners, tell one child in each pair to pretend to have a broken leg. Instruct the other child in each pair to act out ways he or she can help the partner with the broken leg. Kids might help their partners walk, put casts on the broken legs, give partners crutches, or bring partners drinks of water. Encourage kids to switch roles and pretend that one child in each pair has a headache. The other partner should act out ways to help the child with the headache. Continue playing, offering several different scenarios in which one partner in each pair is hurt.

ask • **How did you help your hurt friend?**

• **How did God help Job in our story?**

say God helped Job when Job was hurting. God will also help us when we're hurting. Sometimes God uses other people to help us, just as you helped each other in our game. God always helps us when we're hurting.

Prayers

Action Prayer

Supplies: none

Remind kids that God helped Job, and God will always help us, too. Lead kids in the following responsive prayer.

Teacher: **Dear God, when I've stubbed my toe,**

Children: You help me.

Teacher: **When my mom says "no,"**

Children: You help me.

Teacher: **When I'm feeling sad,**

Children: You help me.

Teacher: **When I hurt real bad,**

Children: You help me.

Teacher: **Thank you, Lord, for loving us!**

In Jesus' name, amen.

snacks

God Takes Care of You

Supplies: 1 bagel half per child, cream cheese, bowls, green food coloring, craft sticks, gummy bears, animal crackers, paper plates

Before class, mix green food coloring into plain cream cheese, and put the cream cheese into several small bowls.

Before you begin this activity, have children wash their hands (or use wet wipes). Give each child a bagel half, a gummy bear, several animal crackers, a paper plate, and a craft stick. Have children use their craft sticks to spread cream cheese on the bagel halves. Then encourage them to put the gummy bears and the animal crackers on the bagels. Tell children that each gummy bear represents Job and the animal crackers represent all the things, including animals, that God gave back to Job because he believed in God and trusted him when he was hurting. When kids have finished putting together their snacks, ask a child to thank God for giving us hope when we are hurting and for helping us be strong like Job. After the prayer, let the children eat their snacks.

 say ▸ **We can have hope in God because we know that God helps us when we're hurting, just as he helped Job.**

songs

Hanging Tough

Supplies: none

You can use this finger play to give your children an example of what it means to be a faithful friend to God, even when times get tough.

Job loved God (hug yourself)

And always took time to pray. (Make praying hands.)

Satan thought if Job's life got tough (hold fists in front of you),

Job's love would go away. (Wave goodbye.)

Satan took away Job's cattle (push arms away and say, "Moo")

And his sheep and house, too. (Push arms away and say, "Baa.")

But Job loved God and kept his faith (fold hands in prayer),

And so can you! (Point to each other.)

DaNieL CHooSes to FoLLoW GoD

Bible Basis:

 Daniel 1:1-20

Put Us to the Test!

Supplies:

Bible, colored construction paper, tape, scissors, stapler

Before class, make a pompom from construction paper for each child. Take three sheets of different colored 8½x11 construction paper and staple them together in one corner. Roll the attached sheets into a tube. Tape the seam. Cut 6-inch slits at one end of the tube. The children will fan the slits to form a pompom they can shake. Make a pompom for yourself also.

Open your Bible to Daniel 1, and show the children the words.

say **Our true Bible story today is about how Daniel and his friends chose to follow God because God knows best. I'm going to need some cheerleaders to help me tell the story. Would all of you be my cheerleaders? First you'll need pompoms.** Hand the children the pompoms you prepared in advance. Show them how to fan out the "fingers" of the pompoms and shake them. **Next, we need to practice our cheer. I'll lead and you follow me.** Demonstrate the following simple cheer:

God knows best! (Shake the pompom with each syllable.)

Put us to the test! (Point to self with pompom.)

Go-o-o-o God! (Wave both hands in the air.)

When it is time for our cheer, I'll say, "Ready?" and you'll say, "OK!" the same way cheerleaders do. Then you follow me in the cheer. Ready? (Children respond "OK!") Repeat the cheer. Practice this several times. **Now we're ready to begin our story.** Have kids sit in a line facing you on the floor with their pompoms in their laps.

Daniel and his three friends were very good. They always chose to serve God because they knew that God knows best. Ready? (Children respond "OK!" and give the cheer along with you.)

One day, a king named Nebuchadnezzar said to his servants, "Go get the best and smartest young men and bring them to me to serve me." The servants went all over, looking high and low for the best people. They took Daniel and his three friends away from their homes. They brought them far away, to where the king lived.

The king kept Daniel and his friends at the palace. The king told the guard to feed Daniel and his friends all the fancy food from the king's own table. But God told Daniel that they shouldn't eat that food. Maybe it wasn't really healthy; maybe the food wasn't good for them.

ask • **What kind of junk foods do we eat sometimes?**

say Well, maybe the king's food was like that. **Daniel wanted to follow God in everything—even when it was hard, even when he was far away from home—because God knows best. Ready?** (Children respond "OK!" and give the cheer along with you.) **So Daniel asked if they could eat the simple food, like vegetables, that God told them to eat. The guard was afraid to go against the king's orders and give them the simple food. He thought they would not look healthy and strong if they didn't eat the king's food. But Daniel knew that God knows best. Ready?** (Children respond "OK!" and give the cheer along with you.) **So Daniel said, "Just try it and put us to the test! Let us eat the simple food for 10 days and see if we don't look stronger and healthier than the other men who eat the king's fancy food." He knew that God knows best. Ready?** (Children respond "OK!" and give the cheer along with you.)

So the guard put them to the test. He gave Daniel and his friends the vegetables and simple food for 10 days.

ask • **At the end of 10 days of eating the food God wanted them to, how do you think Daniel and his friends looked?**

say **Daniel and his friends looked stronger and healthier than the other people who ate the king's fancy food! God knew what was best for them. Ready?** (Children respond "OK!" and give the cheer along with you.) **We follow God in everything—the big things and the small things—because God knows best.**

God blessed Daniel and his friends by helping them learn everything they needed to learn and become very wise. When you are wise, you are smart and you know just what to do. When we follow God, he helps us to be wise. It must have been hard for Daniel to follow God when he was so far from his home, but God helped him! We should always follow God because he knows what is best for us! Ready? (Children respond "OK!" and give the cheer along with you.)

ask • **How did it feel to follow me in our cheer?**

• **Why do you think Daniel chose to follow God?**

• **How do you think God felt when Daniel chose to follow him?**

say **It pleases God when we choose to follow him because God knows best. God loved Daniel very much. God loves us very much, too, and wants us to have good lives. He loves us so much that he sent his Son, Jesus, to help us. Jesus told us how much God loves us—he told us we are God's children! And God's children follow God's rules because God knows best.**

ALLeRGY aLeRt

CRaftS

Veggie Prints

Supplies: celery stalks with leaves, apples, bell peppers, star fruit, knife, plastic forks, tape, paper, newspaper, tempera paint, shallow pans, smocks

Before class, cut vegetables or fruits into shapes the kids can use to make prints. For example, cut apples in half sideways, and make slices of bell peppers or star fruit. Use celery leaves as a paintbrush. Set up a workspace covered with newspapers or a plastic tablecloth. Tape a piece of white paper at each place. Place a smock and a plastic fork at each place. (You can make very simple paint smocks by cutting holes in paper grocery bags for a child's arms and head.)

Gather the children at the workstation you have prepared with newspaper, white papers, and plastic forks. Help the children put on smocks to protect their clothing. Set out sliced vegetables and fruits for the children to dip in washable paint. Place shallow pans of tempera paint at the workstation. Show children how to use plastic forks as handles and dip the slices of fruit into washable paint. Show them how to use the celery leaves as paintbrushes. Help them create prints on their papers.

say ▶ **Just as there are lots of different ways to paint a beautiful picture, there are lots of ways to follow God. We can obey our parents, love our neighbors, and share our toys.**

ask ▶ • **Can you think of another way to choose to follow God in your home?**

say ▶ **Let's choose to follow God this week because God knows best. Take your painting home and tell your family about some ways to follow God.**

GameS

Carrot, Carrot, Who's Got the Carrot?

Supplies: large carrot, CD player, kid-friendly Christian music CD

Talk about different ways to follow God by being kind to others, such as giving someone a pat on the back, helping them with something, or sharing a big smile. Have the children form a circle and sit on the floor. Play the CD as the children pass a carrot among themselves. Stop the music at random and say "Freeze." Ask the child holding the carrot to jump up and call out a way to follow God, either one you just discussed or a new one. Have the other children clap and say, "God knows best!" Repeat until each child has had a chance to share a way to follow God.

say ▶ **Daniel followed God in many ways. He followed God in the big things and the small things. He followed God even when it was hard, and so can we. We can trust what God tells us to do because God knows best.**

Daniel Eats Healthy Foods

Supplies: carrot, potato, celery stalk, green pepper, tomato, and other assorted vegetables, low-fat dressing

Seat the children in a circle. Pass a potato around the circle while saying the words below. Say each line in a rhythmic fashion, and have the children echo the line. At the end of the rhyme, the child holding the potato will say, "Daniel ate potatoes and he became strong."

Use a different vegetable each time you play the game, and change the ending statement accordingly (for example, "Daniel ate carrots…")

After you play the game several times, snack on raw vegetable slices dipped in low-fat ranch dressing.

> **say** **Daniel and his friends had to work for the king.** (Have children echo the line.)
>
> **The king wanted them to eat everything.** (Echo.)
>
> **Daniel said his people could not eat forbidden food.** (Echo.)
>
> **The ruler thought that Daniel was being very rude.** (Echo.)
>
> **Daniel said, "Let me eat food that is good for me.** (Echo.)
>
> **And at the end of 10 days, what a difference you'll see."** (Echo.)
>
> **Daniel and his friend ate the food God OK'd.** (Echo.)
>
> **Daniel was right—what a difference it made!** (Echo.)
>
> **Daniel and his friends looked healthy and strong.** (Echo.)
>
> **By obeying God, they couldn't go wrong!** (Echo.)

Follow the Leader

Supplies: none

Lead the children in a game of Follow the Leader in which they follow you around the room, matching your movements. Remind children that Daniel followed God. Stop at intervals to lead the following chant:

> **God is good,**
>
> **God is best!**
>
> **Follow him 'cause**
>
> **He knows best!**

PRAYERS

Action Prayer

Supplies: none

Remind children that Daniel followed God, even when it was hard. Have children find partners and link arms with their partners. Encourage partners to pray this prayer for each other, repeating each line after you.

 Dear God,

> **Please help my friend follow you**
>
> **Even when it's hard.**
>
> **Thank you that you know what's best for us.**
>
> **In Jesus' name, amen.**

SNACKS

Happy to Follow

Supplies: bananas, grapes, apples, knife, lemon juice, paper plates

Cut round banana slices for eyes, cut grapes in half for noses, cut apple slices for mouths. Store the fruit in lemon juice to prevent browning. Set out paper plates.

Have children wash their hands (or use wet wipes) and then gather together to make the snack. Give each child a small paper plate. Show them how to create happy faces on the plates by using round banana slices for eyes, a half of a grape for a nose, and an apple slice for a mouth. Invite a child to pray and thank God for the food. Then let kids enjoy their snacks.

 • **How do you think Daniel felt when God helped him become wise?**

• **How do you think God feels when we follow him?**

 God is so pleased when we follow him because he loves us and wants the very best for us. God always knows what's best.

Daniel's Friends are safe in the Fiery Furnace

Bible Basis:

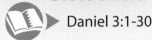

Daniel 3:1-30

A Fiery Fourth

Supplies:

Bible, red and orange paper, scissors, blanket, tape, table

Before class, cut flames from red and orange paper. You'll need enough flames for each child to have one and a few extras for visitors.

Tape a blanket around the sides and back of a table, and place the table in the center of the room.

Open your Bible to Daniel 3, and show children the words.

say **Today's Bible story teaches us that we can stand up for God. Our story is about three young men who were very brave and stood up for God. These three young men were named Shadrach, Meshach, and Abednego.** Ask three children to pretend to be Shadrach, Meshach, and Abednego and to stand next to the table. Ask the rest of the class to sit in front of the table, and give each child a flame.

The king told everyone to bow down before a god that wasn't the real true God. Shadrach, Meshach, and Abednego said that they could only bow down and worship the one and only true God. The king became angry and decided to get rid of the men! He threw them in a fiery furnace. Have the three children crawl under the table, and then have the rest of the children stand up and march around the table waving their flames. Encourage kids to make fire noises, such as "crackle, crackle." As the kids march, choose one child to join the three children under the table.

God took care of Shadrach, Meshach, and Abednego. He even sent someone from heaven to help them. When the king looked into the furnace, he saw an extra person in the fire. Then the king understood that Shadrach, Meshach, and Abednego's God had kept them safe in the fire. The king knew that their God was the one and only true God. So the king had the men taken out of the fire right away. Have the children sit on their flames.

Shadrach, Meshach, and Abednego stood up for God and didn't bow down to the statue, and God saved them.

ask · How do you think Shadrach, Meshach, and Abednego felt when they were thrown into the furnace?

· How do you think they felt when God saved them?

say Shadrach, Meshach, and Abednego would only worship the true God. They did the right thing and obeyed God by not bowing down to the king's false god, even though it made the king angry. Shadrach, Meshach, and Abednego were brave and stood up for God, and God took care of them. We can stand up for God, too.

Jesus also stood up for God when he was on earth. Jesus told others about God, and he helped others get to know God better. We can follow Jesus' example and the example of Shadrach, Meshach, and Abednego. We can stand up for God in our lives!

Bible Experiences

Standing Tall

Supplies: Bible, red crepe paper or strips of fabric, hula hoop, table

Before class, tie the red crepe paper or strips of fabric to the hoop. Save at least one red streamer for each child.

Have kids form a circle and sit down. Open your Bible to Daniel 3, and show children the words.

say Our story is about three young men who were very brave and stood up for God. These three men were named Shadrach, Meshach, and Abednego. Ask three volunteers to pretend to be Shadrach, Meshach, and Abednego and to stand next to the table. Ask the rest of the class to sit in front of the table, and give each child a red streamer.

The king told everyone to bow down before a god that wasn't the real, true God. Shadrach, Meshach, and Abednego loved God and said they would bow down and worship only the real God. This didn't make the king happy at all! In fact, he was so angry that he threw the three men into a fiery, hot furnace!

Have the three children step into the hoop and pull it up around their waists. Encourage the other children to stand up and march around the table, waving their "flames." Tell kids to make fire noises, such as "crackle, crackle." As kids march, choose one child to join the three children in the hoop.

say God took care of Shadrach, Meshach, and Abednego. God even sent someone from heaven to help them! When the king looked into the furnace, he saw an extra person in the fire. Then the king understood that Shadrach, Meshach, and Abednego's God was the only real, true God!

Play this fun game to help children remember the Bible story. Choose three different children to be Shadrach, Meshach, and Abednego. Have the three children step inside the hoop and hold the hoop at their waists so the "flames" are all around them. Choose one child inside the hoop to be the tagger. The tagger doesn't need to hold on to the hoop. The children inside the hoop must move together to help the tagger tag a fourth child with his or her hands. When the tagger tags someone, that child should climb inside the hoop. Then the four kids should immediately drop the hoop so that it falls around their legs. Then they should shout out this chant (encourage other kids to join in as well):

Nebuchadnezzar threw in three,

But I count four! How can that be?

One, two, three, four!

Come on out,

Let's play some more!

Choose three new children, and repeat the game. Then **ask**

- **How do you think the three friends felt when God saved them?**

- **How can you stand up for God like the three friends did?**

say Shadrach, Meshach, and Abednego would worship only the true God. They did the right thing and stood up for God when they chose not to bow down to the fake god—even though they knew they'd get in trouble with the king. We can be brave and stand up for God, too!

CRAFTS

Hot Feet

Supplies: 2 pieces of card stock per child; hole punch; yarn; red, yellow, and orange markers or crayons

Before class, draw flames onto 8½x11-inch pieces of card stock. You'll need two pieces for each child. Punch holes in the corners of each piece of card stock, and cut four 18-inch pieces of yarn for each child.

say Shadrach, Meshach, and Abednego loved the one true God and would not bow down to a pretend god. Even though the king got very angry, the three friends did not change their minds. They stood strong and did what was right.

ask - How do you think Shadrach, Meshach, and Abednego felt when the king told them that they would have to stand in a furnace filled with flames?

- How do you think the king felt when he saw how God protected Shadrach, Meshach, and Abednego?

say Let's make something that will help us think about Shadrach, Meshach, and Abednego standing up for God in the fiery hot furnace.

Give each child two card stock flames. Encourage the kids to color the flames with red, yellow, and orange markers or crayons. When kids have finished coloring, have them string yarn through the holes in the two pieces of card stock. Each child should string one piece of yarn in and out of the top set of holes in each flame and another piece of yarn through the bottom set.

Tie the flames onto each child's legs as if the flames were shin guards.

ask • **Why do you think Shadrach, Meshach, and Abednego stood up for God?**

• **How can you stand up for God?**

Call out each child's name.

• **Can** [name of child] **stand up for God?**

Encourage the child to stand tall and say, "I can stand up for God."

Fiery Furnace

Supplies: red, orange, and yellow tissue paper; building blocks

Have red, orange, and yellow tissue paper ready on a table. Tell the children God saved three men who were thrown into a hot, fiery furnace. Have children help you make some pretend fire. Show children how to crumple the tissue paper to look like flames. Encourage kids to put all three colors together to look even more like flames! Then have children tape the flames to some building blocks and stack the blocks to make a pretend furnace.

PRayeRS

Action Prayer

Supplies: table

Create a simple pretend furnace out of a table. Let the children lay their flames on the floor all around the furnace. Then have the children form pairs, and let the pairs take turns sitting in the fiery furnace as they say the following rhyming prayer:

Lord, help me to be very brave.

I'll stand up for you so others see

You are the God who lives in me.

In Jesus' name, amen.

Snacks

Cheese Flames

Supplies: bread slices, pretzel sticks, squeezable cheese spread

Have children wash their hands (or use wet wipes).

Give each child a piece of bread. Let children squeeze the cheese spread onto the bread slices to create the flames of the fiery furnace. Have children use pretzel sticks to create Shadrach, Meshach, Abednego, and a heavenly visitor in the midst of the flames. Invite a child to pray and thank God for the food. Then let kids enjoy their snacks.

 • **What do you think Shadrach, Meshach, and Abednego thought when they saw a fourth person in the furnace with them?**

 Shadrach, Meshach, and Abednego stood up for God. They did what was right even though it made the king mad. We can stand up for God, too.

Watching Glasses

Supplies: round or oval crackers, whipped cheese, olives, one-inch licorice pieces, plastic spoons, napkins

Give each child two round or oval crackers and a napkin. Help them spread the whipped cheese on the crackers with plastic spoons. Place olives in the centers of the crackers. Give each child a one-inch strip of licorice, and show him or her how to put the licorice between the two crackers to form "glasses." Explain that God doesn't need glasses to see us. As children eat the glasses, remind them that God watches over us when we're scared, just as he was watching over Daniel's friends when they were in the fiery furnace.

Songs

Stand, Stand, Stand

Supplies: none

Remind kids that Daniel's friends stood up for God, and God helped them. Lead children in singing the following song to the tune of "Row, Row, Row Your Boat."

Have kids march in place as they sing.

 Stand, stand, stand for God

No matter what you do.

Even when the going's rough,

God will help you through.

JoNaH

Bible Basis:

 Jonah 1:1–3:10

Supplies:

Bible, boat tickets (create these out of paper), table (overturned to represent a boat), "Nineveh" and "Tarshish" signs with arrows drawn on them pointing in the direction of the different places, tape, spray bottle filled with water, sheet

Before class turn one table upside down to represent the boat. Cover another table with a sheet to represent the fish, and hang the "Nineveh" and "Tarshish" signs.

Open your Bible to Jonah 1, and show children the words.

say **Today's Bible story tells us to do what God wants.**

God told a man named Jonah to go to a city called Nineveh. God told Jonah to warn the people that they should stop doing bad things. Jonah didn't want to do what God told him to do, so he tried to run away from God. Give each child a boat ticket, and have the children sit on the overturned table. **Jonah got on a ship that was headed away from Nineveh.** Point out the signs to Nineveh and to Tarshish, and show the children that Tarshish is in the opposite direction from Nineveh. **God caused a storm that put the ship in danger. The wind blew and the waves splashed.** Have the kids rock back and forth in the make-believe ship as you spray them lightly with water.

ask **• Have you ever been in a storm? What was that like?**

say **Well, Jonah didn't even know about the storm. He was asleep in the bottom of the boat. The sailors woke up Jonah and asked him why God was making this storm. Jonah knew it was because he hadn't done what God wanted. God was trying to get Jonah's attention. Jonah told the men to throw him into the water, and then God would calm the storm. The men didn't want to throw Jonah into the water but the storm kept getting worse. So they threw Jonah overboard.** Have the children climb off the overturned table and pretend that they're swimming. **But as Jonah sank into the water, God sent a giant fish to swallow him.** Direct the kids to crawl under the table that you covered with the sheet and pretend that they're inside a giant fish. **Jonah was in the belly of that fish for three days!**

ask ▸ • What do you think it was like inside the fish?

say ▸ **When Jonah was in the fish's belly, he said a prayer to thank God for saving him. Jonah promised that he'd change his ways. Then God caused the fish to spit Jonah up on the shore.** One at a time, have the children come out from under the table. **God asked Jonah once more to go to Nineveh. This time Jonah obeyed God and went to talk to the people there.** Have the children walk to the Nineveh sign on the wall and say, "Please stop doing bad things! Do what God wants!" **The people listened to Jonah, and they turned away from the bad things they'd done. And Jonah, too, finally learned to do what God wants.**

Have the kids sit in a circle.

ask ▸ • Why did Jonah decide to do what God wanted?

• What are some things you know that God wants you to do?

say ▸ Jonah had to go through some pretty scary things to learn to do what God wants. We can learn from Jonah's story and remember that God wants us to love others and to love God. The Bible helps us to know what God wants us to do. We can also follow Jesus' example and obey God. When Jesus was on earth he obeyed God and followed God's commands. Jesus loved God and wanted to serve and obey God.

Bible Experiences

Whale Adventure

Supplies: white marker, large dark sheet or plastic tablecloth, table

Before class, use a white marker to draw the outline of a whale on a large dark sheet or plastic tablecloth. Drape the sheet over a table, making sure it hangs down to the floor. As each child comes to class, ask if he or she would like to crawl inside the whale. Say that today's Bible story is about a man who lived inside the belly of a whale for three days and nights.

If a child is timid about crawling under the sheet-draped table, you might go inside with him or her. While inside the whale, ask the children what they think it would be like to be inside a huge fish for three days and nights. Talk about the sounds, the movement, the smell, the wetness, and the dark. Ask kids how they'd feel to be alone inside a dark, wet place.

Remind children that God loves them and is always with them. Say that Jonah learned to obey God, and we can learn to obey God, too!

Jonah's Journey

Supplies: Bible-times map

Bring in a Bible-times map and show kids where Jonah was when God called him to preach in Nineveh. Point out the location of Nineveh and the way that Jonah actually went (the opposite direction) before he decided to obey God and go to Nineveh. You can find a Bible-times map in the back of most Bibles, or you can do an Internet search using the words "Nineveh map."

Crafts

Fun Fish

Supplies: small paper lunch bags, 8-inch lengths of yarn, markers, and newsprint

Show children how to make a simple paper-bag fish. Loosely stuff a bag with crumpled newsprint, then tie the open end of the bag shut with the yarn. Leave about an inch of paper bag to flair out at the end—that will be the fish's tail fins. Draw eyes and a mouth at the stuffed end of the bag, and there's your fish!

Remind kids that Jonah was swallowed by a big fish.

Games

Road to Nineveh

Supplies: building blocks

Form two groups of children that will build two cities with building blocks. Have one group of children build Nineveh and the other build Jonah's hometown. Tell the children that the Lord asked Jonah to go to Nineveh. Encourage kids to build a road from one town to the other. Then have kids take turns acting like Jonah. Have them start at Jonah's hometown and then walk slowly toward Nineveh. Then have the kids turn and run quickly back to Jonah's hometown. Remind the children that Jonah chose to run away at first, but we should always do what God wants. Then have children take turns walking briskly to Nineveh from Jonah's hometown.

ask
- **Why do you think Jonah ran away the first time?**
- **What would you have chosen to do?**
- **How do you think God felt when Jonah finally went to Nineveh?**

say It took him awhile, but Jonah realized that he needed to do what God wants. So he went to Nineveh to tell the people there that God's ways are best.

God's Way

Supplies: "Nineveh" and "Tarshish" signs, markers

Draw a smiling face under the word "Nineveh" and a frown under the word "Tarshish." Ask one child to hold up the pictures on one side of the room, and ask the other children to stand on the opposite side of the room. As the child holds up the picture of the smiling face (Nineveh), the other children may walk forward. When the child holds up the frowning face (Tarshish), the others must stop. Have the child alternate the two signs until all of the children have crossed the room. Then all of the kids can hug and say, "Do what God wants."

ask
- **What did you like about this game?**
- **Was it easy or hard to know God's way in the game? What was that like?**

say **In our game, we walked when we saw the smiling face. But in life, we know what God wants us to do by listening to Bible stories and by talking with others who follow Jesus. Do what God wants!**

Snacks

Stuck Inside a Fish

Supplies: pita bread, gummy bears, paper plates

Have your kids prepare a snack and use it to retell the story. Give each child half of a pita bread to represent the big fish and gummy bears to represent Jonah. Have the children form pairs and use the snack foods to tell their partners the story. Then have kids say a prayer, and let them eat their snacks.

ask
- **How do you think Jonah felt when he was inside the fish?**
- **How do you feel when you do something bad?**

say **God loves us and he knows what is best for us. God knew that it was best for Jonah to go to Nineveh. It made God happy when Jonah obeyed him and went to Nineveh. We can obey God and do what God wants, just as Jonah did when he finally went to Nineveh.**

Do What God Wants

Supplies: none

Lead the kids in singing "Do What God Wants" to the tune of "Do Lord." Encourage the kids to join you in singing and doing the motions. Remind kids that Jonah learned to obey God and do what was right.

Do what (march in place)

Our God wants (point up);

His ways are always right! (Palms together, hands "swim" away.)

Do what (march in place)

Our God wants (point up);

His ways are always right! (Palms together, hands "swim" away.)

Do what (march in place)

Our God wants (point up);

His ways are always right! (Palms together, hands "swim" away.)

Yes, the ways of the Lord (point up)

Are right! (Raise both hands high.)

God's Direction Rhyme

Supplies: none

As you teach the children this active rhyme, remind them that God loves us and wants the best for us. That's why we should do what God wants. Say that God knew what was best for Jonah, and God knows what's best for us.

North (point up),

South (point down),

East (point to the children's right),

And west (point to the children's left)—

The ways of the Lord are always best. (Point straight forward with both hands.)

He guides me in my walk each day. (Make a walking motion with your hands.)

Following him is the only way! (Point straight up.)

JONAH COMPLAINS ABOUT GOD'S COMPASSION

Bible Basis:

Jonah 3:10–4:11

A Hot Reminder

Supplies:

Bible, bedsheets, chairs

Before class, make a "shelter" for the children to sit under. Drape a tablecloth or bedsheets over some chairs to make the shelter.

Open your Bible to Jonah 3, and show children the words. Gather all the children under the shelter you made before class.

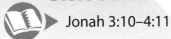 **Today's Bible story tells us that we are to love people who don't know God.** Tell children that when you clap your hands twice, they should say, "Love people who don't know God."

After Jonah went to Nineveh and told all the people about God, they quit doing bad things, and God forgave them. God was so happy! God was happy that Jonah obeyed him and went to Nineveh, and God was happy that the people in Nineveh repented and turned to God. God was patient with Jonah, and God was patient with the people.

But instead of being happy that the people had turned to God, Jonah was angry. Jonah thought that the people should be punished since they had been so bad. Jonah did not love people who don't know God. Clap twice, and have kids shout, "Love people who don't know God."

Jonah left the city and built a shelter. He sat in his shelter to watch for bad things to happen to the people of Nineveh. God was sad because Jonah didn't love the people of Nineveh, not even after the people turned to God. But God was patient with Jonah. God wanted Jonah to repent, turn away from his bad attitude, and love the people of Nineveh. So God made a large vine grow over Jonah's shelter to give him shade while God waited for Jonah to repent. But the next day, a worm came and ate the vine so that it died and withered away. Let's pretend our vine has withered away and we no longer have any shade. Let the children pretend that their index fingers are worms. Show kids how to wiggle their fingers around the sheet and pretend that the worm is eating the shelter. After a few minutes, remove the shelter.

Jonah no longer had any shade out there in the hot sun. The sun beat down on Jonah. Let's pretend that it is very hot.

Jonah still didn't repent, so God sent a wind to blow on Jonah. Have kids blow air at each other. **Jonah was so hot, he thought he would die. But he still didn't want to repent. Jonah was still angry that God had forgiven the people of Nineveh instead of destroying them.** Clap twice, and have kids shout, "Love people who don't know God." **God reminded Jonah that he loved all the people of Nineveh, even though they used to be his enemies. They did bad things before, but the people of Nineveh turned away from their sins, and they followed God's ways. God was glad that they had quit doing bad things. God wanted Jonah to be glad, too, because he should love people who don't know God.** Clap twice, and have kids shout, "Love people who don't know God."

ask • **How did God feel about the people of Nineveh?**

• **How did God want Jonah to feel about the people of Nineveh?**

say Let's remember that God wants us to love people who don't know God, even if they are our enemies.

Lead the children in singing "God Loves Everyone" to the tune of "Deep and Wide."

God loves you. God loves me.

God loves everyone in the whole world.

God wants us to love them, too,

And love the kids that need to know him, too.

(Repeat.)

say **God reminded Jonah that he loves everyone, even those who don't know him. That's why we should also love people who don't know God. Jesus is the very best example of someone who loves people who don't know God. In fact, Jesus even died for all the people who don't know God! When Jesus was on earth, he taught people that didn't know God, and he spent lots of time with those people, too. Because of Jesus, those people did get to know God! And because Jesus died for us, we can know God and spend eternity with God and Jesus in heaven. We can be like Jesus and love people who don't know God.**

BiBLe eXPeRIeNces

Love Everyone!

Supplies: Bible, green construction paper, hair dryer, 1 sock per 2 children, scissors

Before class, cut large leaves out of the green construction paper.

Have kids form a circle and sit down. Open your Bible to Jonah 4, and show children the words.

say ▶ **Jonah was angry with God for being so nice to the people of Nineveh. Jonah wanted God to punish them for all the wrong things they'd done. Jonah didn't think it was fair that God was going to forgive the people of Nineveh and not punish them at all.** Have everyone pretend to pout as Jonah may have pouted.

So Jonah went outside the city and sat down so he could see what God would do to the city. Choose one child to be Jonah and sit down, and have the other kids gather in a circle around the child. **It was very hot outside, and soon Jonah became uncomfortable. God sent a nice leafy plant to shade Jonah from the sun.** Give half of the standing children the green construction paper leaves you made before class. Encourage kids to hold the leaves over "Jonah" and wave them to create a breeze.

Jonah was glad that God sent the plant. But God wanted to teach Jonah a lesson, so he sent a worm to eat the plant. Give the other half of the standing children socks to wear on one of their hands. Encourage children to pretend their sock-covered hand is a worm and to have the worm eat away the plants. After a bit, set the worms and the green construction paper leaves aside.

God also sent a very hot wind to blow on Jonah. Start the hair dryer, and set it on high heat. Blow the hot air toward Jonah and the other kids. **The sun beat down on Jonah's head until he felt very sick. In fact, Jonah felt so sick that he wanted to die!**

Then God said to Jonah, "You are sorry about a plant dying, but you don't care about an entire city dying. I love Nineveh, and I feel sorry for them." God wanted Jonah to understand that God loves all people and wants all people to believe in him and love him. God wants us to love all people. He even wants us to love people who don't know God!

ask ▶ • **Why didn't Jonah want God to forgive the people of Nineveh?**

• **Have you ever been upset because someone didn't get punished for something he or she did wrong? What happened?**

• **Why is it important to show love to people who don't know God?**

• **How can you show love to people who don't know God?**

CRafts

Hearts of Love

Supplies: 5-inch construction paper heart for each child, glitter, sequins, ribbon, stickers, glue

Before class, cut out a 5-inch construction-paper heart for each child.

Give each child a heart. Encourage the children to color and decorate their hearts with decorating supplies such as glitter, sequins, buttons, ribbon, and stickers. Encourage each child to choose a person whom he or she loves and wants to give the heart to. Write the person's name on the back of the heart, and set the heart aside for the child to take home. Tell children that they should love all people—even the people who don't know God. Remind children to take home their hearts and give them to the special people.

Games

Loving People

Supplies: magazines with pictures of kids, canning-lid rings or embroidery hoops

Lay several open magazines on the floor.

> **say** ▶ **God wants us to love all different kinds of people, even people who don't know him.**

Give each child a few canning-lid rings or embroidery hoops. Have children stand and take turns dropping their rings onto the poster to "frame" people's faces. As a child drops a ring, have him or her say, "God loves you!" to the child whose face is mostly in the ring. After everyone has had a few turns, discuss the following questions.

> **ask** ▶ • **How do you think you might show God's love to these people?**
>
> • **How did Jonah feel about the people of Nineveh?**
>
> • **How do you think Jonah could have shown love to the people of Nineveh?**

> **say** ▶ **Jonah was mad because God loved the people of Nineveh even though they had done bad things. But God created the people of Nineveh and loved them. God wanted Jonah to love people who don't know God.**

PRayeRs

Action Prayer

Supplies: blankets, bedsheets

Remind kids that Jonah learned that God loves everyone. Have children find partners. Hand out blankets or bedsheets, and help kids set up partner or small group shelters by draping the sheets over tables. Encourage partners to sit together under their shelters and pray this prayer for each other.

 PRaY **Dear Lord,**

Thank you for loving my friend [partner's name]**.**

Help me love other people, too,

Even those who don't know you.

In Jesus' name, amen.

snacks

Fig Shelter

ALLeRGY aLeRt

Supplies: fig cookies, pretzel sticks, gummy bears

Have children wash their hands (or use wet wipes) and then gather together to make the snack. Give each child one fig cookie, four pretzel sticks, and one gummy bear. Show kids how to poke a pretzel stick into each corner of the cookie to make the legs of the shelter. Then have children put their gummy bears under the shelters to be "Jonah."

ask • **How did Jonah feel as he sat under his shelter?**

• **How did God want Jonah to feel about the people of Nineveh?**

• **How can you love people who don't know God?**

say **Even after Jonah had spoken to the people of Nineveh, he still wanted God to punish them. The Bible doesn't tell us if Jonah ever learned his lesson, but we can love people who don't know God.**

songs

Love God's People

Supplies: none

Sing this song with your children to help them remember that Jonah learned that God loves everyone, and that we should try to love everyone, too. Sing it to the tune of "Frere Jacques."

Love the people (hug yourself)**,**

Love the people (hug yourself)**,**

That don't know God. (Shake your head from side to side.)

That don't know God. (Shake your head from side to side.)

I will love them always. (Hug yourself.)

I will love them always. (Hug yourself.)

You can, too! (Point to others around you.)

You can, too! (Point to others around you.)

an angel appears to Joseph

Bible Basis:

> Isaiah 7:13-14; Matthew 1:18-25

A Dream Come True

Supplies:

Bible, brown paper lunch bags, craft sticks, aluminum foil, glue, construction paper, glitter, markers, crayons

Before class, set out the craft supplies.

Have kids form a circle and sit down. Give each child three brown paper bags and one small craft stick. Encourage kids to use foil, glitter, and white crayons to decorate one brown paper sack as an angel puppet. Tell kids to use the markers and construction paper to decorate one of the other puppets as Joseph and the other puppet as Mary. Have kids draw a baby on the craft stick. Tell kids to use their puppets to act out the story as you tell it.

Open your Bible to Matthew 1, and show children the words.

Say **Joseph was planning to be married to Mary. But when Joseph found out that she was going to have a baby, he was a little worried.** Encourage children to make their Joseph puppets shake their heads and mumble. **Joseph didn't know that Mary was going to have God's Son!**

One night Joseph was asleep. Encourage children to make their Joseph puppets sleep. **While he was sleeping, he had a dream. An angel appeared to him in his dream.** Encourage kids to bring out their angel puppet. **The angel said to Joseph, "Don't be afraid to marry Mary. She loves God, and the baby she will have is God's Son!"** Let children use their angel puppets to repeat the angel's words. **"You should name the baby Jesus because the baby will grow up to save the world."** Encourage kids to have their angel puppets repeat those words. **Then the angel disappeared and Joseph woke up.** Encourage children to have their Joseph puppets wake up.

Joseph believed what the angel said, and he chose to trust God's plans. He married Mary, and when her son was born, they named him Jesus. Encourage children to bring out their Mary puppets and pretend to have Mary and Joseph get married. Then have kids glue the small craft stick "baby Jesus" to their Mary puppets.

When you're finished with the story, have kids sing the following song to the tune of "London Bridge." Choose two kids to be the bridge, and encourage the other kids to walk under the "bridge." At the end of the song, the bridge should collapse and capture one child.

SING
> **Joseph, you can trust God's plans,**
>
> **Trust God's plans, trust God's plans.**
>
> **Joseph, you can trust God's plans**
>
> **Because God loves you!**

When kids capture a student in their arms, tell them to sing the song again, using the captured child's name in place of Joseph's name. Then let the captured child choose another child, and those two children will become the new bridge. Continue playing until each child gets a chance to be captured and play the bridge. Remind children that they can always trust God's plans.

ask
> • **How did Joseph trust God's plans?**
>
> • **How can you trust God's plans for your life?**

BiBLe eXPeRieNCeS

Baby Bunting

Supplies: one 12-inch length of curling ribbon and 1 paper towel per child, scissors, markers, newsprint

Before class, cut curling ribbon into 12-inch lengths.

Set out markers and pieces of newsprint. Show children how to crumple the newsprint into paper wads. Help each child place a paper wad in the center of a paper towel. As children bunch the towel around the paper wad, tie a piece of curling ribbon under the paper wad "head." Use scissors to carefully curl the ribbon under the baby's chin for each child.

Let children use markers to draw faces on their babies. Show children how to cradle and rock their towel babies.

ask
> • **What kinds of things do mothers and fathers do when they take care of a baby?**
>
> • **How do you think Mary and Joseph felt about their baby, Jesus?**

say
> **God had a plan when he sent Jesus to earth as a baby. He knew that Jesus would grow up and do great things. When we believe in Jesus and we're sorry for our sins, we can be forgiven and we can live with God and Jesus forever in heaven. God has good plans, and we can trust God's plans! Let's use our babies to act out this song.**

Lead kids in the following motions as they sing this song to the tune of "Mary Had a Little Lamb."

> **God sent Jesus down to earth** (raise baby, then slowly lower it)**,**
>
> **Down to earth** (raise baby, then slowly lower it)**,**
>
> **Down to earth.** (Raise baby, then slowly lower it.)

God sent Jesus down to earth (raise baby, then slowly lower it)

As a baby. (Rock baby.)

Jesus came to save us all (hold baby in one arm and point to others with other hand)**,**

Save us all (hold baby and point to others)**,**

Save us all. (Hold baby and point to others.)

Jesus came to save us all. (Hold baby and point to others.)

Believe in Jesus. (Hug baby.)

CRafts

Good Hands

Supplies: construction paper, scissors, stapler, tape, pen

Remind kids that Joseph trusted God's good plans, even though he didn't understand all of them.

Let children trace their hands on a sheet of construction paper. Help kids cut out their hand shapes, and staple or tape the two hands together all around the edges, leaving an open space at the top. Write the following rhyme on each child's pair of hands.

I trust you, God. I trust your plans.

It's good to know I'm in good hands.

In Jesus' name, amen.

Encourage kids to talk with their parents about times they're afraid. Their parents can write their fear, and place it inside the hands to remind them that they are safe inside God's loving hands and plans.

Games

Joseph and Mary

Supplies: none

Divide your class into two groups, a "Joseph" group and a "Mary" group. Have the groups stand on opposite ends of the room. Sing "Joseph, Bring Mary Home" to the tune of "The Farmer in the Dell." As you sing, have each "Joseph" walk across the room and take a "Mary" home (back across the room). Have Mary and Joseph sit together, and have Mary pretend to rock a baby.

Joseph, bring Mary home.

Joseph, bring Mary home.

Trust God's plans. You're in good hands.

Joseph, bring Mary home.

(Repeat two times.)

Baby Care

Supplies: baby dolls, plastic baby bottles, small stuffed animals, and other baby supplies such as rattles, pacifiers, and disposable diapers

Before class, set out various baby dolls, plastic baby bottles, small stuffed animals, and other baby supplies (such as rattles, pacifiers, and disposable diapers). Invite children to pretend to care for the babies. Ask what needs a baby has and how to take care of a baby. Tell children that Jesus came to earth as a baby, just as the angel said he would. When Jesus was a baby his mother took care of him.

PRAYERS

Action Prayer

Supplies: newsprint, marker, tape

Before class, draw a large outline of a hand on newsprint and tape it to the floor.

Have each child take a turn standing on the hand you drew before class and saying the following prayer. If you have a large class, make more than one hand or make the hand larger so more than one child can stand inside at a time. Remind children that Joseph trusted God's plans.

 PRay I trust you, God. I trust your plans.

It's good to know I'm in good hands.

In Jesus' name, amen.

SNacKS

Angel Snacks

Supplies: 1 paper plate, 1 small round cookie, and 2 marshmallows per child; marshmallow creme, napkins

say Let's make a snack to help us remember that Jesus came to earth as a baby, just like the angel said he would. Joseph learned that he could trust God's plans, and we can trust God's plans, too!

Have children wash their hands. Then demonstrate how to make a marshmallow angel. Carefully break a small round cookie in half. Lay the two halves, spread apart at the bottom, on a small paper plate. Use marshmallow creme to stick two marshmallows together, one for the angel's head and one for the body. Use the marshmallow creme to stick the angel to the cookie "wings."

Before kids enjoy their snacks, lead them in a prayer. Ask God to help them trust his plans, just as Joseph did when the angel said Jesus would come to earth as a baby.

As kids enjoy their treats, ask the following questions. Encourage all children to contribute their ideas.

ask • Do you think it was hard for Joseph to trust what the angel said? Why or why not?

• What kinds of plans do you think God has for you and your family?

• How does it feel to know that you can trust God's plans?

Encourage kids to show their families how to make snack angels at home. They can use the angels to tell their families how an angel appeared to Joseph.

SONGS

Poetry in Motion

Supplies: 1 small bath towel per child

Give each child a towel. Show kids how to roll up their towels and cradle them like babies. Remind children that Jesus came to earth as a baby, just as the angel said he would.

Practice the following words and motions a couple of times, then begin "Don't You Love to Be a Baby?"

> **Jesus was a baby.** (Cradle the "baby.")
>
> **He grew up to be a man.** (Unroll the towel.)
>
> **Jesus, you're my God.** (Hold the towel over your head.)
>
> **I trust your plans.** (Wrap the towel around yourself.)

Your children will delight in acting out this rhyme over and over.

ask • Why was Joseph afraid?

• Why could he trust God's plans?

say Jesus came to earth as a baby. He was so special because he is also God's very own Son. Jesus wants to be your special friend. You can trust his good plans because Jesus is good and perfect!

John the Baptist Prepares the Way for Jesus

Bible Basis:

> Luke 1

A Welcome Baby

Supplies:

Bible, toy musical instruments (optional)

Have kids form a circle and sit down. Open your Bible to Luke 1, and show children the words. Tell children to pretend to rock a baby every time they hear the word *baby*.

say **Back in Bible times, there was a priest named Zechariah and his wife, Elizabeth. Zechariah and Elizabeth loved God and obeyed him, but they were very sad because they couldn't have a *baby*.** Encourage kids to rock a pretend baby in their arms.

One day Zechariah was working in the Temple—which is like a church—and he suddenly saw an angel of God! The angel told Zechariah that God was going to give him and Elizabeth a *baby*! Encourage kids to rock a pretend baby in their arms. **That was exciting news! But the angel had even more exciting news. The angel told Zechariah that the *baby*** (encourage kids to rock a pretend baby in their arms) **would be a boy and that they should name him John. The angel told Zechariah that John would be a special *baby*** (encourage kids to rock a pretend baby in their arms) **and that he would grow up to help people get ready for Jesus!**

ask • **What are some ways we can get ready for Jesus?**

• **How do you think John helped people get ready for Jesus?**

say **John helped people get ready for Jesus by telling them about Jesus. He also told people that they needed to get their hearts ready for Jesus by telling God about the wrong things they'd done and asking for his forgiveness. Then John would wash the people in water to show that Jesus would forgive the wrong things they'd done. Let's sing a song now about getting ready for Jesus.**

Give children musical instruments such as bells, tambourines, or toy trumpets. If you don't have any instruments, give them anything they can use to make noise! Sing "Are You Ready?" to the tune of "The Battle Hymn of the Republic":

Christmastime is coming;

It's a special time of year.

We must all get ready;

Jesus' birth is almost here.

We must open up our hearts

For the baby, oh, so dear.

Are you ready for our heavenly king?

Everybody's getting ready.

Everybody's getting ready.

Everybody's getting ready,

Ready for our heavenly king.

BiBLe eXPeRieNCeS

Set the Table for a King

Supplies: 1 plastic place setting per child, 1 fancy place setting for Jesus

Before class, prepare a complete plastic place setting (a plate, cup, knife, fork, and spoon) for each child. Prepare one place setting that is fancier than the others. This will be set for Jesus, the special guest. You might also choose to dress up the table with a vase of plastic flowers.

> **say** Let's pretend that Jesus is coming to have lunch with us. Let's get ready!

Give each child the place setting you prepared before class. Show the children how to set the table. When children are finished, make a big deal out of placing the "fancy" setting for Jesus.

When the table is set, pretend to invite Jesus to your special banquet.

> **ask** • What special guests have come to your house?
>
> • How did you prepare for them?
>
> • If Jesus came to your house, how would you prepare for him?

> **say** When we believe in Jesus, he comes to live in our hearts. That's why we need to get our hearts ready for Jesus!

A Place for Baby Jesus

Supplies: none

Children see adults prepare for Christmas by decorating, buying gifts, and trimming the tree. Use this finger play to help them understand that they can get ready for Jesus' coming by making their hearts clean for him. The children will act cleaning up a nursery room for Jesus.

Baby Jesus is coming! Is everything in place? (Draw heart shape on chest.)

We will put away our fighting. (Pretend to pick up something and put it away.)

We will put away our lying. (Repeat motion.)

We will put away our stealing. (Repeat motion.)

These aren't things that baby Jesus would like. (Pretend to rock baby in arms.)

We will paint our room with kindness. (Pretend to paint the air.)

We will give him gifts of love. (Hug yourself.)

We will be ready for baby Jesus. (Pretend to rock baby in arms.)

We will welcome him with love. (Hug yourself.)

Crafts

Baby Quilts

Supplies: Bible, 9x12-inch sheets of paper, markers, scraps of pastel-colored fabric, scissors, glue

Before class, cut fabric scraps into 3-inch squares. Draw twelve 3-inch squares on each sheet of paper.

Give each child a sheet of paper. Have kids write the words from Isaiah 9:6 on the back of the paper. Help children set the fabric squares on the paper, in a pattern, creating a "baby quilt." Let children glue their fabric squares in place. When children have finished, collect craft supplies.

 • **What do people do when they're getting ready for a baby to come?**

• **Why does God want us to be ready for Jesus?**

Read Isaiah 40:3.

 When people are expecting a baby, they make or buy soft blankets that can cover and warm the baby. Keep your blankets in your room to remind you that God prepared for baby Jesus.

Games

Bubble Lesson

Supplies: bottle of bubble solution, a bubble wand for each child

Blow a bubble from the bubble mixture. Catch it with the bubble wand, and hold it up. If the bubble pops, blow and hold another one on your wand.

 Raise your hand when you think this bubble is going to pop. Let's see who can raise a hand closest to the time it pops. Allow the children to raise their hands.

I'll blow bubbles, and you catch one with your wand. Just sit still in your spot, and I'll send some bubbles your way. Be careful not to bump the people sitting near you. Just catch one bubble. If it pops, you can't have another, so be careful with your bubble. Blow small bubbles slowly; catch some for smaller children, and hand the bubbles to them. Play for a while, and see whose bubble lasts the longest.

It's hard to wait for these bubbles, and it's hard to wait for other things to happen, too. That's sort of like how we might get ready for Jesus. While we're waiting for him, let's live the way he wants us to, by telling others about him, going to church, being kind to others, and loving each other. Blow bubbles and let kids try to catch more. When they catch a bubble, have them say one way they can get ready for Jesus.

- -

Great News!

Supplies: none

Sit with children in a circle on the floor. Explain that children will pass around the circle the great news that Jesus is born. You'll say what kind of voice to use as children pass the news. Start by having everyone say, "I bring great news; Jesus is born!" several times. Then tell children that the first time around the circle, they should each whisper the verse to the person on their left.

Begin by whispering the verse to the child sitting to your left. Have that child whisper the verse to the next child and so on until the verse comes back to you. Then vary the way children pass the message. For example, you might shout the verse one time and sing it another.

After children have passed the verse around the circle several times, have them stand and hold hands in a circle.

 • **Why is it important to share the good news that Jesus is born?**

• **Who can you tell about Jesus this week?**

 The angels told the great news that Jesus is born, and we can tell the great news, too!

Snacks

Locusts and Honey Snack

Supplies: celery sticks, cream cheese, pretzels, raisins, plastic knives

Show your class how to make locust snacks from celery sticks, cream cheese, and pretzels. Have the kids use plastic knives to spread cream cheese on the celery sticks and add raisins for eyes. Show the children how to bite the pretzels into legs and use cream cheese to attach them to the celery sticks.

ask • How did John help people get ready for Jesus?

• How can you get ready for Jesus?

say John wanted people to be ready when Jesus came. We need to get ready for Jesus, too. We can get ready for Jesus by asking God to make our hearts clean.

Songs

Time to Get Ready

Supplies: none

Gather the children together in a circle, and teach them this action poem. Remind children that they can get ready for Jesus.

> **John had a job** (hands to mouth as though shouting)**,**
>
> **And we do, too.** (Point thumbs to chest.)
>
> **It's time to get ready** (point to imaginary wristwatch)
>
> **For you-know-who.** (Point up.)
>
> **Let's get excited and give a cheer.** (Clap, then extend right fist above head.)
>
> **Jump for joy—Jesus is here!** (Jump up and down.)

Jesus Is His Name-o

Supplies: none

Sing "Jesus Is His Name-o" to the tune of "Bingo."

> **John the Baptist made the way for the king to come-o.**
>
> **J-E-S-U-S, J-E-S-U-S, J-E-S-U-S,**
>
> **And Jesus is his name-o.**
>
> **God came to earth dressed as a man, and Jesus is his name-o.**
>
> **J-E-S-U-S, J-E-S-U-S, J-E-S-U-S,**
>
> **And Jesus is his name-o.**
>
> **On Christmas Day the king was born, and Jesus is his name-o.**
>
> **J-E-S-U-S, J-E-S-U-S, J-E-S-U-S,**
>
> **And Jesus is his name-o.**
>
> **We thank God for all his love, and Jesus is his name-o.**
>
> **J-E-S-U-S, J-E-S-U-S, J-E-S-U-S,**
>
> **And Jesus is his name-o.**

The Wise Men Come to Worship Jesus

Bible Basis:

 Matthew 2:1-12

Three Wise Men

Supplies:

Bible, three blocks (wrapped in paper), three bows, cotton swabs, vanilla extract, almond extract, gold glitter, glue

Open your Bible to Matthew 2, and show children the words.

say ▶ **Today's Bible story teaches us that we can worship Jesus.**

Before beginning your story, choose children to play the three wise men, Mary, Joseph, Jesus, and King Herod. Have the "three wise men" stand at the front of the class, and have "Mary," "Joseph," "Jesus," and "King Herod" stand off to the side. Explain to the other children that they will pretend to be the chief priests and teachers. When they are asked where the baby king was born, they should shout, "In Bethlehem!" Help the "chief priests and teachers" practice answering in unison.

say ▶ **Today we're going to learn about something special that happened to Jesus when he was about two years old.**

Some wise men lived far away. Point to the wise men. **These wise men were very smart men; they were important people, as important as princes. One of the things they liked to do was study the stars in the sky. One night, they saw something very, very special in the sky.** Have the wise men shade their eyes with their hands, look toward heaven, point, and then jump up and down. **They pointed. Then they jumped up and down. They were so excited!**

They saw a very special star, and they knew it meant that a new baby king was to be born. They knew that this baby king was God. The wise men decided to go to him and worship him. They said, "Let's follow that star and find the new baby king!"

They packed their things, and each wise man took a very expensive gift for the baby king. Give each of the wise men a block with a bow on it. **They took spices and expensive gold. When the wise men were ready for their very long trip, off they went.** Have the wise men walk around the room as you bring King Herod to the front of the class. Have the wise men stop when they reach King Herod.

Finally they came to Jerusalem, where the evil King Herod lived. The wise men asked the king, "Where is the baby king who was born? We saw his star, and we've followed it here." King Herod was angry when he heard that a new baby king had been born. King Herod thought that when the baby grew up, the baby would want to be king and would take his job. He didn't like that thought at all! So King Herod asked the chief priests and teachers if they knew where the baby king was to be born. The chief priests and teachers said, "In Bethlehem." Encourage the chief priests and teachers to shout, "In Bethlehem" with you.

ask • **What would you do if you were King Herod?**

say Well, King Herod called the wise men to him and said, "When you find the baby king, come back and tell me so I can go worship him, too."

The wise men followed the star to Bethlehem. The star stopped over the house where Mary, Joseph, and Jesus lived. Have the wise men walk around the room while Mary, Joseph, and Jesus come to the front of the class. Have King Herod sit down.

When they saw Jesus, the wise men bowed down and worshipped him. Then they gave him the presents they brought. Have the wise men bow down and then give Jesus the gifts.

When it was time for the wise men to go home, God warned them in a dream not to go back to King Herod. So the wise men went home a different way. Have the wise men leave and then sit down.

Have the children sit in a circle with the three gifts in the center.

ask • **How did the wise men worship Jesus?**

say They brought some very special gifts for baby Jesus. Two of the wise men brought very wonderful-smelling gifts. Let's make two of the gifts smell good. Dip a cotton swab in the vanilla extract, and let children wipe the extract on one of the gifts. Dip another cotton swab in the almond extract, and encourage kids to wipe it on a different gift. Then let kids smell the gifts. **The other wise man brought sparkling gold for Jesus. Let's put some gold on the last gift.** Place several drops of glue on the last gift, then pass around a shaker of gold glitter. Encourage each child to shake some gold onto the last gift. When kids have finished, pick up the gift and lightly shake it over a trash can to get rid of any excess glitter. **The wise men worshipped Jesus by bringing him wonderful gifts, but there are many ways to worship Jesus.**

ask • **What are some ways we can worship Jesus?**

say God sees our actions and knows how we feel. God is pleased when we choose to worship him.

BiBLe eXPeRieNCes

Gifts for Jesus

Supplies: gift boxes; gift bags; tissue paper; infant care items such as clothing, bath and feeding items, and toys

Set out gift boxes and bags, tissue paper, and infant care items. Gather children around the supplies. Tell kids that in today's story they will learn about people who brought gifts for the baby Jesus.

Encourage children to choose and wrap gifts that they might have offered to baby Jesus. Remind children that Jesus was a real baby who needed the same love and protection as infants they know.

- -

Amazing Aromas

Supplies: plastic bowls, a variety of spices with distinctive scents and textures, magnifying glass

Put spices in plastic bowls, one spice per bowl. Encourage children to look at the spices and smell them. You might have magnifying glasses available for use in examining the texture of the spices.

CRafts

Scented Boxes

Supplies: small boxes (jewelry size, one per child), glue sticks, four bowls of spices

Set out the bowls of spices. Distribute the boxes. Show kids how to use the glue sticks to put a small amount of glue on each corner of the inside of the boxes. Then have children glue small amounts of spices in the four corners.

ask
- **Why do you think the wise men gave Jesus spices and gold?**
- **How would you feel if you received those gifts today?**
- **What gift would you give to Jesus?**

say **Giving gifts is one wonderful way to worship Jesus, but there are lots of ways to worship Jesus. We can worship Jesus by singing to him, by telling others about him, and by doing the things that Jesus wants us to do. We worship Jesus.**

A Gift for Jesus

Supplies: children's magazines and toy catalogs, scissors, construction paper, glue sticks, ribbon lengths, bows, gift tags

Have children look through magazines for pictures of gifts they would like to give to little Jesus. Remind kids that Jesus was two or three years old, just a little younger than they are. Have each child tear out the picture he or she wants and glue it on a piece of construction paper. Then have the preschoolers make the other side of the paper look like the top of a gift box. Provide bows, the ribbon lengths, and the labeled gift tags.

ask ▸ • What gifts do you like to get?

• Do you think little Jesus might have liked the gifts you like? Why?

say ▸ Jesus was a little child, just like you! I'll bet he really liked getting the gifts the wise men brought to him. We can worship Jesus just as the wise men worshipped Jesus.

Games

Wiggly Worship

Supplies: none

Show kids how to play this variation of Simon Says. Say the phrase "We worship Jesus," then do an action such as clapping your hands. All of the kids will then copy your action. Say the phrase again, then do another action—folding your hands in prayer, for example. All of the kids will then copy the new action. Each time you say the phrase, kids will follow your action. Let each child have an opportunity to lead.

ask ▸ • How did we worship Jesus?

• What are some other ways that we can worship Jesus?

• Why do we worship Jesus?

say ▸ We can worship Jesus by singing, clapping to a beat, and telling others about him. When we worship Jesus, we tell him how much we love him. In our Bible story, the wise men worshipped Jesus, and we can worship Jesus, too.

Follow the Light

Supplies: blocks (one per child), masking tape, baby doll, flashlight

Have the children form a line, shoulder to shoulder, at one end of the classroom, and give each child a block. Ask kids to pretend that the blocks are gifts for Jesus. Put a masking tape "finish line" on the floor some distance from the children. Stand on the other side of the masking tape facing the children, and put a baby doll next to you. Ask the children to pretend that the doll is little Jesus.

say ▶ Today we're going to pretend to be the wise men who followed the star to worship Jesus. Pretend the blocks you're carrying are the presents for Jesus. When I shine this flashlight on your feet, you may follow the light shining on the floor in front of you. But when I turn it off, you have to freeze right where you are. When you reach the line, put your gift in front of little Jesus.

Darken the room as needed, and begin the game. Play until everyone has reached the line and delivered a gift to little Jesus.

ask ▶ • How did you feel following the flashlight to give your gift to Jesus?

• How do you think the wise men felt when they finally found Jesus and gave him their gifts?

• What are some ways we worship Jesus today?

say ▶ Jesus loves us and wants us to show him how much we love him, too. We worship Jesus.

PRayeRS

Worship Jesus

Supplies: none

Have children sit in a circle. Go around the circle and have the kids each tell one way to worship Jesus, such as by praying, helping others, or singing. Remind kids that the wise men worshipped Jesus. Then have the kids repeat each line of the prayer after you.

PRay ▶ Dear God,

Help us worship Jesus every day, in many ways.

In Jesus' name, amen.

- -

Thank You, Jesus

Supplies: none

Remind children that the wise men worshipped Jesus, and we can worship Jesus, too. Ask the children to repeat the lines of this prayer after you.

PRay ▶ Dear Lord Jesus,

We thank you for all the things you've made for us.

We worship you because you are so good.

We give ourselves to you.

In Jesus' name, amen.

Snacks

Sweet, Sparkly Stars

Supplies: bread, star cookie cutters, margarine, knife, colored sugar

Have children wash their hands. Help children to form pairs and then give each pair two slices of bread and a star cookie cutter. Encourage children to help each other press the star cookie cutter into their slices of bread and then pull the remaining edges of the bread away from the cookie cutter until only the star shapes remain. Once children have finished making their star shapes, walk around to each pair and help children spray the star-shaped piece of bread lightly with margarine. This will give the star a gold-colored background and help the sugar sprinkles stick to the bread. While the margarine is still wet, encourage children to decorate their stars by sprinkling them with the colored sugar sprinkles.

Invite one child to pray and thank God for the snack. Then encourage kids to enjoy their sparkling treats.

ask • **Why did the wise men follow the star?**

• **Why do you think the wise men wanted to worship baby Jesus?**

say **The wise men wanted to worship Jesus because they knew he was special. God used a star to lead the wise men to worship Jesus. When we see stars in the night sky or stars used as decorations, we can remember that God wants us to worship Jesus, too.**

Songs

"Three Smart Wise Men" Rhyme

Supplies: none

Lead your class in doing this finger play. Remind children that they can worship Jesus just as the wise men did.

Here are three smart wise men (hold up three fingers)

Looking for a king. (Pretend to put a crown on your head.)

They search and finally find him. (Shade eyes with hand and look all around.)

Three special gifts they bring. (Hold up three fingers, then place them in your other hand and stretch out that hand as if to give.)

JOSEPH TAKES HIS FAMILY to safety in Egypt

STORY 34

Bible Basis:

Matthew 2:13-23

A Timely Trip

Supplies:

Bible, tape, table, sheet, blocks, paper star

Before class, set up three journey destinations: Bethlehem, Egypt, and Nazareth. In the Bethlehem area, tape the star to the wall. In the Egypt area, lay a table on its side, pushed up against the wall for safety, and throw a sheet over the top to create an open tent effect. In the Nazareth area, place blocks (and toy tools if you have them).

Open your Bible to Matthew 2, and show the children the words.

say **Today's Bible story tells us that God guides us. Let's find out how God guided Joseph and showed him where to go with Mary and Jesus so that they would be safe. We're going to go on a journey today, like Mary, Joseph, and Jesus did. Before we start, we need a guide—someone to lead us to Bethlehem.**

ask • **Who will be our guide?** Choose a child to lead the class to the Bethlehem area (that you set up before class). Then sit down.

say **God guided Joseph and Mary to Bethlehem where Jesus was born. Later, the wise men brought gifts to Jesus when he was a small child living in Bethlehem. God knew that mean King Herod wanted to hurt little King Jesus, so God sent an angel to warn the wise men and Joseph. God's angel told Joseph to quickly take Mary and Jesus and go to Egypt where God would care for them and keep them safe. God guided Joseph and his family to Egypt, and God will guide us and care for us, too.**

ask • **Who will be our guide to Egypt?** Choose another child to lead the class to the Egypt area and sit down inside or in front of the tent.

say **God guided Joseph and his family to Egypt. When they got to Egypt, God continued to take care of Joseph, Mary, and Jesus and kept them safe. Back in Bethlehem mean King Herod hunted all over for the baby king, but couldn't find him. King Herod didn't want anyone else to be king except him. Finally, mean King Herod died. Again, God sent his angel to tell Joseph that it was safe to take Mary and Jesus back. This time they were going to a town called**

Nazareth. God guided Joseph and his family to Nazareth, and God will guide us and care for us, too.

ask • **Who will be our guide to Nazareth?** Choose another child to lead the class to the Nazareth area and sit down around the blocks.

say **God guided Joseph and his family to Nazareth. Joseph worked as a carpenter, building many different things from wood. Let's build tables from these blocks.** Have the children take three blocks, and show them how to stand two blocks up and balance one block across the top of the other two.

Through this whole journey, Joseph listened to and trusted God. God was his guide. Now let's sing a song together about God guiding Joseph.

Sing "God Was Joseph's Guide" to the tune of "Row, Row, Row Your Boat":

God was Joseph's guide

Around the countryside.

Joseph trusted in God's plan

Then took them home again.

(Repeat two times.)

ask • **Who guided Joseph to Egypt?**

• **How do you think Joseph felt going to a new place?**

• **How can God guide you?**

say **God was Joseph's guide. God will guide us and take care of us, too.**

Crafts

Beast of Burden

Supplies: 2 spring-loaded clothespins, 1 brown pompom, and 1 craft stick per child; brown construction paper; white glue

Before class, cut two small donkey ears per child from brown construction paper. Glue the two ears onto the top of a brown pompom for each child.

Explain to the children that in Bible times it was common for families to pack all of their bags on a donkey when they went on a long journey. Help the children make their own donkeys by gluing two spring-loaded clothespins to opposite ends of a large craft stick. Have the children squeeze a clothespin open and place a drop of white glue on the inside of the pin. Show them how to place one end of the craft stick inside the clothespin and then let go of the pin. Encourage kids to do this on the other end of their craft sticks with the second clothespin. Give each child one of the pompoms with the donkey ears that you made before class. Instruct the children to glue the pompom to the end of the craft stick to make a head for the donkey. Encourage the children to move their donkeys around the room.

ask • Why did God want Joseph and his family to go to Egypt?

• In what ways has God taken care of your family in the past?

say God loves our families and us. Just like Joseph, we can trust God to guide us and take care of us.

Games

Guided Journeys

Supplies: rope, 1 paper plate per 3 or 4 children

Set out ropes about 8 feet long and paper plates to use for steering wheels. Have kids work in groups of three or four children each called "families." Let the families each choose a guide, then tie the rope loosely around the guide's waist. Give the guides the paper plate steering wheels, and have them tell their families an imaginary place they will guide them to and then lead their families around the playing area.

Sing "God Knows the Way" to the tune of "The Farmer in the Dell" as they lead each other around.

sing I'm packing for a trip.

I'm packing for a trip.

God guides me and cares for me.

I'm packing for a trip.

I'll follow high and low.

I'll follow high and low.

God guides me and cares for me.

I'll follow high and low.

He knows the way to go.

He knows the way to go.

God guides me and cares for me.

He knows the way to go.

Sing the song again, and let kids take turns being the leader or guide for their families. When all the children have had a chance to guide their families, bring the families back into a circle, and ask the following questions.

ask • Where did you guide your family?

• Where did God guide Joseph and his family?

• How has God cared for and guided your real family?

say God guided Jesus' family, and God guides us.

PRAYERS

Action Prayer

Supplies: sheet, play clothes, toys

Have children fill the sheet with play clothes and a few other classroom toys they might take if they were moving. Have the children take turns pretending to be Joseph and Mary and packing for their trip. Allow children to take turns (in small groups of four to six) walking with the sheet as they repeat the following prayer after you.

 PRay **Thank you, God,**

For guiding Joseph

And keeping Jesus safe.

Thank you for guiding us.

In Jesus' name, amen.

snacks

Caring Buddies

Supplies: 1 paper plate, 1 graham cracker, and 1 craft stick per child; frosting; gumdrops

Before class, arrange with another class to have snacks together at the same time. Have the teacher from the other class prepare this same activity snack so kids will feel like they can "trust you" for the same snack.

Tell kids that they are making a snack for another class and can't eat this one. You may have to remind some children during this activity not to eat any of the ingredients by adding the simple words "trust me."

Before the children begin, have them wash their hands or use wet wipes. Give each child a paper plate and craft stick. Let the children place a graham cracker on the plate to represent a cart that may have carried belongings while traveling. Place about a tablespoon of frosting on each plate, and show children how to use the craft sticks to spread the frosting on their graham crackers. Then give each child four gumdrops or other small, soft candies to represent the angel God sent, Joseph, Mary, and Jesus, and have children stick the candy to the frosting.

Let the children line up and meet the other teacher and class in a neutral place so kids will be surprised when they see that the other class has the same snack for them as the one they brought. Remind the children that Joseph trusted God to care for his family, just as they trusted you to have a snack to eat. Invite one child to pray for the snack.

Jesus Heals a Paralyzed Man

Bible Basis:

 Mark 2:1-12

A Helpless Man

Supplies:

Bible, two tables with an opening between them, sheet (covering the opening of the tables), towel, small pieces of cloth

Open your Bible to Mark 2, and show children the words.

say ▶ **Today's Bible story teaches us that Jesus forgives us.**

Gather the children around the story scene, near the opening between the tables.

say ▶ **Jesus went to the town of Capernaum. When the people heard he was there, they all wanted to see him. So many people came that there was no more room for them inside the house where he was teaching. The people wanted to see and hear Jesus so much that they even crowded around the outside of the door. Have children squeeze in under the tables.** Have the children who won't fit under the tables sit around the outside.

Four men brought their friend to see Jesus. Their friend couldn't walk, so the four men carried him on a mat. The mat may have looked something like this towel. The four men wanted Jesus to heal their friend. Choose four children to pull a smaller child on the towel to the house scene.

When the men got to the house where Jesus was teaching, they couldn't get in. There were too many people there already! This was a problem!

ask ▶ • **How do you think the four men could get their friend to Jesus so Jesus could heal him?**

say ▶ **Because they couldn't carry the man inside, the friends decided to carry him up to the flat roof. Then they lowered the man's mat down through the ceiling. Since it's not safe for us to climb on top of our table "house," we'll make some room for our sick friend to lie down under the tables with Jesus.** Have the "four friends" carefully pull aside the sheet to reveal the opening to view "Jesus." Help the children under the table make room for the "sick friend," and have that child lie down inside the "house" where Jesus is.

When Jesus saw the hurt man and the faith of his friends, he said to him, "Son, your sins are forgiven." Jesus forgave the man and made him feel clean again. Then Jesus told the man to get up from his mat and walk. Have the child lying on the towel come out and walk around the tables. Then have the children gather in a circle and sit down.

ask ▸ • Imagine that Jesus just forgave and healed you. What would you feel like doing?

say ▸ I bet the man in the story did those things. One thing we know for sure is that the man didn't need his mat anymore! Give each child a small piece of cloth. When Jesus heals and forgives us, we don't need to worry about all the wrong things we've done, just as the man in the story didn't need to worry about his mat anymore. Go around the circle and have the children pray and thank Jesus for taking away the bad things they've done so they don't have to worry about them anymore.

We don't know what the man's sin was, but we do know that Jesus forgave him. Even the crowds of people were happy that Jesus forgave the man and healed him. Jesus told them that because he was God, only he had the power to forgive sins. Being forgiven of our sins gives us a clean and wonderful feeling. Jesus can forgive all of us.

BiBLe eXPeRiences

Through the Roof

Supplies: paper with outline of a house on it, yarn pieces, cutout figure of a man, cutout figure of a mat, double stick tape, glue

Set out the yarn pieces, the papers (along with the cutout figures of the man and mat), double-stick tape, and glue.

Have children each take a paper figure and tape it on top of the mat. Then have children each glue one end of a piece of yarn to the back of the mat and glue the other end to the roof of the house. Let children form pairs and pretend to raise and lower the man to Jesus as they take turns retelling the Bible story.

ask ▸ • In today's Bible story, why did the friends lower the sick man through the roof?

• Who can you tell the story to when you go home?

• What can you tell that person about Jesus' forgiveness?

say ▸ The friends in the story brought the man to Jesus to be healed. What great friends! The best thing we can do for our friends is tell them about Jesus. Jesus loves us and he forgives us. Jesus wants us to live forever in heaven with him.

Crafts

Clean Again

Supplies: smocks, construction paper, finger paints

Have children wear smocks and stand around a table. Give each child a piece of construction paper. Set finger paints on the table. Encourage the children to each finger-paint a scene from the Bible story on their piece of construction paper. After the children have finished, have them wash their hands. Then give each child another piece of construction paper. Show children how to put the piece of paper on top of their finger-paint creation and then lift the paper up. The paper should show a reverse print. Set the papers in a safe place to dry.

ask
- **What was your favorite part in the Bible story?**
- **When has Jesus forgiven your sins? What happened?**
- **How do you feel when Jesus forgives your sin?**

say Jesus loves us and wants to forgive our sins. When we believe in Jesus, we know that Jesus will forgive our sins and help us live in heaven forever.

Encourage each child to keep one of the pictures and give the other one to a friend or family member. Tell kids they can use the pictures to tell people about today's Bible story.

Games

Forgiveness Mats

Supplies: old bath or beach towel for each child to use as a mat

You'll need an old bath towel or beach towel for every three kids to use as a mat. If you don't have enough towels, you can use folded sheets or blankets. Clear the area of furniture.

Help the kids form trios, and give each group a "mat." Have the kids take turns pretending to be the paralyzed man and the friends who bring the man to Jesus. Have two of the children in each group pull the third child on the towel to the other side of the room. When they get there, the two children will say, "Jesus forgives you," then the "sick man" will pick up the towel and walk with the friends back to the starting point. When they get back, have the children affirm each other with high fives or pats on the back and say, "Thanks for being an awesome friend!"

ask
- **What did Jesus do for the sick man?**
- **What does Jesus do for us?**

say In our story, the sick man couldn't walk, so his friends carried him to Jesus on a mat. Jesus forgave the man for his sins, then he healed him. Aren't you glad that Jesus forgives us, too?

PRAYERS

Forgiveness Prayer

Supplies: none

Have the kids say, "Jesus forgives us" after each line of the prayer:

> **Dear God,**
>
> **I'm sorry when I do wrong.** (Jesus forgives us.)
>
> **I'm sorry when I don't obey.** (Jesus forgives us.)
>
> **I'm sorry when I hurt my friends.** (Jesus forgives us.)
>
> **I'm sorry when I'm mad all day.** (Jesus forgives us.)
>
> **Thank you, God, for loving me.** (Jesus forgives us.)

Then close the prayer by having the children say with you, "In Jesus' name, amen."

SNACKS

Surrounded

Supplies: warm water, cups, hot chocolate mix, plastic spoons, miniature marshmallows, large marshmallows

Set out a cup of not-too-hot water for each child, hot chocolate mix, plastic spoons, miniature marshmallows, and large marshmallows.

Ask the kids to wash their hands before preparing the snacks. Have them stir hot chocolate mix into the water so that the water turns brown—like the house in the story. Have the kids each put a large marshmallow in their cup to represent Jesus. Then have the children sprinkle some miniature marshmallows on top, as the four friends and the paralyzed man who went to Jesus. Encourage the children to sip the hot chocolate and talk about the good friends in the story.

ask
- **How did the men help their friend?**
- **How can we help our friends?**

say **The men helped their friend get to Jesus, and Jesus healed the man and forgave his sins. We can help our friends get to know Jesus, too. Jesus forgave the man in the Bible story, and Jesus forgives us, too.**

Construction Site

Supplies: bread, plastic knives, softened cream cheese, coconut or chow mein noodles, round cookie cutters, small round cookies

Have children wash their hands and gather around your snack table.

say ▶ **Today we learned that Jesus healed a paralyzed man after his friends lowered him through the roof of a house. Let's make our own roofs so we can act out the Bible story and remember that Jesus forgives us!**

Give each child a slice of bread. Help children use knives to spread the softened cream cheese on their bread slices. Then show kids how to sprinkle the bread with coconut or chow mein noodles. Explain that when Jesus was on earth, roofs were made of thatch, which looked a lot like straw.

Go around the room and help each child use the cookie cutter to cut a whole in his or her bread "roof." Review the Bible story as you cut the holes. Then give each child a cookie, and show children how to pretend to lower their cookie people through the holes in the roofs.

ask ▶ • **Why did the paralyzed man's friends lower him through the roof?**

• **Why did Jesus forgive and heal the paralyzed man?**

• **Why does Jesus forgive us?**

say ▶ **Jesus forgives us because he loves us. Let's thank God for sending Jesus to forgive us.**

Before children enjoy their snacks, lead them in this prayer: **Dear God, thank you for sending Jesus to forgive us. In Jesus' name, amen.**

SONGS

Sing a Rhyme

Supplies: none

Remind kids that Jesus forgave the paralyzed man's sins. Lead the children in singing the rhyme "Jesus, Please Forgive" to the tune of "Jesus Loves Me." Remind children that Jesus forgives them.

sing ▶ **Jesus, please forgive my sins.**

Wash me clean and fresh again.

Jesus, tell me what to do

When I need to feel brand-new!

Yes, Jesus loves me.

Yes, Jesus loves me.

Yes, Jesus loves me.

The Bible tells me so.

Jesus Calms a Storm

Bible Basis:

Mark 4:35-41

Supplies:

Bible

Open your Bible to Mark 4, and show children the words.

say ▸ **Today's Bible story teaches us that Jesus helps us when we're afraid.**

Our story is about a storm. Before we start our story, let's practice making storm noises.

Help the children form four groups (reserve one child for a special-effects job), and assign a sound effect to each group. Be sure that each child has a part. Have children in one group make thunder sounds by clapping their hands. Have another group blow or whistle to imitate the sound of wind. Have another group suggest rain by saying "drip, drip" and a fourth group suggest waves by saying "splash, splash." Assign to the special-effects child the job of turning the lights on and off to suggest lightning. Have children practice the sound and light effects on cue before beginning the story.

say ▸ **We learned that Jesus preached to the people. Jesus went from place to place to preach and heal people. In today's story, Jesus and his disciples got on a boat to cross the Sea of Galilee.**

A furious, frightening storm came up on the sea. There were loud claps of thunder (clap)**, the wind was howling** (blow)**, the rain began to fall** (say "drip, drip")**, the waves lapped over the boat** (say "splash, splash")**, and the lightning flashed** (turn the lights on and then off)**.**

ask ▸ • **How do you think the disciples felt?**

• **How do you feel when you hear thunder and see lightning?**

say ▸ **Jesus had given God all his worries. He wasn't afraid. He was fast asleep on the boat. The loud, terrifying storm didn't even wake him up, not the thunder** (clap)**, not the strong wind** (blow)**, not the rain** ("drip, drip")**, the waves** ("splash, splash")**, or the flashing of the lightning** (flash the lights)**. The disciples had probably been out on the lake before when storms came up, but they had never seen one that made them so scared.**

ask ▸ • **What do you think they did?**

Have all the kids make their storm sounds at the same time.

say ▶ Well, the disciples finally remembered that Jesus was with them, so they woke him up. Jesus wasn't even scared, not one little bit! He simply got up and spoke right to the wind and waves. He said, "Quiet! Be still!" And the storm stopped. All of a sudden everything was quiet.

Have kids stop their storm sounds. Pause to listen to the silence.

The disciples had never seen anyone who had that kind of power before. Jesus reminded them not to be afraid. He would always be with them.

The same is true for us. Jesus will always be with us to help us when we're afraid. He can take away all of our worries and fears. Jesus helps us when we're afraid.

ask ▶ • What were the disciples afraid of?

• When have you been afraid? What happened?

say ▶ Turn to a friend, and tell your friend some ways Jesus can help you when you're afraid.

BiBLe eXPeRieNCeS

Blowing Storm

Supplies: several large towels, plastic tubs and buckets filled ⅓ of the way with water, eggbeaters, whisks, small toy boats

Lay the towels on the floor. Place plastic tubs or buckets on top of the towels. Set eggbeaters, whisks, and small toy boats on the floor.

Remind children that the Bible tells us how Jesus calmed a storm. Encourage children to place the boats on the water and then cause a storm by blowing and stirring the water with the whisks and eggbeaters. In real storms, water always has whitecaps! To create this effect, drop a few drops of dish soap in the water and stir with the whisks or eggbeaters.

- -

Give God Your Worries

Supplies: paper with "Jesus" written across the top, pencils, carbon paper

Distribute the "Jesus" pages. Have the children use pencils to draw pictures on the carbon paper of things that make them afraid. When they've finished, have them lift the carbon paper and see that they have given their worries to Jesus. Remind them that the disciples were afraid during a storm, but Jesus helped them by calming the storm. Say that Jesus helps us when we're afraid and we can give him our worries.

ask ▶ • What are some things you worry about?

• How do you feel when you worry?

• What does God want us to do?

say ▶ Jesus wants us to give our worries to him because he will help us when we're afraid.

Crafts

Fears and Worries

Supplies: paper, strips of blue ribbon, glue, smiling face stickers

Distribute the paper, and have kids write their names on them. Give kids the strips of ribbon. Have children each wind a piece of ribbon around their finger and lay the ribbon on the page so it looks like waves in the storm. Have the children form pairs, and let the partners show each other frightened faces to show how the disciples may have looked in the storm. Ask children to tell their partners something that they're afraid of, such as stormy weather or being alone in the dark.

The children can then straighten the ribbons and glue them flat across their pages, like the water after Jesus calmed the wind and waves. Have the children stick the smiling face stickers to their pages.

ask > • **What were the disciples afraid of in the Bible story?**

> • **What is something that you're afraid of?**

> • **How did Jesus help the disciples when they were afraid?**

> • **How can you ask Jesus to help you when you're afraid?**

say > **Jesus helped the disciples when he calmed the wind and the waves! Jesus loves us and he helps us when we're afraid. Let's trust him this week to help us when we need him.**

Games

Stormy Seas

Supplies: bedsheet or tablecloth, foam ball

Gather children around a bedsheet or tablecloth. Have everyone hold onto the edge of the sheet, lift it waist high, and pull the sheet taut. Place a foam ball in the middle of the sheet to represent the boat in the Bible story.

say > **Let's pretend that this ball is the boat that Jesus and his disciples were on during the storm. When we move the sheet gently up and down, we can make waves like the waves in our Bible story.** Have children practice gently making waves. **See how the little boat is being tossed up and down by the waves? The disciples must have been scared! But Jesus helps us when we're afraid, and he calmed that storm right down.** Have children stop moving the sheet so the "storm" stops.

Teach children this rhyme to say as they use the sheet to create and calm the storm:

> **Sailing on the sea so slow** (move the sheet gently from side to side)**,**

> **Then the wind began to blow.** (Move the sheet very softly up and down.)

> **Soon the waves went up and down.** (Move the sheet a little more up and down.)

The disciples all began to frown. (Move the sheet a little more up and down.)

But Jesus helps us when we're afraid. (Begin to slow the movement of the sheet.)

"Be still" was all he had to say. (Slow the movement of the sheet.)

The wind and the waves would crash no more (stop moving the sheet)**,**

And the little boat sailed on to shore. (Move the sheet gently from side to side.)

 **ask** • **When are you afraid?**

• **How can this story remind you that Jesus helps us when we're afraid?**

say **Just as Jesus calmed the storm and helped his disciples when they were afraid, Jesus helps us when we're afraid, too. The next time you're afraid, think of this story and ask Jesus to help you. He will!**

PRAYERS

Standing Here

Supplies: none

Teach this rhyming prayer to your class. Have children substitute other things they're afraid of. For example, a child might say, "When dogs bark, I have a fear" or "When in the water, I have a fear." Repeat the prayer as often as children want to include their fears.

PRay **Dear God,**

When in the dark, I have a fear.

Help me feel you standing here.

In Jesus' name, amen.

snacks

Banana Boat Snack

Supplies: paper plates, bananas, pretzel sticks, fruit leather

Have the children create boats from banana halves (cut lengthwise), pretzel sticks, and fruit leather sails. Have the kids lay their banana halves on their plates, push the pretzel sticks through the fruit sails, and push the pretzels into the bananas. Remind children that, in the Bible story, Jesus calmed the sea and helped the disciples when they were afraid.

ask • **When do you feel afraid?**

• **How can you trust Jesus when you're afraid?**

say **Jesus helps us when we're afraid. We can pray to him when we're afraid, and he will help us.**

"Jesus Helps" Rhyme

Supplies: none

Read the following action rhyme to the children, and teach them the motions. Then have the children stand as they act out the words. Remind children that Jesus helps them when they're afraid.

Jesus said to his disciples, "Let's go to the other side. (Point thumb out to the side.)

And now we must get in the boat and over the water ride." (Pretend to get into a boat and start rowing.)

While Jesus slept, a storm did start and the wind began to howl. (Swirl hands and arms over your head as you spin around and howl gently.)

The men on board were frightened, so their faces had a scowl. (Make a frightened, scowling face.)

"Wake up, wake up now, dear Jesus, for we are really afraid." (Put hands on face in front of eyes in fear.)

"Fear not," said Jesus as he stopped the winds and waves. (Hold up one hand in a "stop" gesture.)

"Jesus helps us when we're afraid," the disciples said. "It's true!" (Nod head.)

And "Jesus helps us when we're afraid" is also true for you! (Point to others in room.)

Fishermen are astonished by a Miraculous Catch

Bible Basis:

Luke 5:1-11

I Caught You!

Supplies:

Bible, large blue sheet, 2 laundry baskets, fishing net, construction paper

Before class, cut simple fish shapes from construction paper. Spread a large blue sheet on the floor, and put the baskets near it.

Have kids form a circle and sit down. Open your Bible to Luke 5, and show children the words.

say **Today we'll learn that Jesus wants us to follow him.**

One day Jesus was standing by a lake, teaching a large crowd of people. Have children crowd around you. **It got so crowded on the shore that Jesus almost got pushed into the water. Jesus saw Peter in his boat, so Jesus told Peter to take him out into the middle of the lake.** Push one of the baskets into the "water," and have kids climb in with you.

After Jesus finished teaching the crowd, he told Peter to go out even farther into the water to catch some fish. Peter was very tired because he'd been up fishing all night long, and he hadn't caught a single fish! But Peter followed Jesus' instructions and went out into the water. Encourage kids to get out and push the "boat" farther into the water.

Peter threw his net into the water, and guess what happened? Have kids throw the net over the side of the boat and into the water. **Peter caught so many fish that he couldn't even pull the net back into the boat!** Toss the paper fish into the net. **Peter had to call his friends James and John to bring another boat to help him bring in all those fish.**

James and John brought their boat up next to Peter's boat. Encourage half of the kids to push the other basket into the water. **There were so many fish that the boats started to sink!** Pretend to act afraid, and encourage kids to push the boats back to the shore. **The men were surprised by all of the fish they'd caught, but Jesus told them that if they followed him, they could fish for people instead of for fish.**

ask • What do you think Jesus meant when he said the men would fish for people?

say Jesus was telling Peter, James, and John that they could tell other people about Jesus and "catch" them by helping them believe in Jesus. Let's play a game now in which we'll catch people!

Have children get into groups of four, and have two of the children form a bridge with their hands so the others can go under. Sing this song to the tune of "London Bridge":

> Jesus says to come follow him,
>
> Follow him, follow him.
>
> Jesus says to come follow him,
>
> **Catching people.** (Have the pair bring the bridge down and catch the child in the "bridge" between their arms.)

say Peter, James, and John left their fishing boats and followed Jesus. Jesus wants us to follow him, too.

ask • Why did Peter, James, and John choose to follow Jesus?

• Why do you want to follow Jesus?

• How can you follow Jesus in your life?

say We can follow Jesus by believing in him, by obeying his words, and by telling others about him. Jesus wants us to follow him!

CRafts

Love Fishes

Supplies: large and small construction paper hearts for each child, glue sticks, markers or crayons

Give each child a large and a small paper heart. Demonstrate how to glue the hearts together to make a fish shape. This is best done by overlapping the points of the large and small heart. The small heart forms the fish's tail, and the large heart forms the body. Children can use the markers to each add an eye to their fish.

ask • Who caught fish after obeying Jesus?

• How do you feel when you obey?

• Who are some people you need to obey?

say These fish can remind you of how good it is to obey. It's most important that we obey Jesus. But Jesus wants us to obey our parents and teachers, too. You can give your fish to someone to say, "I love you" and "I will obey you."

Games

Fish Net

Supplies: none

Remind kids that Jesus helped the disciples catch a lot of fish one day.

Choose one child to be the "fish." Have the other children form a "net" by standing in a circle and holding hands. Have the fish stand in the middle of the circle and try to escape by "swimming" between people or breaking through their hands. Give the fish about 30 seconds to escape the net. If the fish breaks free, have all of the other children drop hands and swim to tag him or her. Then choose a new fish to stand inside the net. If the fish doesn't break through the net in 30 seconds, call time and choose a new fish.

Cast Your Net

Supplies: beach towel

Have all the children stand in a circle. Choose two children standing together to be the fishers. Leave their spaces open. If you have a large group, make the opening about one-quarter of your circle. Have the fishers stand in the middle and hold the beach towel on both ends and practice swinging it up and over their heads. You may need to help them.

Chant the follow rhyme as the children march to the left without closing the circle.

> **Fished all night and what did we get?**
>
> **Not one fish in this great big net!**

Have the fishers swing the net into the empty space. Then chant the next verse as children march to the right.

> **Here comes Jesus on the shore.**
>
> **He says, "On the other side, you'll catch more!"**

Have the fishers swing the net the other way over two children standing in the circle. These children will become the new fishers. Continue until everyone has had a chance to be a fisher.

Lots of Fish

Supplies: colored construction paper, scissors

Before class, cut fish out of construction paper. Make the fish a variety of colors and sizes.

Have the children sort the fish in different ways: by colors, size, or specific patterns such as two of one color then two of another color, or one large then one small. Encourage counting skills by having children count the fish as they work. Tell them that the fisherman obeyed Jesus and caught a lot of fish.

Story 37: Fishermen Are Astonished by a Miraculous Catch

PRayeRS

Action Prayer

Supplies: none

Before you pray, show the children how to make the thumbs-up sign. Tell them that this sign means "good job." As children pray, have them point up to Jesus to begin the prayer and then give the thumbs-up sign when saying "best I can."

PRay **Dear God,**

Obeying Jesus is my plan. (Point up to Jesus.)

I'll do the very best I can! (Thumbs up.)

In Jesus' name, amen! (Shout, "AMEN!")

Around-the-World Prayers

Supplies: large map of the world, fish stickers, blindfold

Show children the world map.

Say **This is the world that God made. Jesus wants us to follow him so we can share him with everyone, all over the world.**

Give stickers to the children one at a time, blindfold the children, spin them around, and let them place their stickers on the map. As you spin the children, say this rhyme:

God is here; God is there.

God made our world. God is everywhere!

After a child has placed a sticker, help him or her say this prayer: **God, bless the people in** [name of area] **and help them to follow Jesus.**

snacks

Fish Food Snack

Supplies: fish crackers, napkins

Have the children wash their hands or use wet wipes. Let each child take a handful of fish crackers and place them on a napkin.

ask • **What happened when the fishermen obeyed Jesus?**

• **How can you obey Jesus?**

Say **When Jesus told Peter and his friends where to fish, the nets were so full they could barely count the fish. Let's thank God for the many fish he gave us, then count our fish as we eat them.** Invite one child to pray for the snack.

"Jelly" Fish

Supplies: white bread; heart-shaped cookie cutters; assorted, different colored jellies; paper plates; napkins

Set out jellies, plates, bread, plastic spoons, and small heart-shaped cookie cutters.

Have children cut the bread with the cookie cutter, then spread jelly on each piece of bread. Point out that when you turn the heart-shape on its side, it looks like a fish. (The pointed end is the face, the rounded end represents the fins.)

say **We made our fish. In our Bible story, the fishermen caught their fish.**

ask **• How many fish did the men catch after they obeyed Jesus?**

• How can you follow and obey Jesus like the fishermen in our story?

say **Let's thank God for the many fish he gave us. Invite one child to pray for the snack.**

SonGS

God Calls Us

Supplies: none

Remind children that the disciples followed Jesus and obeyed him. Play a game of Follow the Leader as you teach children this song to the tune of "Old MacDonald."

God calls us to follow him
Every single day!
God calls us to follow him.
He'll lead us all the way.

Follow God!
He loves you, too!
Do just what he says to do.

God calls us to follow him
Every single day!

God calls us to obey him
Every single day!
God calls us to obey him
He wants us to obey.

Obey God!
He loves you, too!
Do just what he says to do.

God call us to obey him
Every single day!

Jesus Tells the Parable of the Lost Son

Bible Basis:

▶ Luke 15:11-32

So Much to See and Do

Supplies:

Bible, poster board, marker, action figures to represent the father and the son, heart sticker, gold coins, double-sided tape, crayons, washable brown inkpad, wet wipes

Before class, create a poster with a picture of a house in one corner, a city in the middle, and a pigsty in an opposite corner of the house. Draw a wide path from the house to the city and from the city to the pigsty.

Open your Bible to Luke 15:11-32, and show the children the words.

say ▶ **Today's Bible story tells us that God is loving and forgiving. Let's hear a story that Jesus told about a father who loved and forgave his son.**

There once was a father who had two sons. The father loved his sons very much. Ask a child to place the heart sticker on the father. **The father's youngest son didn't want to live at home anymore. The youngest son said, "Give me a lot of money, Dad, so I can go away from here."**

ask ▶ • **How do you think the father felt when the son said that?**

say ▶ **The son's words made the father sad, but he gave the son some money.** Have a few children each take a plastic coin from the father's pile and use double-sided tape to stick it on the son. **Then the son left his father's home. He went far away to another city.** Have several other children use crayons to color the path the son took from the father's home to the city.

In the city, the son spent all his money on the wrong kinds of things. Have a few children take the coins off the son and place them on the city with double-sided tape. **When he ran out of money, he had to get a job. The only job he could do was feed pigs.** Have one child move the son along the path to the pigsty. Ask each child to place a thumb on the ink pad, then make "muddy" thumbprints in the pigsty. Let children clean their thumbs with wet wipes.

It wasn't a very good job. The son was so hungry that he even thought about eating the pigs' food! All of a sudden, the son realized that even his father's servants were living better than he was. The son realized how much he'd hurt his father by leaving home.

He decided to go back home and tell his father, "I'm sorry." Have a child move the son along the path from the pigsty back to the father's house. His father saw him and ran to him. Place the father next to the son. The father hugged his son and kissed him. The son said, "I hurt you, Dad. I'm so sorry!" Then the father said, "I love you, son. I forgive you."

ask
- When have you felt bad because you've done something wrong?
- How do you think the son felt when his father forgave him?
- How can you show others that you've forgiven them?

say Just as the father in the story loved and forgave his son, our God is loving and forgiving toward us.

BiBLe eXPeRiences

Loving Homes

Supplies: connecting blocks

Place connecting blocks where children can easily reach them. Encourage children to use the blocks to build homes like the young son might have gone back to. As children work, remind them that God is loving and forgiving.

ask
- How do you feel when you see your home after a long trip?
- How do you think the young son felt when his father welcomed him home?
- How can we show God that we are thankful for his love and forgiveness?

Home and Away

Supplies: blocks, action figures to represent the father and son

Encourage the children to use blocks to build the father's home and a far-off town. Give them the father and son figures to act out the story.

ask
- How do you think God feels when you do something wrong?
- How can you thank God for forgiving you?

say The father loved and forgave his son. When we do something wrong, we can tell God we're sorry. God is loving and forgiving toward us.

Crafts

Piggy Project

Supplies: large and small paper plates, staplers, pink chenille wire, newspaper, glue, crayons, pink paint

say ▸ **In today's Bible story, the son who left home ran into some trouble, didn't he? In fact, things got so bad that he ended up feeding pigs for a living. Let's make a piggy project to help us remember this Bible story!**

Help each child staple the rims of two large plates together with the curved sides out, so that a pillow-shape is created. Leave an opening along one edge. Staple a chenille wire to one of the plates, and then let the child crumple and stuff newspaper into the opening before closing the edge with more staples. The child may curl the chenille wire as a tail.

Show children how to glue the smaller plate to the edge of the plate opposite the tail as a face for the pig. Let children use crayons to draw eyes, a mouth, and other features on the pigs' faces. Instruct them to staple the ears to the top of the front plate. Then let kids dab pink paint onto their pigs and set them aside to dry.

say ▸ **These pigs can remind you that even though the son in our story messed up, his father still loved and forgave him. Parents are wonderful like that! Take your piggy projects home and give them to your parents with a big hug for always forgiving you!**

Welcome Home Greeting

Supplies: 12x18-inch piece of construction paper with the words "Welcome Home!" printed on it (one per child), magazine pictures of happy people, scissors, glue, crayons

Let children choose pictures to glue on their papers. They may also draw cheerful pictures.

ask ▸ • **Has someone you loved ever been away for a long time? If so, what was that like?**

▸ • **When someone comes home after being away for a while, how do you celebrate?**

say ▸ **God celebrates every time one of his children comes to him. You can put this greeting on a door at home to welcome a parent home from work or to welcome a visitor. When you welcome someone, you can remember the son in the story and his loving and forgiving father.**

PRAYERS

Body Formation Prayer

Supplies: none

Have kids lie on the floor head to toe, and help them form a giant heart shape with their bodies. Tell the children that their heart is like God's love for us. Remind kids that God forgives us and always loves us as the father forgave his son in the Bible story. Then lead the children in the following prayer:

Thank you God for your love.

Thank you God for your forgiveness.

In Jesus' name, amen.

Forgiveness Prayer

Supplies: none

Before praying, talk with the children about how important it is to tell God we're sorry when we do something wrong. Remind them that in the story, the son told the father he was sorry for leaving and the father forgave the son. God is loving and forgiving just as the father in the story was.

Have the children repeat after you the lines to the following prayer.

Thank you, God, for loving me

And also for forgiving me.

Help me try to do what's right

So I'm close to you all day and night.

In Jesus' name, amen.

Story 38: Jesus Tells the Parable of the Lost Son

snacks

Mixed-Up Snacks

Supplies: bowls, plastic spoons, refried beans, mild salsa (or diced tomatoes), corn, sour cream, cheese, tortilla chips

Have children wash their hands or use wet wipes. Set up an assembly line of containers with foods such as refried beans, mild salsa (or diced tomatoes), corn, sour cream, and cheese, and put a small spoon in each bowl or jar. Give each child a bowl, and direct kids to go through the line to make their snacks.

say ▶ **The son in our Bible story fed the pigs a mixture of all kinds of food. It may have looked a little like this. Let's thank God for loving us and for providing our snacks today.** Invite one child to pray for the snacks.

Have kids sit down to eat, and set out tortilla chips for children to eat with their mixed-up snacks. As kids enjoy eating the food, remind them that the young son was so hungry that he wanted to eat even the leftovers that were given to the pigs to eat.

Mud!

Supplies: instant chocolate pudding, milk, covered container, small cups, plastic spoons

Have the children wash their hands (or use wet wipes) and then sit down to prepare the snack.

say ▶ **In our story today, the young son ended up feeding pigs. He was so hungry that he almost ate the pigs' food. Pigs love to roll in the mud. For our snack today, we are going to make pretend mud to eat.**

In a large container pour a package of instant chocolate pudding. Add the milk and cover with a lid. Let the children take turns shaking the container until the pudding is set (about five minutes). Pour the pudding into small cups and let sit while you discuss the questions.

ask ▶ • **How do you think the son felt when he was taking care of the pigs?**

• **How would you feel if that was your job?**

say ▶ **Let's thank God for loving and forgiving us and for providing our snack.** Invite one child to pray for the snack, and then let kids enjoy their "mud."

Jesus Came to Die for Us

Bible Basis:

 Luke 19:28-40; 23:1-49

Supplies:

Bible, coats, jackets or sweaters

Open your Bible to Luke 19:28-40; 23:1-49, and show the children the words.

say ▸ **Today's Bible story tells us that Jesus died for us.**

Our Bible story begins as Jesus and his disciples were going from place to place preaching and teaching. When Jesus and his disciples were about to go into Jerusalem, Jesus sent his disciples ahead to get a young donkey that he could ride. During Bible times, kings and other royal people often rode donkeys to show that they would bring peace to the people. Jesus wanted to show that he was the King of kings, sent from God to bring peace and forgiveness for people's sins, as a prophet had promised a long time before.

ask ▸ **• How do you think the people felt to be so close to such an important person as Jesus?**

say ▸ **Show me how you think the people might have reacted when they saw Jesus coming.** Pause for the children to react. **The people were so excited to see Jesus that many of them threw their coats on the ground for the young donkey to walk on so he wouldn't get his hooves dirty. They treated Jesus like a king.**

We celebrate in many ways when someone does something extra special. We might cheer, clap, stomp our feet, or whistle. The people in Jesus' day did the same thing, and they celebrated with a procession or a parade. Let's act out a parade like the one the people had for Jesus.

Bring out the coats, jackets, and sweaters, and have each child choose an item to wear. Have children form groups with an even number in each group (four or six children to a group might work best). Let each of the groups choose a child to be the Donkey and another child to be Jesus. Let the Donkey get on all fours, then have Jesus carefully sit on the Donkey's back. Let the other children each take off the clothing item and lay it on the floor in front of the Donkey. As each child puts his or her coat on the floor, have that child say something he or she likes about Jesus. Have the Donkey carry Jesus across the clothing, and then continue the Bible story.

say ▶ Many people were glad to see Jesus entering Jerusalem on a donkey. But some people were not so happy to see Jesus. Some of the people were jealous and became angry with Jesus, so they asked the leaders to arrest him.

Jesus was arrested. The guards were mean, and they hurt Jesus very badly. Then they took Jesus to a man named Pilate who was kind of like the judges we have today. Pilate's job was to decide if Jesus had done anything wrong. The people said that Jesus had told everyone not to pay their taxes and that Jesus told people he was Christ, the King of kings.

ask ▶ • Do you think Jesus had really done anything wrong? Why or why not?

say ▶ Pilate said that Jesus hadn't done anything wrong and that he should be set free, but the people were so angry that they wouldn't listen. Have kids put their hands over their ears, pretend not to listen, then take their hands away.

Pilate then sent Jesus to a man named Herod to let Herod decide what would happen to Jesus. Herod agreed that Jesus had done nothing to deserve death, but the angry crowd demanded that Jesus die.

ask ▶ • What would you have said to Herod or Pilate about Jesus?

say ▶ The people took Jesus to a hill with two criminals who had done some very bad things. The people hung Jesus on a cross to die alongside the criminals. They continued to call Jesus names and gave him vinegar to drink when he was thirsty. Jesus hung on the cross until he died.

ask ▶ • How do you think Jesus' friends felt when Jesus died?

say ▶ Even though dying on a cross was a terrible thing that happened to Jesus, Jesus knew God's plan. Just before Jesus died, he prayed and asked God to forgive all the people for their sins because they didn't realize what they were doing. Because Jesus died for us, our sins are forgiven, and we can live with him in heaven. The most exciting part of God's plan for his Son was that Jesus didn't stay dead!

BiBLe eXPeRiences

A Picture Parade

Supplies: sidewalk chalk

When it's time to begin, lead your children to an area where kids can each safely use a small portion of a pathway. (Make sure to have plenty of adult supervision.) Call this pathway their Picture Parade. Give children each a piece of sidewalk chalk, show them where they can draw their pictures, and instruct them to draw pictures about today's

Bible story. Remind kids that the people celebrated Jesus as the King of kings by giving a parade; tell kids they can create a picture parade and celebrate Jesus by drawing pictures that remind them of the Bible story. Encourage kids to sign their names near their pictures.

When the children have finished the pictures, gather the class together, and let children each tell about their Bible story pictures.

ask • **What are some things you remember about the Bible story?**

• **Why do you think the people wanted to celebrate and honor Jesus?**

• **What do you like to celebrate about Jesus?**

say **Jesus wanted people to know that he was the King of kings, the Son of God. We can celebrate and tell others that Jesus died for us.**

At the end of class, invite the parents to view the children's works of art.

CRafts

A Bitter Drink for a King

Supplies: paper, markers, cotton swabs, vinegar, small bowls

Distribute the paper and markers. Instruct the kids to use the markers to draw a hill and a cross on the hill. Then have each of the children dip a cotton swab into the vinegar and dab the vinegar onto the cross.

say **The cross is a symbol that reminds us that Jesus died for our sins. This vinegar smells yucky—just like our sins are yucky to God. When Jesus died for our sins, he forgave us, and he took away our yucky sins.**

ask • **What is something you've done that might make Jesus sad?**

• **Have you asked Jesus to forgive your sins? Why or why not? Would you like to?**

say **Even though some of the people were mean to Jesus, Jesus still loved the people and wanted God to forgive them. Jesus was willing to die on the cross for us and even for the sins of mean people. Jesus died for us because he loves us.**

Cross Reminders

Supplies: wide craft sticks (two per child), glue, markers, wooden pinch clothes pins, square note paper, magnetic tape

say **In today's lesson, we're learning that Jesus died for us. That's such an important thing to remember, let's make a craft that we can look at every day!**

Explain that people often write notes to help them remember important things. Say that kids will be making note-pad reminders to help them remember that Jesus died on the cross for us.

Give each child two wide craft sticks. Help kids use craft glue to attach the sticks in the shape of a cross. Help kids use markers to write, "Jesus died for us" on their crosses.

Then give each child a wooden pinch clothespin, and use craft glue to attach the clothespin to the cross, pinch-side facing down. Give each child a small stack of square note paper, and help kids clip the paper in the clothespin. Finally, attach a strip of magnetic tape to the back of each cross.

say ▸ **Take these note holders home, and hang them on your refrigerators. That way, every time someone in your family writes a reminder note or opens the refrigerator, they'll remember that Jesus died for us!**

PRAYeRS

Cloaks of Praise Prayer

Supplies: coats or dress up clothes

Have children each choose a coat or other item of dress-up clothing and put on the item. Then instruct kids to take turns removing the items and laying them on the floor. Remind kids how people laid their coats in the road as Jesus passed by to show how much they loved Jesus. Then lead kids in saying the following prayer.

PRay ▸ **Dear Jesus,**
Thank you for dying for me
And forgiving my sins.
In Jesus' name, amen.

snacKS

Donkey Trail Mix

aLLeRGY aLeRt

Supplies: paper towel, frosted-wheat cereal, cups, water

Have the children wash their hands (or use wet wipes), and then let kids sit down to prepare their snacks. Remind the children that Jesus rode into Jerusalem on a young donkey. Tell kids that donkeys like to eat hay and drink lots of water.

Give children each a paper towel with a few frosted-wheat cereal pieces, and let kids pretend that the cereal is the donkey's hay. Then pass out cups of water. Let the children make donkey sounds while they wait for others to be served.

ask ▸ • **Do you think the donkey had any idea how special Jesus was? Why or why not?**

say ▸ **The young donkey had a very special job to do for Jesus. Maybe he was rewarded with a special treat to eat. Let's eat our snack and remember that soon after the donkey's special job was over, Jesus would die for our sins. Bow your heads and let's pray.**

Have the children repeat the following prayer before they eat their snacks.

PRay ▸ **Dear God, thank you for sending your Son, Jesus, to die for our sins. Please bless this food. In Jesus' name, amen.**

Jesus appears to Mary

Bible Basis:

 John 20:1-18

Emotional News

Supplies:

Bible, Bible-times costume or woman guest dressed up as Mary, 1 small box and 1 piece of construction paper per child, markers, stapler or tape

Before class, draw a happy face on one side of each box, a sad face on another side, a scared face on another side, and an excited face on one side.

Have kids form a circle and sit down. Open your Bible to John 20:1-18, and show children the words. If you weren't able to greet kids wearing the Bible-times costume, take a minute now to put it on over your clothes.

say **Hello, everyone! My name is Mary. I've come to tell you about what I saw when I visited Jesus' tomb.**

You see, Jesus was a good friend of mine. I loved him very much, and I traveled with him and his disciples. I knew that Jesus was special, and I even knew that he was the promised one from God. Being with Jesus made me happy. Encourage kids to hold up the happy side of their box.

ask • **Who do you think Jesus was?**

• **How do you feel when you spend time with Jesus?**

say **Well, now I believe, I know, that Jesus is the Son of God. Let me tell you about what happened when I visited Jesus' tomb.**

I was so sad after Jesus died. Encourage kids to hold up the sad side of their box. **For three days I wept and cried because they had killed him.**

Then, on the third day, I went to his tomb and found that the stone had been rolled away! I was scared and didn't know what to do. Encourage children to hold up the scared side of their box. **So I ran back and got two of Jesus' disciples. They came to find the tomb open as well and went running away to tell the other disciples. I stood outside the tomb crying because I thought someone had stolen Jesus' body, and that made me very sad.** Encourage children to hold up the sad side of their box.

I turned to leave and saw someone standing behind me. I thought it was the gardener, so I asked him if he had taken Jesus' body. Then the man said my name. "Mary!" he said. And I knew. I knew as soon as he said my name that it was Jesus. Can you imagine how excited I was? Encourage children to hold up the excited side of their box. **Jesus is alive!**

ask ▸ • **How does it make you feel to know that Jesus is alive?**

say ▸ **I laughed and cried and hugged Jesus! I was just so happy!**
Encourage children to hold up the happy side of their box.

Then Jesus said to me, "Don't cling to me…go find my brothers and tell them that I am going to my Father and your Father, to my God and your God."

Jesus was telling me that soon he'd be going to heaven to be with God. Jesus wanted me to go and tell his disciples and others that Jesus is alive and is going back to his Father in heaven.

That's why I'm here today. I'm so excited to tell you my story! Encourage children to hold up the excited side of their box. **I wanted you to know that Jesus is alive! Now you can go and tell others the good news!**

ask ▸ • **Whom can you tell that Jesus is alive?**

• **What else can you tell people about Jesus?**

say ▸ **It's important to tell others about Jesus. See how many people you can talk to about Jesus this week!**

Crafts

Easter Place Mats

Supplies: 1 sheet of construction paper per child, stickers, crayons

Give each child a piece of construction paper. Make stickers and crayons available. Let children create place mats that celebrate Easter and the fact that Jesus is alive. Encourage children to use these as they eat dinner later in the day and to tell their families what they learned about Jesus today.

ask ▸ • **How can we celebrate that Jesus is alive?**

• **Who can you show your place mat to and tell that Jesus is alive?**

say ▸ **Easter is a day to celebrate and show how happy we are that Jesus is alive!**

Mighty Megaphones

Supplies: construction paper, markers and crayons, tape

Give each child a piece of construction paper and some markers and crayons. Tell kids to decorate one side of their construction paper with pictures from Jesus' life. When kids are finished drawing and coloring, help them roll their construction paper—with the pictures on the outside—into megaphones. Tape the paper in place.

say ▸ **Now you can use your megaphones to shout out the good news that Jesus is alive!**

Games

Alive Today!

Supplies: Bible

Have the children form a circle and sit down. Open your Bible to Romans 5:8, and show children the words.

say ▸ **Romans 5:8 says that Jesus died for us. That means that Jesus died to take the punishment for the wrong things we do. The good news is that Jesus came back to life. Jesus is alive! Let's say that verse together.** Lead children in saying: **Jesus died for us.**

Have children form trios. Have two of the children face each other and clasp hands (as if playing "London Bridge"). Have the third child stand in the middle of their hands as if he or she has been captured.

Have all the children softly say together, "Jesus died for us." Then have those clasping hands lift their hands to release the captured child as everyone shouts, "Jesus is alive!" Play several times so that each child has a turn at both roles.

Prayers

Who Needs to Know?

Supplies: empty plastic egg

Have children stand in a circle. Ask them to think of people who need to know that Jesus is alive. Tell children that they will toss a large empty plastic egg to each other and say the person's name during the prayer.

Dear God,

Help us to tell the exciting news that Jesus is alive to all our friends. Let each child toss the empty egg to one another and say the name of his or her person. Have kids continue tossing the egg until they all have had a chance to say their person's name. **In Jesus' name, amen.**

snacks

Empty Tomb

Supplies: pita bread, teddy bear crackers, napkins

Have the children wash their hands (or use wet wipes) and then sit down to prepare the snack. Give each child a napkin, a half piece of pita (or pocket) bread, and several teddy bear crackers. Have children place the teddy bears inside the pita bread just as Jesus was placed inside the tomb. Then have children remove the teddy bears to make a tomb as empty as Jesus' tomb. Remind children that Jesus' tomb was empty because Jesus is alive. Allow children to eat their bread and crackers.

 • **How did Mary feel when she saw that Jesus was alive?**

• **What good news can you tell others on Easter?**

 Jesus' tomb was empty because Jesus is alive! That's great news! Let's thank God for bringing Jesus to life and for providing our snack. Invite one child to pray for the snack.

Songs

Spread the Good News

Supplies: none

Use this song to get your children excited about telling other about Jesus. This song is sung to the tune of "Old MacDonald."

Spread the good news everywhere. (Hold arms up and turn in a circle.)

Jesus is alive! (Pat hands against a partner's hands.)

Take the good news here and there. (Point around the room.)

Jesus is alive. (Pat hands against a partner's.)

Step-step-hop. (Step, step, hop.)

Don't be slow. (Wave "come on.")

Right foot, left foot (step with right foot, then left foot),

Do-si-do! (Cross arms over chest, then circle around partner.)

Spread the good news everywhere. (Hold arms up, and turn in a circle.)

Jesus is alive. (Pat hands against a partner's.)

Jesus Returns to Heaven

Bible Basis:

 Matthew 28:16-20; Acts 1:1-11

Come to Jesus

Supplies:

picture of Jesus, Bible

Have the children form a circle and sit down. Place a picture of Jesus in front of you. Open your Bible to Matthew 28:19-20, and show children the words.

say **Our verse from the Bible says, "Therefore go and make disciples of all nations, baptizing them in the name of the Father and of the Son and of the Holy Spirit, and teaching them to obey everything I have commanded you. And surely I am with you always, to the very end of the age." That means we can teach the world about Jesus. Let's say that together.** Lead the children in repeating the age-appropriate verse with you: We can teach the world about Jesus.

Jesus isn't just for you and me—he's for everyone everywhere! Jesus wants us to tell everyone—the whole world—about him. We're going to sing a song about telling the whole world about Jesus. I have a picture of Jesus that each of you will get to take to a class friend. You will tell your friend about Jesus as we sing.

Have the children stand in a large circle as they sing. Choose one child to take the picture of Jesus to a friend in the circle and show it to him or her. Let that child take Jesus to another child. Continue having the children "share" Jesus with everyone until everyone has had a turn to bring Jesus to a friend, repeating the song if you have a large class.

Sing "Go Tell" to the tune of "When the Saints Go Marching In." Encourage children to join in when they learn the words.

> **Go tell the world**
>
> **That Jesus cares,**
>
> **That Jesus died and rose again.**
>
> **Don't be afraid 'cause he is with you.**
>
> **So go and tell the world today!**
>
> *(Repeat.)*

After the game, have children return to the circle and sit down.

say > You just showed each other Jesus. Another way we can show each other Jesus is by talking about him and telling people about the wonderful things he does.

ask > • Who have you told about Jesus?

> • What can you tell someone about Jesus?

say > Jesus wants us to teach other people about him. Let's tell the whole world about Jesus!

BiBLe eXPeRiences

Up, Up, Up

Supplies: poster board, Bible, age-appropriate magazines, glue sticks

Open your Bible to Matthew 28, and show the children the words.

say > **Today's Bible story teaches us to tell the world about Jesus. We're going to learn about Jesus going back to heaven. I'll need you to help me tell the story. You'll be using your bodies, so let's get warmed up first.** Lead children in wiggling around and stretching.

> **Remember that Jesus died on a cross and came back to life.** Have kids stand up and hold their arms out from their sides. **When Jesus came back to life, he spent some more time with his disciples. But soon it was time for Jesus to go back to heaven to be with God.**

> **Jesus went to the top of a high mountain. Jesus' friends climbed up the mountain.** Have children pretend to be climbing up a mountain. **When they got to the top of the mountain, Jesus said to his friends, "While I am gone, I want you to go and tell the whole world about me."** Have children cup their hands around their mouths, turn to each other, and pretend to tell each other about Jesus. **Then an amazing thing happened. Jesus started to go up, up, up into the sky. He went up into a cloud and back into heaven without wings or a plane or anything! That was a miracle!** Have children point up to the sky.

> **Suddenly there were two men dressed in white standing beside Jesus' friends. They were angels. The angels said, "Why do you stand here looking into the sky? Jesus will come back someday."** Have children look at each other and say, "Tell everybody!"

> **Jesus' friends were so surprised at what they saw! They wanted to tell the whole world about Jesus and his love.** Have children run to three people and say, "Jesus loves you!"

> **Good job! Thanks for all of your help!**

ask > • **How do you think Jesus' friends felt when they saw him go back into heaven?**

> • **How do you think they felt about telling other people about Jesus?**

> • **What are some ways you can tell other people about Jesus?**

Say ▶ **The very last thing Jesus said before he went to heaven was that we should tell the world about him. There are lots of ways we can tell other people about Jesus. Let's look through this magazine and find some ways that we can tell others about Jesus.** Give the children several age-appropriate magazines. Encourage kids to find and tear out pictures of ways to tell others the good news of Jesus. The children might look for pictures of mouths, hands, writing utensils, paper, microphones, or people doing nice things for others. **Let's glue our pictures onto this poster board to remind us that we can use all these things to tell the world about Jesus.** Help children use glue sticks to glue the magazine pictures onto the poster board.

All Around The World

Supplies: globes, maps, travel guides, travel brochures, atlases, travel paraphernalia

Before class, setup a "travel center" in one corner of the room. Set out globes, maps, travel guides, travel brochures, atlases, and any other travel paraphernalia you may have. As kids arrive, direct them to the center. Let them look through the books and explore the pictures of other places. Encourage kids to talk about the differences between the people, the clothes, the food, and the environment of the places in the books and pictures. Remind kids that Jesus wants them to tell the world about his love.

CRafts

Tell the World Megaphone

Supplies: 1 piece of construction paper per child, magazines, glue sticks, tape, telephone, letter, e-mail, picture of Jesus, book about Jesus

Remind the children that we are to tell the world about Jesus. Show the children the telephone, the letter, the e-mail, the picture, and the book, and ask them how they could use each of these different things to tell someone about Jesus. Give each child a piece of construction paper. Have them look through the magazines for pictures of ways they can tell people about Jesus and then tear the pictures out. Next, encourage kids to glue the pictures to the piece of construction paper in a mosaic pattern. Finally, show them how to roll and tape the construction paper to make megaphones. Encourage them to talk through their megaphones and tell one another things they know about Jesus.

ask ▶ • **Who are we supposed to tell the world about?**

• **What is one thing you can tell someone about Jesus?**

Games

Tell the World

Supplies: pictures of children from around the world

Before class, gather pictures of children from around the world, enough for each child to have one. Hide the pictures around the room.

Have kids search for the pictures you hid before class. When they find a picture, have them each say to the person in the picture, "Jesus loves you!" After the children find their pictures, gather kids together to 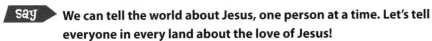 **ask** the following questions:

- **Who can we tell about Jesus?**
- **What is the good news we share?**

say **We can tell the world about Jesus, one person at a time. Let's tell everyone in every land about the love of Jesus!**

Share the News

Supplies: Bible, plastic egg

Have the children sit in a circle. Read aloud Matthew 28:19a, and have children repeat it after you.

ask **• Who should we follow?**

• Why is it important for everyone to follow Jesus?

say **This verse tells us that Jesus wants us to share his good news with others so they'll learn to follow him, too. Let's pretend our circle is the world while we play a following game!**

Choose one child to be the Leader and give him or her a plastic egg. Instruct the leader to walk around the circle as you lead children in this song to the tune of "Did You Ever See a Lassie?"

> **We will go and make disciples,**
>
> **Disciples, disciples.**
>
> **We will go and make disciples,**
>
> **All over the world!**

When the song ends, have the Leader stop and give the plastic egg to the child nearest him or her. Instruct that child to follow the Leader around the circle while children sing the song again. Then have the Follower give the egg to the person nearest him or her when the song ends. Continue playing, singing the song a little faster each time, until the entire class is following the Leader.

Close in prayer asking God to help us share the good news so others follow Jesus like us.

PRAYERS

Action Prayer

Supplies: pictures of children from around the world

Give each child a picture. Have children sit in a circle holding their pictures.

say ▸ **Jesus asked his friends to tell the whole world about him. He wants us to tell everyone about him, too. Let's pray and use these pictures of children from other countries to help us remember to tell everyone about Jesus.**

pray ▸ **Dear God,**

Thank you for sending us Jesus. Have kids hold their pictures up. **Be with these children in our pictures. Please send someone to tell them that Jesus loves them, too. Help us tell everyone we know that Jesus loves them and is coming back for all of us. In Jesus' name, amen.**

snacks

Into the Clouds

Supplies: small paper plates, plastic spoons, blue gelatin powder, whipped topping, elf-shaped cookies

Have children wash their hands or use wet wipes. Give each child a plate. Have kids spoon a small dollop of whipped topping onto the plate and then sprinkle one spoonful of gelatin powder over the whipped topping to make it look like a cloud. Then give each child an elf-shaped cookie to represent Jesus. Encourage kids to stand their cookies up in the "clouds." Invite one child to pray and thank God for the snacks. As kids are eating, remind them that they can tell the world about Jesus.

ask ▸ • **Where was Jesus going when he went up into the cloud?**

• **How do you think his friends felt when they saw him leaving?**

say ▸ **Before Jesus went back to heaven, he asked us to tell the world about him. We can tell the world about Jesus, one person at a time. Let's start today!**

GOD SENDS HIS HOLY SPIRIT

Bible Basis:

 Acts 2:1-21; 3:12-19

A Special Person

Supplies:

Bible, red tissue paper (one square per child)

Open your Bible to Acts 2, and show children the words.

say **Today's Bible story tells about the time God gave us the Holy Spirit. As you listen to the story, I want you to wave your red tissue paper high in the air every time I say "Holy Spirit." Let's try it.** Practice saying "Holy Spirit" as the children wave their tissue paper squares. **Imagine the red squares are flames blowing in the wind.**

In our Bible story, Jesus' disciples were together in a secret room in Jerusalem. They could hear the sound of people's voices outside, and the people were speaking in many different languages. Crowds of people were in the streets because it was a special day. It was the feast of Pentecost. People came from all over the world to attend the celebration.

On that day, the disciples were praying together in a room. They remembered that Jesus said they would teach people all over the world about him. But Jesus told them to wait until God sent them the Holy Spirit (have children wave the red tissues)**. God would send the Holy Spirit** (have children wave the red tissues) **to be with them and to give them power to tell everyone about him. Could this be the day, they wondered?**

While the disciples were praying, they heard a strange sound. It was even louder than the voices in the street. It was the sound of a great wind. It grew louder and louder, and it filled the house where they were praying. The disciples looked at each other, and they saw what looked like little fiery flames, kind of like our pieces of tissue. The flames seemed to be sitting on the top of each person's head!

ask **• Why do you think God sent the wind and the flames?**

say **God knew that the disciples couldn't see the Holy Spirit** (have children wave the red tissues)**, so he sent the wind so they could hear and feel him. And he sent the flames of fire so they could see him,**

The Humongous Book of Preschool Ideas 2   205

also. The disciples knew the Holy Spirit (have children wave the red tissues) **had come to be their friend and be with them.**

God gave them the Holy Spirit (have children wave tissues) **to be their teacher and friend and to help them tell others about him. He helped the disciples that day speak to thousands of people about Jesus. The Holy Spirit** (have children wave the red tissues) **gave them the power to speak to people in their own languages. Lots and lots of people believed in Jesus that day.**

 ask • **What do you think it would be like to talk to someone in another language?**

• **How do you think the disciples felt when lots and lots of people began to believe in Jesus?**

• **Who can the Holy Spirit help you tell about Jesus?**

say **The wind is a nice reminder that God gives us the Holy Spirit** (have children wave the red tissues)**. Every time the wind blows, we can remember that God gives us the Holy Spirit** (have children wave the red tissues) **to be our friend and to help us tell others about Jesus. God gives us the Holy Spirit** (have children wave the red tissues) **to help us, to comfort us when we're scared, to teach us, and to be our friend.**

BiBLe eXPeRienCeS

"The Holy Spirit" Chant

Supplies: blindfold, paper fan

Have the children stand in a circle. Choose one child to be blindfolded and stand in the middle of the circle. Choose another child to fan the blindfolded child using the paper fan. Have the blindfolded child move toward the fan while the other children chant this rhyme:

> **The Holy Spirit is our friend.**
>
> **Holy Spirit, come on in!**

When the blindfolded child touches the child with the fan, that child becomes the blindfolded child.

"Handy" Search

Supplies: box, several pairs of mittens or gloves, blindfold

Gather the children around the box of gloves. Select one child to be the searcher. Give that child a glove or mitten and have him or her put it on. Then blindfold the child and have him or her feel through the gloves in the box to find the right match for his or her glove. Encourage the other kids to shout out hints and encouragement as the child looks for the other glove. Once the child finds the glove, encourage the child to take off the blindfold and put the glove on his or her hand.

say ▶ **When you put your hand inside the glove, your hand fills up the glove.** Return one glove to the box and let the next child take a turn. Play until all the children have had a chance to find a matching glove.

ask ▶ • **What happens to a glove when you put your hand inside?**

• **What happened to the people in today's story?**

• **What kinds of things does the Holy Spirit help us do?**

say ▶ **Just as our hands filled the inside of these gloves, God gives us the Holy Spirit to fill the inside of our lives with comfort and strength. The Holy Spirit helps us do the right thing, and the Holy Spirit helps us tell others about Jesus.**

- -

I Know Jesus

Supplies: paper, crayons

Guide the children to a table where you have placed paper and crayons. Encourage each of the children to draw on a separate sheet of paper anything they know about Jesus. A child could draw a heart to show Jesus loves us, a cross to show Jesus died for us, and so on. Then have kids use their papers to "teach" one another what they know about Jesus. Tell children that's why God gives us the Holy Spirit—to teach us about Jesus who loves us so!

CRafts

Pouring Out the Spirit

Supplies: newspaper, crayons, Styrofoam cups, pitchers of water, towels, various sizes of measuring cups, droppers

Cover a table with newspaper. Set out crayons, Styrofoam cups, pitchers of water, towels, various sizes of measuring cups, and droppers.

say ▶ **Peter told the crowd that God had promised he'd "pour out" his Holy Spirit. That means the Holy Spirit fills us, lives in us, and helps us tell everyone about Jesus' love!**

Have kids color the cups to look like a crowd of people—old and young, men and women, with different colors of hair, skin, and eyes. Then let the kids have fun using a variety of utensils to fill the cups with water. As they fill each cup, have them repeat, "God gives us the Holy Spirit."

ask ▶ • **What did God give the believers in the story?**

• **What does God give us?**

• **What does the Holy Spirit help us do?**

say ▶ **God gives us the Holy Spirit. The Holy Spirit fills us and helps us live like Jesus would want us to. The Holy Spirit helps us tell everyone about Jesus so we all will be saved and live forever in heaven!**

PRayeRS

Flaming Prayer

Supplies: flashlight

Shine the flashlight on each child, and have everyone pray with you:

> **Thanks, God, for giving your Holy Spirit to help** [child's name]**.**

Then have everyone close by praying:

> **In Jesus' name, amen.**

- -

Action Prayer

Supplies: none

Have the children sit in a circle. Tell them you're going to thank God for sending the Holy Spirit. Tell them to pop up when they hear their names. Encourage the whole class to say the prayer with you as you pray for each child.

 **PRay** **Thank you, God, for sending the Holy Spirit to help** [child's name]**.**

> **In Jesus' name, amen.**

SnacKS

 **alleRGY aleRt**

Disciple Treats

Supplies: small dishes or trays, red and brown (a mixture of red and green) food coloring, large marshmallows, cotton swabs, toothpicks, graham crackers

Set out small trays or dishes of food coloring, which the children will use as paint. Give each child two large marshmallows, half a cotton swab, and three toothpicks. Have children each use a toothpick to connect their marshmallows. Then have them each paint a face on their marshmallow "disciple" by dipping the end of a toothpick in the brown food coloring. Have each child push half a cotton swab into the top marshmallow so the cotton is sticking out of the top and push a toothpick through the bottom marshmallow to make arms. When the children have finished, have them gather in a circle holding their snacks, and remind them that God gives us the Holy Spirit.

asK • **Who remembers our story and what happened to the disciples' heads when the Holy Spirit came?**

After the children respond, allow them to dip the cotton swabs at the top of their "disciples" in the red food coloring. Show the children how to carefully take apart their snack to eat it. Provide graham crackers to go with the marshmallow disciples.

CHRISTiaNS CaRe foR oNe aNotHeR

Bible Basis:

 Acts 2:42-47

Together Time

Supplies:

Bible, 1 classroom toy per child, age-appropriate worship CD, CD player, snacks

 **+ aLLeRGy aLeRt**

Before class, prepare a snack for each child.

Have kids form a circle and sit down. Give each person a toy from the classroom.

say ▶ **Each of you is holding a toy. We're going to use these to play a game called Musical Toys. When the music plays, pass the toy you're holding to the person to your right, and keep passing the toys around the circle until the music stops.** Show kids which way is toward the right. **When the music stops, stop passing the toys and hold on to the toy in your hand. When the music starts again, continue passing the toys around until the music stops again.**

Play an age-appropriate worship CD for several seconds, and then stop it. Begin the music again, and continue playing for several minutes.

ask ▶ • **How did it feel to keep giving away toys you wished you could keep?**

• **How do you think children who don't have any toys feel?**

Collect the toys and place them out of the way. Open your Bible to Acts 2:42-47, and show children the words.

say ▶ **I want to tell you a true story about some people who lived a long time ago. This story is found in the Bible, in the book of Acts. These people had just heard about how much Jesus loved them, and they wanted to show their love for Jesus in some special ways.**

ask ▶ • **How do you show other people how much you love Jesus?**

say ▶ **Lots of people started to believe in Jesus, and all those people formed a group. They loved each other so much, and they spent time together worshipping Jesus, praying together, and learning more about Jesus. These people were celebrating Jesus together. We can celebrate Jesus together, too.**

Begin the CD again, and encourage kids to stand up and sing, twirl, jump, clap, and celebrate together. After the song is over, ask kids to come back to the circle.

say > **These people also shared everything they had with each other, just as we were sharing our toys in the game we played earlier. They sold everything they owned and shared the money they made with people in need. They wanted to show their love to others and help them learn about Jesus, too!**

ask > **• How can you show Jesus' love to others?**

> **• How can you help other people learn about Jesus?**

say > **The people in the Bible story worshipped together at church, and they shared meals together at home.** Pass around the snack that you prepared before class. **You see, we're celebrating Jesus together right now! It's wonderful to know that we have such good friends here at church and that we can celebrate and worship Jesus together!**

ask > **• How can you celebrate Jesus with your family when you're at home?**

> **• How can you celebrate Jesus when you're with your friends?**

say > **God wants us to be like the people in our Bible story and celebrate Jesus together!**

BiBLe eXPeRieNCeS

Overflowing Love

Supplies: 1 clear cup of water and 1 golf ball per child, pitcher of water, shallow pans or pie plates

Before class, fill one clear cup per child with water. Set the cups inside shallow pans or pie plates so that spilling is not a problem during the activity.

Help your children understand that when they do good things for others, love overflows from them to the people they help. Gather kids around the cups of water that you prepared before class. Help kids experience what "overflowing" means by giving each child a golf ball and a clear cup filled with water.

Have children take the balls in and out of the water, observing what happens to the level of the water. Explain that the ball is like the good things they can do for others. Say that Jesus' love and kindness can flow out of us to the people around us, just as the water flows out of the cups.

ask > **• What are some nice things you can do for others?**

> **• Why does Jesus want us to do nice things?**

say > **When we do nice things for others, Jesus' love flows out of us! And Jesus will help us do good things for others.**

CRafts

A World of Love

Supplies: globe; lightweight white modeling clay; washable blue, green, and red markers; wet wipes; small straws; one 15-inch piece of string per child

Before class, cut a 15-inch piece of string for each child.

Show kids a globe (or an aerial picture of Earth). Explain that the globe represents all the people and places in the whole world. Tell kids that they are going to make small globe necklaces as a reminder to tell the world about Jesus.

Give each child a gumball-sized piece of clay. Have kids flatten the clay and then use the blue and green markers to color on the clay. When kids have finished coloring, tell them to twist, turn, and finally roll the clay back into a ball to make a globe.

Have the children flatten the balls into disks with the side of their fists. Use a straw to poke a hole near the top part of the disk, and let the children insert the string. Ask each child to draw a red cross in the middle of the disk. Use the wet wipes to clean off kids' hands, and then help children tie the ends of the string into a knot. Tell the children to let the clay dry overnight before they wear the necklaces.

say ▸ **God helps us do good things for others. We have a whole world full of people who need good things, but the most important good thing everyone needs is Jesus. Look at your globe necklace and then look at a friend's necklace. Everybody's necklace is different, just like people are different. But one thing is the same with all of us—Jesus loves us!**

ask ▸ **• Why do you think we put crosses on our globe necklaces?**

say ▸ **Jesus died on a cross so we could be forgiven for the bad things we do. That's how much he loves us! And then three days later, he rose again! When we believe in Jesus, he's with us wherever we go in the world. And people all over the world need to hear about Jesus.**

ask ▸ **• Who can you tell about Jesus this week?**

say ▸ **In our Bible story, the people told everyone they knew about Jesus, and the news about him spread all over the world. After your necklace dries, you can wear it to remind you to tell everyone about Jesus!**

Games

Surprise Sacks

Supplies: 6 lunch bags, bread, bandages, toy people, doll clothing, toy house, coins

Before class, put each of the following items in six different lunch bags: bread, bandages, toy people, doll clothing, toy house, and coins. As children enter, allow them to take turns feeling objects inside each of the paper bags and guessing what's inside without looking. Tell children people use these items to do good for others. Remind kids that the people in the Bible story shared with each other and did good things for each other.

PRAYERS

Action Prayer

Supplies: none

Have the children go to the far corners of the room and sing the following prayer to the tune of "Alouette" as they come together to hold hands.

> **Dear God, help me to encourage**
> **Others to do good things for you.**
> **I will do good things for you.** (I will do good things for you.)
> **Do good things.** (Do good things.)
> **Ooooooh!**
>
> **Dear God, help me to encourage**
> **Others to do good things for you.**
> **I will do good things for you.** (I will do good things for you.)
> **Do good things.** (Do good things.)
> **Ooooooh!**
>
> **Dear God, help me to encourage.**
> **I will do good things for you.**
> **In Jesus' name, amen.**

SNACKS

Sharing Is Caring

Supplies: 1 cup per child, 2 different small snacks (crackers, pretzels, raisins, or M&M's)

If you plan to use raisins as part of the activity, cut the raisins in half to avoid a potential choking hazard.

Have the children wash their hands (or use wet wipes) and then sit down to prepare the snack. Give each child a small disposable cup, and then give half of the children a double portion of one small snack, such as little crackers or pretzels. Give the other half of the children a double portion of another small snack, such as raisins or M&M's. Have children show their care for each other by giving each other part of their snacks. When they've finished sharing, each child should have somewhat equal portions of both snacks. Invite one child to pray for the snack.

ask ▸ • How did it feel to be a giver?

• How did it feel to be a getter?

• What can you share at home?

say ▸ It feels good to share. It also feels good to be cared about. God helps us do good things for others, just as he helped the people in our Bible story.

SONGS

We Can Teach

Supplies: none

Have the children form a circle and hold hands. Pick one child to stand in the center of the circle and clap as you move around him or her. Lead the children in singing "We Can Teach" to the tune of "The Farmer in the Dell."

> **We can teach the world.**
>
> **We can teach the world.**
>
> **Teach all about Jesus.**
>
> **Now who will we teach?**

Like in "The Farmer in the Dell," the child in the middle chooses someone to join him or her and then tells that child something about Jesus. The children in the middle continue to clap as the children in the circle move around them and sing again. The next child in the middle then chooses someone else to come to the center and tells him or her something about Jesus. When the last child is chosen and you are left to circle around the children, finish the song with the following verse:

> **We can teach the world.**
>
> **We can teach the world.**
>
> **Teach all about Jesus.**
>
> **Now let's all shout hooray!**
>
> **"Hooray!"** (Together, with hands up.)

ask ▸ • Why is it good to teach about Jesus?

• Who can you teach about Jesus?

say ▸ The world is a big place, but we can teach one friend at a time until everyone knows about Jesus. We teach by the things we say and do. God helps us do good things for others. That's one way we can teach about Jesus.

PHILIP TELLS THE ETHIOPIAN ABOUT JESUS

Bible Basis:

Acts 8:26-40

Philip Tells All

Supplies:

Bible, masking tape, pan of sand, pan of water, 3 toy people, rectangular block

Before class, use masking tape to outline a chariot on the floor that is large enough for children to stand or sit inside. Place a pan of sand, a pan of water, three plastic people, and a rectangular block close by.

Open your Bible to Acts 8, and show children the words. Invite the children to sit in the "chariot."

say **Today's Bible story teaches us that we can listen to God.**

During Bible times, some people rode in chariots. Chariots were carts that were pulled by horses. The man in our Bible story rode in a chariot, so let's pretend to ride in one, too.

Explain to the children what each prop represents: the pan of sand is the desert; the three plastic people are the angel, the Ethiopian, and Philip; and the rectangular block is the chariot. Choose children to take turns moving the figures as you direct them. Make sure every child has a turn.

say **One day an angel of God** (have a child hold up the "angel") **said to a man named Philip** (have a child hold up "Philip")**, "Go to Gaza."**

So Philip headed down the desert road (have a child walk Philip along in the pan of sand)**. Along the way he met an Ethiopian man** (have a child hold up the "Ethiopian") **who was riding in a chariot** (have a child place the Ethiopian on the block and set it in the sand)**. The Ethiopian was a very important man. He took care of all of the Queen's money. The Ethiopian was on his way home from worshipping and was reading Scriptures.** (Have a child drive the "chariot" slowly along the road.)

The angel (have a child hold up the angel again) **told Philip to go over to the chariot** (have a child move Philip near the block)**. When Philip got near the chariot, he could hear the man reading God's words from the scroll. Philip asked the Ethiopian if he understood what he was reading. The Ethiopian said he couldn't understand**

the Scriptures unless someone told him what the words meant. **The Ethiopian invited Philip to sit in the chariot with him** (have a child place the Philip figure on the block with the Ethiopian figure). **The Ethiopian had been reading about Jesus, but he didn't understand. So Philip told the Ethiopian all about Jesus.**

As they traveled down the road (have the child continue to move the block in the sand)**, they came to some water. The Ethiopian asked Philip if he could be baptized. The Ethiopian loved Jesus with all his heart and wanted to obey him by doing what the Scriptures said to do. Both Philip and the Ethiopian got out of the chariot** (have a child take both figures off the block) **and went down into the water** (have the child place the figures in the pan of water)**. Philip baptized the Ethiopian that very day. When Philip and the Ethiopian came out of the water, Philip went where God told him to go, and the Ethiopian went on his way rejoicing. He was so happy!**

ask
- **What are some ways we can show God we're happy about what he did in today's story?**

- **What's one thing God has done for you that makes you happy?**

say
In our story, Philip listened to God by obeying the angel and doing what he was told. The Ethiopian listened to God by reading the Scriptures and listening to Philip tell him about Jesus. We can listen to God just as Philip and the Ethiopian did.

When we love God with all our heart, we want to listen to his words, just as the Ethiopian listened to Philip and to God. Ask your parents this week if they will read to you from the Bible the way Philip read to the Ethiopian.

BiBLe eXPeRieNCeS

Chariots

Supplies: 1 large foam cup per 2 children, 4 craft sticks per child, card stock, craft glue, scissors, fine-tipped markers

Before class, cut the foam cups in half. Make two small slits side by side in the top curved part of each cup and two small slits side by side in the bottom flat part of each cup. Cut two 2-inch wheels out of card stock for each child.

Give each child half of a foam cup. Show children how to glue the wheels to the sides of their cup. Then give each child two craft sticks, and encourage kids to use the markers to draw faces and clothes on the sticks so they look like Philip and the Ethiopian. Show kids how to carefully slide the craft sticks into the holes on top. Then show children how to slide the remaining two craft sticks into the end holes to make the bars that the horses would be hooked to. Encourage children to use the craft to act out the Bible story.

• What did Philip tell the Ethiopian when they were riding in the chariot?

• Who can you tell about Jesus?

• What will you say about Jesus?

say Philip listened to God and told the Ethiopian about Jesus. We can listen to God, too, and we can tell others about Jesus.

Games

Chariot Tag

Supplies: none

Ask for one volunteer to be Philip.

say **The Bible tells us about a man named Philip who ran after a man is his chariot to tell him about Jesus. Today** [child's name] **will be Philip. The rest of you will get down on your hands and knees and crawl around the room on all fours like chariots. When Philip tags you, sit down and wait until all of the other chariots have been tagged. We'll choose a new Philip and play several times.**

Prayers

Listen Up!

Supplies: Bible

Have kids sit in a circle on the floor with you.

say **When God told Philip to teach the Ethiopian about Jesus, Philip listened and obeyed. It's important for us to listen to God, too. This prayer can help!**

Explain that you'll begin the prayer by whispering in the ear of the person next to you something God wants us to do. That person will whisper the message to the next person, and so on, until the message goes around the circle and comes back to you. Then you'll whisper another message.

Whisper several things God wants us to do, such as tell others about Jesus, love each other, forgive each other, and listen to God. Close the prayer by saying: **We love you, God. In Jesus' name, amen!**

SNACKS

Listening Ears

Supplies: 1 sugar cookie, 1 tablespoon of icing, and 1 plastic knife per child; 2 apple slices per child; chocolate chips

Give each child a round sugar cookie with a small amount of icing in the middle. Show the children how to use plastic knives to spread the icing all around the cookie. Provide chocolate chips to use as eyes, a nose, and a mouth. Finally, give each child two apple slices to place on either side of the cookie to represent ears. As the children enjoy their snack, remind them that we can listen to God, just as Philip did.

SONGS

We Can Listen to God

Supplies: none

Lead the children in singing "We Can Listen to God" to the tune of "Oh, Be Careful." Remind kids that Philip listened to God and obeyed him.

We can listen to God every day.

We can listen to God every day.

We can listen to God and obey his holy Word.

We can listen to God every day.

The Philip Rhyme

Supplies: none

 Let's do an action rhyme together. The rhyme tells how Philip told the Ethiopian about Jesus.

Philip heard God's angel say "go" (put hand to ear, and then point with finger)**,**

And he went on down that sandy road. (Pretend to walk.)

Along the way there came a man ("walk" two fingers in the other hand)

Who wanted to know about God's plan. (Shrug shoulders with palms up.)

Well, Philip told him about Jesus and living in his way. (Point to heaven.)

The Ethiopian heard what Philip said and followed God that day. (Put hands to ears, and then point to heaven.)

PAUL TEACHES ABOUT SPIRITUAL GIFTS

Bible Basis:

 1 Corinthians 12:4-27

Gifts From God

Supplies:

Bible

Open your Bible to 1 Corinthians 12:4-27, and show children the words.

say **Today we're learning that God gives us different gifts. We're not talking about the clothes or toys you get on your birthday. God's gifts are way better that that! You never outgrow God's gifts as you do clothes, and you never get tired of God's gifts as you might a toy.**

God's gifts are inside of us. Each one of us is special, and God gives everyone who believes in Jesus a special gift! We can all use our different gifts to praise God and do his good work. The Bible tells us to think of it like this:

A body has lots of different parts that all work together, right? The eyes see (point to your eyes)**, the ears hear** (point to one ear)**, the feet walk** (stomp in place)**, and the hands can wave to your friends** (hold up your hands and wave to the class)**. But all of those are part of the same body!**

Help children form four groups, and have each group go to a different corner of the room. The four groups will be the Eyes, the Ears, the Feet, and the Hands. Explain that you'll call each group to the center of the room and tell the children something their group can do to praise and honor God with their body part. Then they can act out what you tell them.

Call the Eyes to the center of the room first.

say **The eyes can look all around. Put your curled fingers up to your eyes like binoculars, and use them to look all around the room.** Lead children in the action. **The eyes can always be on the lookout for friends to help!**

Have the Eyes return to their corner. Then call the Ears to the center of the room.

say **The ears can always be listening for friends in trouble.** Lead children in cupping their hands to their ears and turning in a circle. **The ears can be good listeners when a friend is sad or needs someone to talk to!**

Have the Ears return to their corner, then call the Feet.

say **The feet can walk all around.** Lead children in stomping their feet as they turn in a circle. **The feet can walk right up to a friend who needs help!**

Have the Feet return to their corner, then call the Hands.

say **The hands can do lots of things.** Lead children in hugging themselves as they turn in a circle. **The hands can give a hurting friend a great big hug!**

Have the Hands return to their corner.

say **See? Each part of the body can do a special job for God. And guess what? They can all work together! Let's see what that's like.**

Have all four groups come to the center of the room, but have children stay in their groups. Teach children this rhyme, leading groups in the appropriate actions:

> **Do you have eyes to see?** (Lead the Eyes in using pretend binoculars.)
>
> **Then look for friends in need.** (Lead the Eyes in using pretend binoculars.)
>
> **We all have gifts** (spread your arms open wide)
>
> **To use for God.** (Point to heaven.)
>
> **Wouldn't you agree?** (Nod your head up and down.)
>
>
> **Do you have ears to hear?** (Lead the Ears in cupping their hands to their ears.)
>
> **Then listen to a friend.** (Lead the Ears in cupping their hands to their ears.)
>
> **We all have gifts** (spread your arms open wide)
>
> **To use for God.** (Point to heaven.)
>
> **Wouldn't you agree?** (Nod your head up and down.)
>
>
> **Do you have feet to walk?** (Lead the Feet in stomping in place.)
>
> **Then walk up to a friend.** (Lead the Feet in stomping in place.)
>
> **We all have gifts** (spread your arms open wide)
>
> **To use for God.** (Point to heaven.)
>
> **Wouldn't you agree?** (Nod your head up and down.)
>
>
> **Do you have hands to hug?** (Lead the Hands in hugging themselves.)
>
> **Then hug a friend who's sad.** (Lead the Hands in hugging themselves.)
>
> **We all have gifts** (spread your arms open wide)
>
> **To use for God.** (Point to heaven.)
>
> **Wouldn't you agree?** (Nod your head up and down.)

Explain that during the first two lines of the last stanza, all groups will perform their actions.

> **Do you have eyes and ears?** (Have all groups do their motions.)
>
> **And feet and hands?** (Have all groups do their motions.)
>
> **We all have gifts** (spread your arms open wide)
>
> **To use for God.** (Point to heaven.)
>
> **Wouldn't you agree?** (Nod your head up and down.)

Lead children in a big round of applause for everyone's participation.

 God gives us different gifts. And we can all use our different gifts to praise and serve God. Some of us might be good at sharing. We can use that gift to share our toys and show God's love to our friends. Some of us might be good at drawing. We can draw a picture to show God how much we love him. And we can all be good at caring for others. Remember? We can use our eyes and ears and feet and hands to serve God. We can use all the things we're good at to serve God.

Just as all the different parts of the body work together, we can all work together for God!

BiBLe eXPeRieNCeS

Beautiful Bouquet

Supplies: Bible, vase, water, fresh-cut flowers

Before class, partially fill the vase with water. Make sure you have a flower for each child, plus a few extras for visitors.

Open your Bible to 1 Corinthians 12:1-13.

 God has given each of us a special gift or talent. Think of a gift or talent God has given you. Pause. **God gives us gifts so we can serve him. You've already thought of a gift God has given you—now think of how you can use that gift to serve God.**

When you're sure each child has thought of an idea, gather kids around the vase.

 Just as individual flowers can make a beautiful bouquet, we can all make a difference in God's kingdom by using our gifts to serve God. When it's your turn, choose a flower to add to the bouquet. As you put the flower in the vase, tell us what gift you thought of and how you can use it to serve God.

After each child has added a flower to the bouquet, pray: **Lord, thank you for the gifts you've given each person in this room. Help us all to use our gifts to serve you so we can make a beautiful bouquet of love and service. In Jesus' name, amen.**

CRAFTS

Self-Portraits

Supplies: Bible, paper plates, fine-tipped markers, crayons, glue, yarn

Open your Bible to 1 Corinthians 12:1-13.

say ▶ **God gives us gifts so we can serve him. We're all special in some way because that's the way God made us. Let's make self-portraits to remind us of the gifts and talents God has given us to use to serve him.**

Give each child a paper plate, and tell kids to decorate their plates to look like their own faces. Kids can use markers and crayons to draw facial features and then glue yarn to the top as hair.

Encourage kids to take their self-portraits home to remind them that God gives us gifts so we can serve him.

Games

Hands and Feet

Supplies: none

Explain that the goal of the game is for children to get to the other side of the room and back. But each child can use only one foot!

Ask children how they think they will be able to get across the room on only one foot. Then explain that children will work in pairs. They will link arms, and then, together, they will have two feet! Encourage kids to practice linking arms with partners and hopping forward together. When the kids are ready, let each pair travel across the room and back as the rest of the class cheers the pair on.

After the game, gather everyone in a circle on the floor.

ask ▶ **• What was it like to work with your partner in this game?**

• How can we all work together to serve God?

say ▶ **Just as you worked together in our game, we can work together to serve God. God gives us different gifts to use, but we can all use our gifts to serve God!**

Our Bodies

Supplies: various posters depicting how the body works

Bring in posters of how the body works, and hang the posters on the wall at children's eye level. Show the kids the posters, and point out how amazing the human body is. Point out that God made all the big and little body parts to work together. Encourage kids to look at the posters and talk about how special their bodies are. Lead kids in demonstrating how various parts of their bodies work. For example, kids could wiggle their fingers in the air to show how their fingers work, stomp their feet, and open and shut their eyes.

Tell children that God gives us different gifts. Just as there are many parts of the body, there are many different gifts that God gives people. Tell kids that we can use our gifts together to serve God!

PRAYERS

He Gave Us Us

Supplies: none

say ▶ **God gave us bodies that we can use to serve him. Let's stand up and thank God for the bodies he's given us.**

Have kids spread out. Tell them to repeat the words after you and follow your motions. Be sensitive to any children with physical challenges in your class. Don't use any motions they can't do.

Thanks, God, for our hands. (Wave hands in the air.)

Thanks, God, for our feet. (Wiggle a foot in the air.)

Thanks, God, for our elbows. (Flop your elbows out at your sides.)

Thanks, God, for our knees. (March with your knees going high.)

Thanks, God, for our heads. (Roll your head around and around.)

Thanks, God, for our hips. (Wiggle your hips.)

Thanks, God, for our seats. (Sit down on the floor in a circle.)

snacks

Muffin Heads

Supplies: 1 English muffin half per child, soft cream cheese, plastic knives, paper plates, raisins, orange and apple slices, string licorice

Before class, cut string licorice into 2-inch lengths.

Have children wash their hands (or use wet wipes) and then sit down to prepare their snacks.

Set out plastic knives, softened cream cheese, raisins, orange and apple slices, and string licorice pieces. Give each child an English muffin half on a small paper plate.

Encourage each child to make a face on his or her muffin "head." First, have children spread the muffins with cream cheese. Then let them add orange- or apple-slice mouths, raisin eyes and noses, and licorice eyebrows. When everyone has finished, let each child show the face to the rest of the class.

Story 45: Paul Teaches About Spiritual Gifts

say Wow! Each face you made is different! That reminds me of how each person God makes is different. God gives us different gifts that we can use to serve him. Let's thank God for giving us different gifts and for giving us this yummy snack. Choose a child to pray for the snack.

Songs

Good Gifts

Supplies: none

Remind children that God gives each of us good gifts to use for him. Then lead kids in singing the following song to the tune of "Mary Had a Little Lamb."

> **God gives me good gifts to use,**
>
> **Gifts to use, gifts to use.**
>
> **God gives me good gifts to use.**
>
> **I'll use my gifts for God.**

For more amazing resources

visit us at
group.com...

...or call us at
1-800-447-1070!

Also available at your favorite Christian Retailer.